# HIGH PROFITS WITHOUT RISK

**How You Can Earn More
Than 50% on Your Investment
With Absolute Safety**

# HIGH PROFITS WITHOUT RISK

**How You Can Earn More Than 50% on Your Investment With Absolute Safety**

77-3574

by
## Howard E. Deutch, J.D., C.P.A.

JEFREN PUBLISHING COMPANY
1216 Holy Cross, Monroeville, Pennsylvania 15146

THE OZARKS REGIONAL LIBRARY
217 EAST DICKSON STREET
FAYETTEVILLE, ARK. 72701

The author gratefully acknowledges permission to reprint the advertisements appearing on pages 69 and 70. The advertisements originally appeared in the October 8, 1975 issue of *Coin World*, copyright© 1975 by Amos Press, Inc., Sidney, Ohio.

Copyright© 1976

By Howard E. Deutch

All rights reserved. No part of this book may be reproduced or transmitted in any form or by any means, electronic or mechanical, including photocopying, recording, or by any information storage and retrieval system now known or to be invented, without permission in writing from the publisher, except by a reviewer who may quote brief passages in connection with a review written for inclusion in a magazine, newspaper, or broadcast.

FIRST EDITION

Published by

JEFREN PUBLISHING COMPANY
1216 Holy Cross
Monroeville, Pennsylvania 15146

---

Library of Congress Cataloging in Publication Data

Deutch, Howard E      1932-
   High profits without risk.

   Includes index.
   1. Coins, American.    2. Coins as an investment.
I. Title.
CJ1832.D48      737.4'9'73      76-19925
ISBN 0-917244-01-X

---

International Standard Book Number: 0-917244-01-X

Printed in the United States of America

TO ROSILYN, KAREN, AND JEFFREY

*For putting up with a part-time husband and father*
*during the two years it took to write this book*

*The happiest time in any man's life is when he is in red-hot pursuit of a dollar with a reasonable prospect of overtaking it.*

JOSH BILLINGS

# TO THE READER

In 1948, I answered a small advertisement which promised me the secret to riches for just a couple of dollars. And I received, for my two dollars, a small booklet which said that the way to make a great deal of money was to invest in rolls of uncirculated coins. I did not take the author's advice.

In 1974, for some unexplained reason, I thought about the small booklet that I had read twenty-six years earlier and I wondered if the advice had been correct. So I set about to research what had happened to values of uncirculated coins in the interim. This book is the result of that research.

Howard E. Deutch
July 12, 1976

P.S. If I had taken the author's advice in 1948, I would have realized a return on my investment of more than 1,400%. I hope you will not wait twenty-six years as I did.

## ACKNOWLEDGMENTS

I wish to express my sincere thanks to Martin Ashkin, George Cohen, Miles Thomson, and Rosilyn Deutch for their many valuable suggestions.

Special thanks are also due to my wife Rosilyn for typing and to my daughter Karen and my son Jeffrey for proofreading the many versions of the manuscript of this book.

H.E.D.

# Contents

12/Contents

# Tables

# 16/Tables

# Introduction

*October. This is one of the peculiarly*
*dangerous months to speculate in stocks.*
*The others are July, January, September,*
*April, November, May, March, June, December,*
*August and February.*

SAMUEL LANGHORNE CLEMENS (MARK TWAIN):
Pudd'nhead Wilson

## Why People Invest

Every day people just like you put their money into all kinds of "investments." Their goals are many:

- to make a great deal of money

- to protect the purchasing power of their money (as a hedge against inflation)

- to set up a retirement fund

- to pay for a child's education or wedding

*Most of these people will see their investment shrink — or disappear entirely.* That's because these people aren't really investing. They're speculating.

## Speculation

According to Webster's New World Dictionary, *speculate* means: "to take part in any risky venture on the chance of making huge profits." All speculation has one thing in common — you risk the loss of some or all of your money.

If you want to speculate, there are hundreds of ways to do so. Some of the more popular things in which you can speculate are:

| | |
|---|---|
| art objects and antiques | options |
| cattle feeding and breeding | rare coins |
| commodity futures | rare stamps |
| diamonds | real estate |
| equipment leasing | scotch whiskey |
| foreign currency | silver |
| gold | syndications |
| mutual funds | warrants |
| oil and gas drilling | wine |

## The Stock Market

One of the most common kinds of speculation is the stock market (although the stockbrokers would like you to think of stocks as an investment). A graphic illustration of speculation that produced tremendous losses was the recent performance of the stock market. On January 11, 1973 the Dow Jones Industrial Average reached an all-time high of 1051.71. Exactly two years later, on January 10, 1975, the "Dow" had dropped to 658.79 — a loss of 37%. During that same two-year period the performance of the other stock market averages was even worse:

Standard & Poor's Composite Stock Index dropped 39%

The NYSE composite of all stocks traded
on the New York Stock Exchange      dropped 41%

The Amex composite of all stocks traded
on the American Stock Exchange      dropped 42%

The Value Line composite of approximately
1550 stocks      dropped 51%

But there is another kind of risk in the stock market that is even more hazardous — the risk that you will be *completely wiped out*. Ask any of the people who own stock in Equity Funding, Home-Stake Production Company, Four Seasons Nursing Centers, or Penn Central Railroad. As a result of this kind of risk, many people now feel that stocks shouldn't be called "securities," but rather "insecurities."

**THIS BOOK IS NOT ABOUT SPECULATING. IT IS ABOUT INVESTING.**

### Elements of an Ideal Investment

The ideal investment is one that has the following elements:

- no possibility of loss of investment
- high yield (profit)
- easy to buy (available in every city)
- easy to sell (constant demand — millions of potential buyers)
- no commissions or fees when bought or sold
- no taxes while holding (such as real estate taxes)
- low tax when sold (capital gains)

- easy to determine most profitable time to sell
- no minimum investment required

## The Only Ideal Investment

There is only one investment I know of that contains *all* the elements of an ideal investment. *That investment is current-year uncirculated coins.* Millions of people collect coins. And millions more speculate in coins. But very few *invest* in coins. The only way you can make huge profits *without any risk* is to *invest* in coins. But not just any coins. Most coins in which people "invest" are as risky as the stock market.

## Making a "Killing"

In the stock market, people who make a "killing" take a big risk. They have to select a stock that is going to go up, they have to know when to buy (before it goes up), and they have to know when to sell (at or near its "high"). *And only a handful make any substantial profits.* Most lose money (some lose *most* of their investment).

While there is no guarantee of a "killing" in current-year uncirculated coin investments, history shows that there have been "killings" — and there are likely to be more. But even without a "killing", *current-year uncirculated coin investments have outperformed, and should continue to outperform, the stock market and just about every other investment you can think of.*

## What This Book Will Do For You

This book will show you how to make money by investing in rolls of current-year uncirculated coins. It will tell you:

- which coins to buy (and which coins not to buy)

- how to buy them at their face value
- how to preserve and protect them
- how and when to sell them for maximum profits
- to whom to sell them
- how much to sell them for

This book will *prove* that — if the future is anything like the past — your investment should increase by *more than 50% each year*. And this book will show you how to do all this without risking your investment. That's right, by following the instructions that are contained in these pages *you cannot lose one penny of your investment*.

THIS BOOK DOES NOT CONTAIN THE USUAL WARNING THAT YOU SHOULD ONLY INVEST AMOUNTS THAT YOU CAN AFFORD TO LOSE — BECAUSE THERE IS NO WAY THAT YOUR INVESTMENT IN ROLLS OF CURRENT-YEAR UNCIRCULATED COINS CAN EVER BE WORTH LESS THAN THE AMOUNT YOU PAID FOR THEM.

# HIGH PROFITS WITHOUT RISK

## How You Can Earn More Than 50% on Your Investment With Absolute Safety

# Chapter 1

# Uncirculated Coin Rolls

*If thou wouldst keep money, save money;*
*If thou wouldst reap money, sow money.*

THOMAS FULLER, *Gnomologia.* No. 2721

## Stock Market Profits vs. Uncirculated Coin Profits

On February 21, 1973, the New York Stock Exchange ran a full page advertisement in the Wall Street Journal proclaiming that, if $10,000 had been invested on December 31, 1949 in the composite index of all common stocks listed on the New York Stock Exchange and if all dividends over those 23 years had been reinvested, on December 31, 1972 (when the Dow Jones Industrial Average was near the highest point in its history) "the $10,000 would have grown to approximately $140,000."

That's very impressive until you consider that, if the same $10,000 had been invested on December 31, 1949 in a composite (equal dollar amounts) of all uncirculated coins that were minted in that year, by December 31, 1972 the $10,000 *would have grown to approximately $261,700.*

The advertisement went on to say: "There's always a risk in buying common stocks." *They weren't kidding*! On April 2, 1974, the New York Stock Exchange ran another full page advertisement in which they boasted that the same $10,000 (with dividends reinvested) would, by December 31, 1973, have grown to 117,000. *If you had held this stock investment only one more year you would have lost $23,000.* However, if you had held the same uncirculated coin roll investment for one more year, *you would have gained more than $119,000* (the same $10,000 investment in uncirculated coin rolls increased in value from $261,700 at December 31, 1972 to $381,500 at December 31, 1973).

These comparisons are interesting, but they aren't very practical. They assume a single investment made on a single date. December 31, 1949 might have been an unusually good time to invest. But suppose you had invested your money in a different year or had held your investment for a different length of time. How would your investment have performed then?

**Periodic Investments in Stocks, Corporate Bonds, and Uncirculated Coin Rolls**

Let's look at a hypothetical investment of $100 per year in stocks and corporate bonds *over varying numbers of years* and compare it with the same investment in rolls of current-year uncirculated coins.

| $100 invested each year beginning December 31, | Number of years invest-ment held | Total amount invested | Value at December 31, 1973 of | | |
|---|---|---|---|---|---|
| | | | Stocks[1] | Corporate Bonds[2] | Uncirculated Coin Rolls[3] |
| 1963 | 10 | $1,000 | $ 1,800 | $1,260 | $ 2,189 |
| 1958 | 15 | 1,500 | 3,120 | 2,220 | 3,561 |
| 1953 | 20 | 2,000 | 6,320 | 3,040 | 6,076 |
| 1948 | 25 | 2,500 | 10,063 | 4,000 | 16,493 |
| 1943 | 30 | 3,000 | 13,710 | 5,160 | 25,479 |

Wait a minute! Maybe it's misleading to show results for 1973. Maybe 1973 was an unusually good year for uncirculated coins. What would have happened if you had made the same investment of $100 per year over periods of 10, 15, 20, 25, or 30 years ending, not in 1973, but in some other year? Would the results have been the same?

The following table illustrates the same investment of $100 per year over periods of from 10 to 30 years ending in 1966, 1971, and 1975 and compares the results with those at the end of 1973.

---

[1]Based on actual rates of return from Standard & Poor's Composite Stock Index for the periods indicated. See Roger G. Ibbotson and Rex A. Singuefield, *Stocks, Bonds, Bills And Inflation: The Past And The Future* (Chicago: University of Chicago's Center for Research in Security Prices, 1974), pp. 123-125.

[2]Based on annual returns from high grade, long term corporate bonds for the periods indicated. Ibbotson and Singuefield, *op. cit.*, pp. 128-130.

[3]Based on average prices that dealers were *paying* for such coin rolls at the end of 1973.

| $100 invested each year for | Total amount invested | Value of Uncirculated Coin Rolls at December 31, | | | |
|---|---|---|---|---|---|
| | | 1973 | 1966 | 1971 | 1975 |
| 10 years | $1,000 | $2,189 | $2,095 | $1,664 | $2,240 |
| 15 years | 1,500 | 3,561 | 6,856 | 2,715 | 3,925 |
| 20 years | 2,000 | 6,076 | 16,029 | 5,259 | 6,132 |
| 25 years | 2,500 | 16,493 | 26,747 | 11,314 | 12,410 |
| 30 years | 3,000 | 25,479 | 60,880 | 18,482 | 19,414 |

Notice how values of uncirculated coin rolls fluctuate. You will receive a greater profit if you sell your coin rolls in some years than if you sell them in other years. But how can you know when to sell to maximize your profit? Stock market "investors" have been trying to answer this question for hundreds of years — with little success. However, for uncirculated coin roll investors there is a simple, foolproof method that tells you when to sell to maximize your profits. See Chapter 3 for details.

## Some Coin Rolls are More Profitable Than Others

The amounts in the preceding table are based on an assumed investment in a *composite* (equal dollar amounts) of all uncirculated coins minted in those years. An analysis of the performance of the coin rolls of each denomination (divided equally among the coins produced by the various mints) tells a more interesting — and profitable — story.

| $100 invested in current-year uncirculated rolls of the indicated coin each year for | Total amount invested | Value of Uncirculated Coin Rolls[4] at December 31, | | | |
|---|---|---|---|---|---|
| | | 1973 | 1966 | 1971 | 1975 |
| **10 years** | | | | | |
| cents | $1,000 | $3,862 | $4,030 | $3,174 | $3,928 |
| nickels | 1,000 | 1,498 | 1,912 | 1,199 | 1,687 |
| dimes | 1,000 | 1,410 | 1,372 | 1,129 | 1,638 |
| quarters | 1,000 | 1,518 | 1,296 | 1,091 | 1,430 |
| half-dollars | 1,000 | 2,657 | 1,865 | 1,727 | 2,517 |
| **15 years** | | | | | |
| cents | 1,500 | 6,412 | 14,365 | 5,124 | 6,949 |
| nickels | 1,500 | 2,302 | 8,356 | 2,031 | 2,392 |
| dimes | 1,500 | 2,517 | 3,819 | 1,874 | 3,212 |
| quarters | 1,500 | 2,665 | 3,088 | 1,767 | 2,930 |
| half-dollars | 1,500 | 3,911 | 4,651 | 2,779 | 4,140 |
| **20 years** | | | | | |
| cents | 2,000 | 10,724 | 27,547 | 9,679 | 10,757 |
| nickels | 2,000 | 4,139 | 25,891 | 5,062 | 3,662 |
| dimes | 2,000 | 4,445 | 9,440 | 3,395 | 5,018 |
| quarters | 2,000 | 4,420 | 6,106 | 3,051 | 4,789 |
| half-dollars | 2,000 | 6,651 | 11,161 | 5,108 | 6,432 |
| **25 years** | | | | | |
| cents | 2,500 | 23,451 | 46,839 | 16,660 | 20,435 |
| nickels | 2,500 | 18,302 | 47,722 | 15,211 | 13,552 |
| dimes | 2,500 | 14,936 | 14,003 | 8,198 | 7,869 |
| quarters | 2,500 | 8,927 | 9,498 | 5,606 | 7,251 |
| half-dollars | 2,500 | 16,849 | 15,673 | 10,893 | 12,943 |
| **30 years** | | | | | |
| cents | 3,000 | 33,748 | 86,697 | 29,156 | 31,102 |
| nickels | 3,000 | 29,374 | 97,825 | 29,183 | 18,350 |
| dimes | 3,000 | 20,357 | 28,508 | 10,817 | 17,013 |
| quarters | 3,000 | 12,974 | 57,777 | 8,091 | 12,331 |
| half-dollars | 3,000 | 30,943 | 33,592 | 15,165 | 18,275 |

[4]These are average prices that dealers were *paying* for the coin rolls in the years indicated. All mints did not produce each denomination of coin in every year. Value of coins minted nearest missing date (average of before and after) has been used for value of coin rolls assumed to have been purchased in that year.

## Graphs Showing Price Movement of Uncirculated Coins

Up to this point we have only been considering periodic investments in uncirculated coin rolls. Now let's see how a one-time purchase of these same coin rolls has increased in value over varying periods of time.

The graphs on the following pages show the price movement of an initial purchase of $100 face value of uncirculated rolls of each of the coins that were minted between 1935 and 1974 (except S[5] nickels, S dimes, S quarters, and S half-dollars, which are no longer minted for general circulation). The prices are the average prices that dealers were *paying* for the coin rolls.

---

[5]The meaning of *P*, *D*, or *S* in front of a coin denomination (such as S nickels, *P* cents, etc.) is explained in Chapter 2.

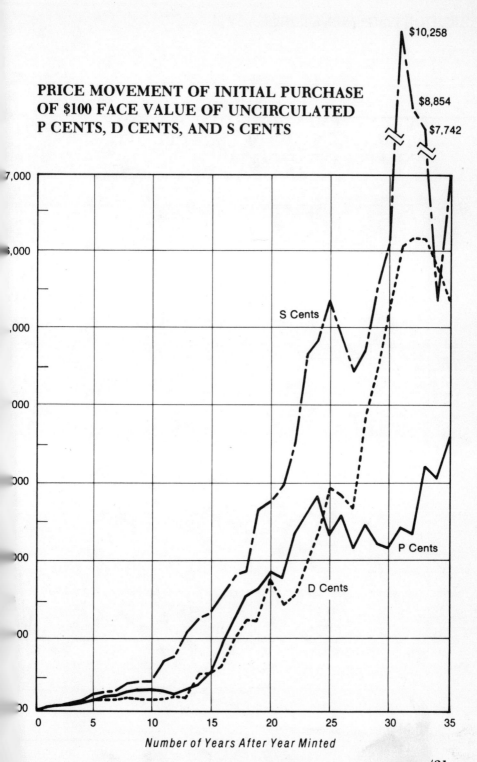

PRICE MOVEMENT OF INITIAL PURCHASE
OF $100 FACE VALUE OF UNCIRCULATED
P CENTS, D CENTS, AND S CENTS

$10,258

$8,854

$7,742

S Cents

P Cents

D Cents

*Number of Years After Year Minted*

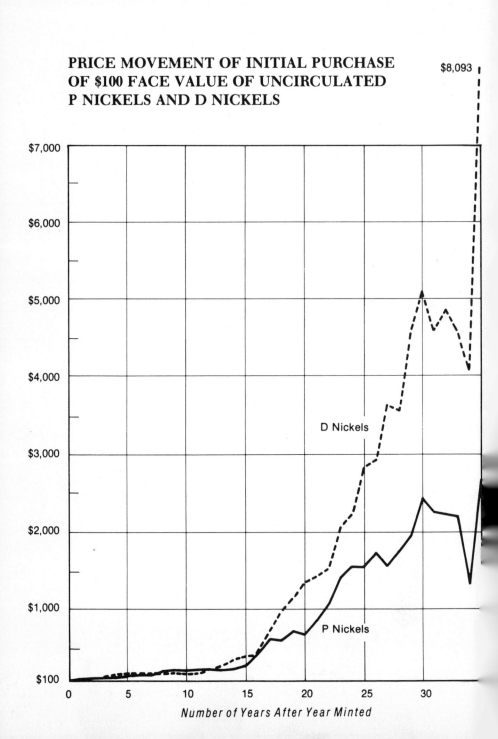

**PRICE MOVEMENT OF INITIAL PURCHASE OF $100 FACE VALUE OF UNCIRCULATED P NICKELS AND D NICKELS**

$8,093

D Nickels

P Nickels

*Number of Years After Year Minted*

## PRICE MOVEMENT OF INITIAL PURCHASE
## OF $100 FACE VALUE OF UNCIRCULATED
## P DIMES AND D DIMES

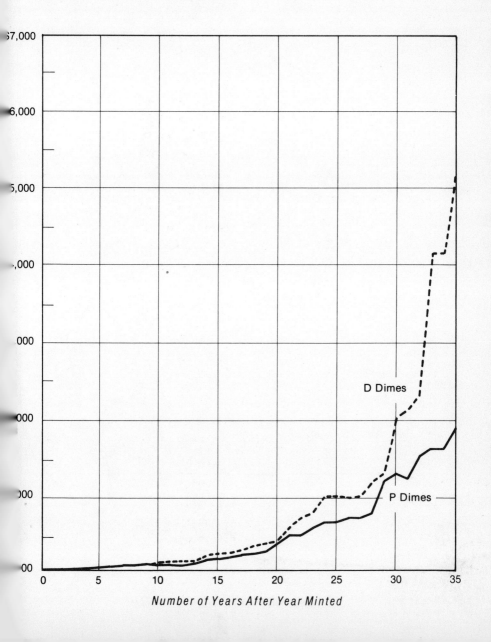

Number of Years After Year Minted

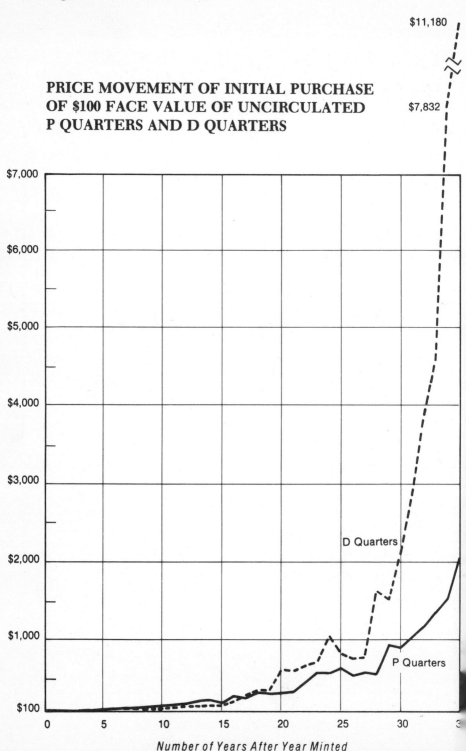

PRICE MOVEMENT OF INITIAL PURCHASE
OF $100 FACE VALUE OF UNCIRCULATED
P QUARTERS AND D QUARTERS

$11,180

$7,832

D Quarters

P Quarters

Number of Years After Year Minted

## PRICE MOVEMENT OF INITIAL PURCHASE
## OF $100 FACE VALUE OF UNCIRCULATED
## P HALF-DOLLARS AND D HALF-DOLLARS

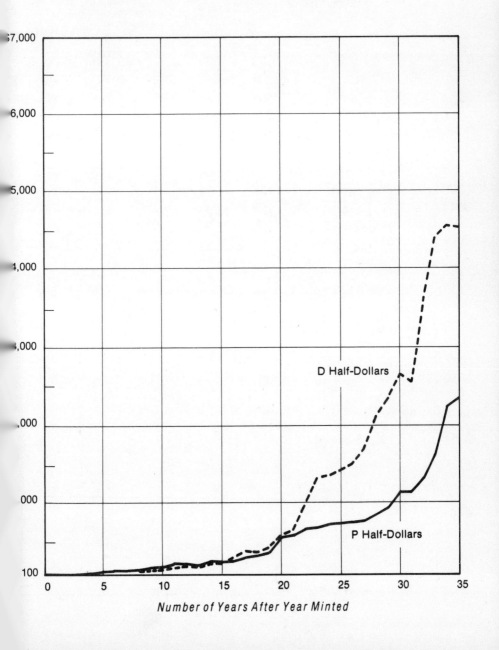

*Number of Years After Year Minted*

These graphs show that $100 invested in coin rolls of each
denomination and mintage (except those that are no longer
minted for general circulation) would have been worth the
following amounts:

| | Number of Years After Year Minted | | | | |
| | 10 | 15 | 20 | 25 | 30 |
|---|---|---|---|---|---|
| P cents | $352 | $ 590 | $1,872 | $2,380 | $2,184 |
| D cents | 208 | 546 | 1,778 | 2,964 | 5,110 |
| S cents | 468 | 1,326 | 2,730 | 5,304 | 6,084 |
| P nickels | 203 | 291 | 695 | 1,577 | 2,418 |
| D nickels | 166 | 415 | 1,349 | 2,822 | 5,084 |
| P dimes | 158 | 233 | 442 | 711 | 1,343 |
| D dimes | 166 | 288 | 474 | 1,027 | 2,054 |
| P quarters | 152 | 219 | 342 | 625 | 931 |
| D quarters | 129 | 190 | 623 | 851 | 2,109 |
| P half-dollars | 171 | 241 | 559 | 732 | 1,102 |
| D half-dollars | 152 | 228 | 570 | 1,444 | 2,687 |

Note that the figures shown above are based on average
prices that dealers were *paying* for such coin rolls. Higher
prices would have been realized if the coins had been sold to
private buyers rather than to dealers.

# Chapter 2

# The Basics

*What disease is so desperate which mony*
*may not medicine?*
*what wound so deadly which coin can not cure?*

GEORGE PETTIE, Petite Pallace

Throughout this book I will be using some terms that are probably unfamiliar to you. Therefore, I have included this chapter to explain certain basic information about coins.

## Rolls of Coins

Standard quantities of the various denomination coins are normally rolled in paper wrappers to make counting and handling easier. Standard coin rolls contain:

| Denomination | Quantity | Face Value |
|---|---|---|
| cents | 50 | $ .50 |
| nickels | 40 | 2.00 |
| dimes | 50 | 5.00 |
| quarters | 40 | 10.00 |
| half-dollars | 20 | 10.00 |

Some coin collectors collect single coins and some collect coin rolls. The term *coin roll* refers to a quantity of coins — not necessarily a paper-wrapped roll. As a matter of fact, many *coin rolls* are really plastic tubes or other holders that contain the quantity of coins that would be included in a paper-wrapped roll.

It is unwise to keep your coins in their original paper wrappers or in most of the plastic tubes or other holders that are widely used because the paper or plastic often creates a chemical reaction that causes damage to the coins over a period of time. Methods of protecting your coins are discussed in detail in Chapter 6.

## Mints and Mint Marks

All U.S. coins are manufactured at one of the three presently operating mints which are located in Philadelphia, Pennsylvania; Denver, Colorado; and San Francisco, California. The Bureau of the Mint distributes coins for general circulation to the more than 6,200 national and state banks that belong to the Federal Reserve System through the facilities of the twelve Federal Reserve Banks. Banks that do not belong to the Federal Reserve System get coins from member banks.

Coins produced at the Philadelphia mint (since 1946) do not have a mint mark, although such coins are usually referred to by the letter *P* (*P* cents, *P* nickels, etc.). Coins produced at the Denver mint carry the letter *D* and those produced at the San Francisco mint carry the letter *S*.

### Location of Mint Marks on Recently Minted Coins

CENTS — on the obverse (head side) of the coin under the date

| NICKELS | — on the obverse of the coin between the date and Jefferson's hair |
|---|---|
| DIMES | — on the obverse of the coin above the date |
| QUARTERS | — on the obverse of the coin at the right of Washington's hair ribbon |
| HALF-DOLLARS | — on the obverse of the coin above the date |

## Condition of Coins

Coins are generally classified as follows:

CHOICE BRILLIANT UNCIRCULATED (CH.BU)
An uncirculated coin that has greater definition and brilliance than average uncirculated coins of the same denomination and mintage.

UNCIRCULATED (UNC) OR BRILLIANT UNCIRCULATED (BU)
New condition. Regular mint striking but never placed in circulation. Coin retains original polish — no scratch marks or imperfections. Older pieces may be tarnished or "toned."

ABOUT UNCIRCULATED (AU)
Nearly new condition. A coin that has had a slight amount of circulation and shows only a trace of wear.

EXTREMELY FINE (EF or XF)
Circulated coin showing slight wear only on the high spots.

VERY FINE (VF)
Noticeable wear on the high spots but most details clearly visible.

FINE (F)
Significant wear on the high spots and some wear on the low spots. A fair amount of detail is visible.

VERY GOOD (VG)
Basic features clear but minimum of detail visible.

GOOD (G)
Basic features outlined and date visible. Rim of coin usually worn down to the tops of letters.

The condition of a coin has a tremendous effect on its value. Generally, an UNCIRCULATED coin is worth from two to ten times as much as the same coin in EXTREMELY FINE condition and as much as *three hundred times* as much as the same coin in GOOD condition.

# Chapter 3

# The Magic of AAPP

*Remember that money is of a prolific generating nature. Money can beget money, and its offspring can beget more.*

BENJAMIN FRANKLIN, *Letters: To My Friend, A.B.*


## Which is More Profitable?

Suppose you could invest $100 for up to twenty years and could have it produce either:

CHOICE A — a total profit of 300% at the end of 20 years; or

CHOICE B — a total profit of 200% at the end of 10 years.

Which would you choose? Choice A, which is a total profit of 300%, sounds great. But, if it takes 20 years to earn a 300% return on your money, you will have only received an average annual profit of 15%. Choice B, which produces a lesser total profit of 200% over a shorter period of time, is the better choice because it produces a higher average annual profit (20%). And, at the end of the 10-year period, your money is again available to reinvest and earn more profits. If, over the second ten years, your original investment and accumulated profits only earn half the percentage of profit that you earned during the first ten years, you will have earned a total profit over the twenty-year period of $500 as compared with only $300 under Choice A.

### Average Annual Profit Percentage

The key to high profits, then, is not the total profit that you receive over a period of years, but the Average Annual Profit that you receive. The higher Average Annual Profit Percentage (AAPP) will *always* produce the greatest profit for you.

I've been talking about annual profit of 20%. Does this seem unattainable? After all, in October 1974 when Pacific Telephone and Telegraph Co. offered notes that yielded only 9.1% annual profit, people nearly came to blows trying to buy them. How, then, can I talk about annual profit of 20%? Well, 20% average annual profit is not only attainable, it is *too low a profit target.* You should be able to realize more than 50% annual profit on your investment — *you should at least double your money every two years!*

Most people are skeptical of claims of such high profits. And they should be! But healthy skepticism should be accompanied by an open mind. Apply *your* open mind to the balance of this chapter. Then *you* decide.

### AAPP Tables

Appendix IV contains AAPP tables of all the coins that were minted in each year from 1935 to 1974 (except S nickels, S dimes, S quarters, and S half-dollars which, on the date this book was written, were no longer minted for general circulation). These tables show the percentage of average annual profit that you would have received on your investment if you had purchased the uncirculated coin rolls in the year minted and had sold any of them up to forty years later. The figures are based on average wholesale prices that dealers were *paying* for the coin rolls in each of those years. You would have received *even more* if you had sold them to private parties at "retail" — more about this in chapter 5.

If you study the AAPP tables you will see that, while the AAPP *usually* increases as the holding period increases, *there are declines in some years.* This fluctuation in the AAPP from year to year is the key to maximizing your profits.

### Seven Rules for High Profits Without Risk

You can earn an average annual profit on your investment of more than 50% a year by following these seven simple steps:

1. Invest as much as you can in rolls of current-year uncirculated coins (see Chapter 4).

2. Protect the coins so that they retain their uncirculated condition (see Chapter 6).

3. Check the coin newspapers once or twice a year and keep a record of the prices that dealers are paying for your coin rolls (see Chapter 4 for names and addresses of the two major coin newspapers). Adjust these prices to "wholesale" by multiplying them by the Wholesale Price Factors shown in Chapter 5.

4. Calculate the Average Annual Profit Percentage that you would receive if you sold your coins at the wholesale price (see Chapter 9).

5. Set a minimum AAPP goal. Suggested minimum goals are:

| | |
|---|---|
| cents | 75% |
| nickels | 50% |
| dimes | 50% |
| quarters | 50% |
| half-dollars | 50% |

You can establish any minimum AAPP goal you wish. But remember — the higher your goal, the longer you must hold your coin rolls to reach it. If you don't mind waiting thirty or forty years (in some instances) to reap the rewards, you might set a minimum AAPP goal of 100% or 200% or more. It's up to you.

6. Keep your coins for at least four years after the date minted (to give the coin-investing public and the dealers a chance to establish values for the coin rolls) and as long thereafter as the AAPP stays below your minimum goal.

7. Do not sell your coins when the AAPP reaches your minimum goal. Continue to hold them until the AAPP dips below the previous year's AAPP (but remains at or above your minimum goal). Then sell. If the AAPP drops below your minimum goal, hold your coins until the AAPP again reaches your minimum goal and continue to hold until it drops below a previously attained high (which is at or above your minimum goal).

## Example No. One:   440% Profit in Eight Years

Let's see if the "Seven Rules" really work. Look at the P nickel table on page 171. Let's follow the progress of the 1956 P nickel. In the fourth year it showed an AAPP of 58 (above our minimum goal of 50). In the fifth year the AAPP dropped to 34 (not only below the previous high of 58, but also below our minimum goal of 50). Therefore, in accordance with Rule Seven, we did not sell. In the sixth year the AAPP dropped further to 25. Then, in the seventh year, the AAPP reached 81 (comfortably above our minimum goal of 50). In the eighth year the AAPP dropped to 55 — below its previous AAPP of 81 but still above our minimum goal of 50. This was the SELL SIGNAL. If you had sold in the eighth year you would have realized an average annual profit of 55% on your investment — that's a total profit over the eight-year holding period of 440%. Or, stated another way, a $100 investment (during 1956) in 1956 P nickels could have been sold eight years later for $540 ($100 return of investment plus $440 profit).

## Example No. Two:   2,088% Profit in Nine Years

Now look at the P cent table on page 159 and follow the progress of the 1952 P cent. In the fourth year it showed an AAPP of 28 — far below our minimum goal of 75. By the sixth year the AAPP had reached 113, surpassing our minimum goal. In the seventh year the AAPP rose to 264 and in the eighth year it rose further to 300. Then, in the ninth year, the AAPP dropped to 232, which was below the previous year's AAPP but still above our minimum goal of 75. This was the SELL SIGNAL. If you had sold in the ninth year you would have realized an average annual profit of 232% on your investment — that's a total profit over the nine-year holding period of 2,088%. A $100 investment (during 1952) in 1952 P cents could have been sold nine years later for $2,188 ($100 return of investment plus $2,088 profit).

**Example No. Three:   28,740% Profit in Fifteen Years**

Let's look at one more. Look at the D nickel table on pages 175 and 176 and follow the progress of the 1950 D nickel. In the fourth year it showed an AAPP of 30 (below our minimum goal of 50). But then it started to move steadily up — from 57 in the fifth year to a remarkable 2,809 in the fourteenth year. In the fifteenth year the AAPP dropped to 1,916, which was below the previous year's AAPP but still above our minimum goal of 50. This was the SELL SIGNAL. If you had sold in the fifteenth year you would have realized an average annual profit of 1,916% on your investment — that's a total profit over the fifteen-year holding period of 28,740%. A $100 investment (during 1950) in 1950 D nickels could have been sold fifteen years later for $28,840 ($100 return of investment plus $28,740 profit).

**Some Coins Are Slow Starters**

Some coins take many years to begin their profit rise. The 1945 P nickel is an example of such a coin. During the first thirteen years after it was minted, the AAPP of the 1945 P nickel fluctuated between 2 and 7 (see tables on pages 171 and 172). In the fourteenth year it suddenly jumped to 73, and in the fifteenth year it rose further to 75. In the sixteenth year the AAPP dropped to 48 (below our minimum goal of 50). But then it started to move up — from 55 in the seventeenth year to 333 in the nineteenth year. In the twentieth year the AAPP dropped to 203. If you had sold your rolls of uncirculated 1945 *P* nickels in the twentieth year you would have realized an average annual profit of 203% on your investment — that's a total profit over the twenty-year holding period of 4,060%.

## Purpose of the Seven Rules

Notice that none of these coin rolls would have been sold at its *highest* AAPP. That is not the purpose of the "Seven Rules". *The purpose of the "Seven Rules" is to prevent you from selling while the value of your coin rolls is increasing and to force you to sell when prices start to fall.*

## Results of Application of the Seven Rules Over a 40 Year Period

The following pages show what would have happened if you had applied the "Seven Rules" to all the coins that were minted between 1935 and 1974 (except S nickels, S dimes, S quarters, and S half-dollars which, on the date this book was written, were no longer minted for general circulation).

The tables show the number of years you would have held each investment, the AAPP at which you would have sold, and the total profit that you would have received *for each $100 invested*. Don't be misled by some of the lower "Total Profit For Each $100 Invested" figures. For example, the 1958 *P* cent, which produced only $834 total profit in six years, was a much better investment than the 1943 *P* cent which produced $1,848 total profit in twenty-two years. The 1958 *P* cent produced $139 profit each year of the six year holding period while the 1943 *P* cent only produced $84 profit each year of its twenty-two year holding period.

# P Cent

## Minimum AAPP Goal: 75%

| Year Minted | Number of Years Held | AAPP Realized | Total Profit for Each $100 Invested |
|---|---|---|---|
| 1935 | 29 | 279% | $8,091 |
| 1936 | 25 | 171% | 4,275 |
| 1937 | 24 | 113% | 2,712 |
| 1938 | 21 | 285% | 5,985 |
| 1939 | 22 | 109% | 2,398 |
| 1940 | 21 | 122% | 2,562 |
| 1941 | 23 | 233% | 5,359 |
| 1942 | 19 | 89% | 1,691 |
| 1943 | 22 | 84% | 1,848 |
| 1944 | Holding at December 31, 1975 | | |
| 1945 | 16 | 101% | 1,616 |
| 1946 | Holding at December 31, 1975 | | |
| 1947 | 14 | 249% | 3,486 |
| 1948 | 13 | 196% | 2,548 |
| 1949 | 12 | 239% | 2,868 |
| 1950 | 11 | 175% | 1,925 |
| 1951 | 9 | 336% | 3,024 |
| 1952 | 9 | 232% | 2,088 |
| 1953 | 8 | 114% | 912 |
| 1954 | 7 | 264% | 1,848 |
| 1955 | 6 | 126% | 756 |
| 1956 | 8 | 105% | 840 |
| 1957 | 7 | 108% | 756 |
| 1958 | 6 | 139% | 834 |
| 1959 | Holding at December 31, 1975 | | |
| 1960 | Holding at December 31, 1975 | | |
| 1961 | Holding at December 31, 1975 | | |
| 1962 | Holding at December 31, 1975 | | |
| 1963 | Holding at December 31, 1975 | | |
| 1964 | Holding at December 31, 1975 | | |
| 1965 | Holding at December 31, 1975 | | |
| 1966 | Holding at December 31, 1975 | | |
| 1967 | Holding at December 31, 1975 | | |
| 1968 | Holding at December 31, 1975 | | |
| 1969 | 6 | 117% | 702 |
| 1970 | Holding at December 31, 1975 | | |
| 1971 | Holding at December 31, 1975 | | |
| 1972 | Holding at December 31, 1975 | | |
| 1973 | Holding at December 31, 1975 | | |
| 1974 | Holding at December 31, 1975 | | |

# D Cent

## Minimum AAPP Goal: 75%

| Year Minted | Number of Years Held | AAPP Realized | Total Profit for Each $100 Invested |
|---|---|---|---|
| 1935 | 25 | 230% | $ 5,750 |
| 1936 | 25 | 171% | 4,275 |
| 1937 | 22 | 109% | 2,398 |
| 1938 | 26 | 806% | 20,956 |
| 1939 | 25 | 1,494% | 37,350 |
| 1940 | 20 | 135% | 2,700 |
| 1941 | 19 | 122% | 2,318 |
| 1942 | 23 | 97% | 2,231 |
| 1943 | 18 | 85% | 1,530 |
| 1944 | Holding at December 31, 1975 | | |
| 1945 | 19 | 159% | 3,021 |
| 1946 | 19 | 122% | 2,318 |
| 1947 | 13 | 118% | 1,534 |
| 1948 | 12 | 141% | 1,692 |
| 1949 | 6 | 81% | 486 |
| 1950 | 11 | 104% | 1,144 |
| 1951 | 10 | 84% | 840 |
| 1952 | 9 | 76% | 684 |
| 1953 | 8 | 85% | 680 |
| 1954 | 7 | 86% | 602 |
| 1955 | 6 | 107% | 642 |
| 1956 | Holding at December 31, 1975 | | |
| 1957 | Holding at December 31, 1975 | | |
| 1958 | Holding at December 31, 1975 | | |
| 1959 | Holding at December 31, 1975 | | |
| 1960 | Holding at December 31, 1975 | | |
| 1961 | Holding at December 31, 1975 | | |
| 1962 | Holding at December 31, 1975 | | |
| 1963 | Holding at December 31, 1975 | | |
| 1964 | Holding at December 31, 1975 | | |
| 1968 | Holding at December 31, 1975 | | |
| 1969 | Holding at December 31, 1975 | | |
| 1970 | Holding at December 31, 1975 | | |
| 1971 | Holding at December 31, 1975 | | |
| 1972 | Holding at December 31, 1975 | | |
| 1973 | Holding at December 31, 1975 | | |
| 1974 | Holding at December 31, 1975 | | |

# S Cent

## Minimum AAPP Goal: 75%

| Year Minted | Number of Years Held | AAPP Realized | Total Profit for Each $100 Invested |
|---|---|---|---|
| 1935 | 29 | 1,072% | $31,088 |
| 1936 | 25 | 246% | 6,150 |
| 1937 | 24 | 155% | 3,720 |
| 1938 | 26 | 1,076% | 27,976 |
| 1939 | 22 | 155% | 3,410 |
| | | | |
| 1940 | 24 | 256% | 6,144 |
| 1941 | 23 | 403% | 9,269 |
| 1942 | 5 | 160% | 800 |
| 1943 | 13 | 88% | 1,144 |
| 1944 | 21 | 125% | 2,625 |
| | | | |
| 1945 | 16 | 82% | 1,312 |
| 1946 | 19 | 97% | 1,843 |
| 1947 | 13 | 148% | 1,924 |
| 1948 | 13 | 232% | 3,016 |
| 1949 | 12 | 414% | 4,968 |
| | | | |
| 1950 | 11 | 246% | 2,706 |
| 1951 | 10 | 458% | 4,580 |
| 1952 | 9 | 318% | 2,862 |
| 1953 | 8 | 212% | 1,696 |
| 1954 | 7 | 142% | 994 |
| | | | |
| 1955 | 9 | 648% | 5,832 |
| 1968 | Holding at December 31, 1975 | | |
| 1969 | Holding at December 31, 1975 | | |
| 1970 | Holding at December 31, 1975 | | |
| 1971 | Holding at December 31, 1975 | | |
| | | | |
| 1972 | Holding at December 31, 1975 | | |
| 1973 | Holding at December 31, 1975 | | |
| 1974 | Holding at December 31, 1975 | | |

77-3574

# P Nickel

## Minimum AAPP Goal: 50%

| Year Minted | Number of Years Held | AAPP Realized | Total Profit for Each $100 Invested |
|---|---|---|---|
| 1935 | 25 | 54% | $1,350 |
| 1936 | 24 | 56% | 1,344 |
| 1937 | 28 | 211% | 5,908 |
| 1938 | 23 | 77% | 1,771 |
| 1939 | 18 | 64% | 1,152 |
| 1940 | Holding | at December 31, | 1975 |
| 1941 | Holding | at December 31, | 1975 |
| *1942 | 20 | 57% | 1,140 |
| **1942 | 19 | 187% | 3,553 |
| 1943 | 22 | 123% | 2,706 |
| 1944 | 17 | 62% | 1,054 |
| 1945 | 20 | 203% | 4,060 |
| 1946 | Holding | at December 31, | 1975 |
| 1947 | Holding | at December 31, | 1975 |
| 1948 | Holding | at December 31, | 1975 |
| 1949 | 12 | 75% | 900 |
| 1950 | 5 | 76% | 380 |
| 1951 | 10 | 56% | 560 |
| 1952 | 9 | 53% | 477 |
| 1953 | 11 | 63% | 693 |
| 1954 | 10 | 52% | 520 |
| 1955 | 6 | 232% | 1,392 |
| 1956 | 8 | 55% | 440 |
| 1957 | 7 | 72% | 504 |
| 1958 | 6 | 239% | 1,434 |
| 1959 | 5 | 96% | 480 |
| 1960 | Holding | at December 31, | 1975 |
| 1961 | Holding | at December 31, | 1975 |
| 1962 | Holding | at December 31, | 1975 |
| 1963 | Holding | at December 31, | 1975 |
| 1964 | Holding | at December 31, | 1975 |
| 1965 | Holding | at December 31, | 1975 |
| 1966 | Holding | at December 31, | 1975 |
| 1967 | Holding | at December 31, | 1975 |
| 1971 | Holding | at December 31, | 1975 |
| 1972 | Holding | at December 31, | 1975 |
| 1973 | Holding | at December 31, | 1975 |
| 1974 | Holding | at December 31, | 1975 |

*Pre-War (made of nickel)
**Wartime alloy

THE OZARKS REGIONAL LIBRARY
217 EAST DICKSON STREET
FAYETTEVILLE, ARK. 72701

# D Nickel

## Minimum AAPP Goal: 50%

| Year Minted | Number of Years Held | AAPP Realized | Total Profit for Each $100 Invested |
|---|---|---|---|
| 1935 | 23 | 86% | $ 1,978 |
| 1936 | 29 | 175% | 5,075 |
| 1937 | 28 | 182% | 5,096 |
| *1938 | 27 | 173% | 4,671 |
| **1938 | 23 | 149% | 3,427 |
| 1939 | 5 | 146% | 730 |
| 1940 | 21 | 69% | 1,449 |
| 1941 | 21 | 60% | 1,260 |
| 1942 | 6 | 260% | 1,560 |
| 1943 | 18 | 82% | 1,476 |
| 1944 | 17 | 62% | 1,054 |
| 1945 | 20 | 120% | 2,400 |
| 1946 | 20 | 62% | 1,240 |
| 1947 | 18 | 75% | 1,350 |
| 1948 | 17 | 122% | 2,074 |
| 1949 | 13 | 63% | 819 |
| 1950 | 15 | 1,916% | 28,740 |
| 1951 | 10 | 135% | 1,350 |
| 1952 | 9 | 335% | 3,015 |
| 1953 | 11 | 63% | 693 |
| 1954 | Holding at December 31, 1975 | | |
| 1955 | 9 | 81% | 729 |
| 1956 | Holding at December 31, 1975 | | |
| 1957 | Holding at December 31, 1975 | | |
| 1958 | Holding at December 31, 1975 | | |
| 1959 | Holding at December 31, 1975 | | |
| 1960 | Holding at December 31, 1975 | | |
| 1961 | Holding at December 31, 1975 | | |
| 1962 | Holding at December 31, 1975 | | |
| 1963 | Holding at December 31, 1975 | | |
| 1964 | Holding at December 31, 1975 | | |
| 1968 | Holding at December 31, 1975 | | |
| 1969 | Holding at December 31, 1975 | | |
| 1970 | Holding at December 31, 1975 | | |
| 1971 | Holding at December 31, 1975 | | |
| 1972 | Holding at December 31, 1975 | | |
| 1973 | Holding at December 31, 1975 | | |
| 1974 | Holding at December 31, 1975 | | |

*Buffalo nickel
**Jefferson nickel

# P Dime

## Minimum AAPP Goal: 50%

| Year Minted | Number of Years Held | AAPP Realized | Total Profit for Each $100 Invested |
|---|---|---|---|
| 1935 | 30 | 57% | $1,710 |
| 1936 | 39 | 80% | 3,120 |
| 1937 | Holding at December 31, 1975 | | |
| 1938 | 32 | 50% | 1,600 |
| 1939 | Holding at December 31, 1975 | | |
| 1940 | Holding at December 31, 1975 | | |
| 1941 | Holding at December 31, 1975 | | |
| 1942 | Holding at December 31, 1975 | | |
| 1943 | Holding at December 31, 1975 | | |
| 1944 | Holding at December 31, 1975 | | |
| 1945 | 30 | 59% | 1,770 |
| 1946 | Holding at December 31, 1975 | | |
| 1947 | 17 | 59% | 1,003 |
| 1948 | 13 | 65% | 845 |
| 1949 | 7 | 51% | 357 |
| 1950 | 6 | 57% | 342 |
| 1951 | 13 | 90% | 1,170 |
| 1952 | Holding at December 31, 1975 | | |
| 1953 | 11 | 70% | 770 |
| 1954 | Holding at December 31, 1975 | | |
| 1955 | 6 | 52% | 312 |
| 1956 | Holding at December 31, 1975 | | |
| 1957 | Holding at December 31, 1975 | | |
| 1958 | 7 | 70% | 490 |
| 1959 | Holding at December 31, 1975 | | |
| 1960 | Holding at December 31, 1975 | | |
| 1961 | Holding at December 31, 1975 | | |
| 1962 | Holding at December 31, 1975 | | |
| 1963 | Holding at December 31, 1975 | | |
| 1964 | Holding at December 31, 1975 | | |
| 1965 | Holding at December 31, 1975 | | |
| 1966 | Holding at December 31, 1975 | | |
| 1967 | Holding at December 31, 1975 | | |
| 1968 | Holding at December 31, 1975 | | |
| 1969 | Holding at December 31, 1975 | | |
| 1970 | Holding at December 31, 1975 | | |
| 1971 | Holding at December 31, 1975 | | |
| 1972 | Holding at December 31, 1975 | | |
| 1973 | Holding at December 31, 1975 | | |
| 1974 | Holding at December 31, 1975 | | |

# D Dime

## Minimum AAPP Goal: 50%

| Year Minted | Number of Years Held | AAPP Realized | Total Profit for Each $100 Invested |
|---|---|---|---|
| 1935 | 31 | 545% | $16,895 |
| 1936 | 30 | 300% | 9,000 |
| 1937 | 25 | 81% | 2,025 |
| 1938 | 28 | 236% | 6,608 |
| 1939 | Holding at December 31, 1975 | | |
| 1940 | 35 | 135% | 4,725 |
| 1941 | 25 | 72% | 1,800 |
| 1942 | Holding at December 31, 1975 | | |
| 1943 | 32 | 60% | 1,920 |
| 1944 | 31 | 62% | 1,922 |
| 1945 | 30 | 65% | 1,950 |
| 1946 | Holding at December 31, 1975 | | |
| 1947 | Holding at December 31, 1975 | | |
| 1948 | 17 | 50% | 850 |
| 1949 | 13 | 59% | 767 |
| 1950 | 21 | 62% | 1,302 |
| 1951 | Holding at December 31, 1975 | | |
| 1952 | Holding at December 31, 1975 | | |
| 1953 | Holding at December 31, 1975 | | |
| 1954 | Holding at December 31, 1975 | | |
| 1955 | 10 | 93% | 930 |
| 1956 | Holding at December 31, 1975 | | |
| 1957 | Holding at December 31, 1975 | | |
| 1958 | Holding at December 31, 1975 | | |
| 1959 | Holding at December 31, 1975 | | |
| 1960 | Holding at December 31, 1975 | | |
| 1961 | Holding at December 31, 1975 | | |
| 1962 | Holding at December 31, 1975 | | |
| 1963 | Holding at December 31, 1975 | | |
| 1964 | Holding at December 31, 1975 | | |
| 1968 | Holding at December 31, 1975 | | |
| 1969 | Holding at December 31, 1975 | | |
| 1970 | Holding at December 31, 1975 | | |
| 1971 | Holding at December 31, 1975 | | |
| 1972 | Holding at December 31, 1975 | | |
| 1973 | Holding at December 31, 1975 | | |
| 1974 | Holding at December 31, 1975 | | |

# P Quarter

## Minimum AAPP Goal: 50%

| Year Minted | Number of Years Held | AAPP Realized | Total Profit for Each $100 Invested |
|---|---|---|---|
| 1935 | 30 | 60% | $1,800 |
| 1936 | 30 | 66% | 1,980 |
| 1937 | 24 | 51% | 1,224 |
| 1938 | 22 | 182% | 4,004 |
| 1939 | 25 | 66% | 1,650 |
| 1940 | 25 | 78% | 1,950 |
| 1941 | Holding | at December 31, | 1975 |
| 1942 | Holding | at December 31, | 1975 |
| 1943 | Holding | at December 31, | 1975 |
| 1944 | Holding | at December 31, | 1975 |
| 1945 | Holding | at December 31, | 1975 |
| 1946 | Holding | at December 31, | 1975 |
| 1947 | Holding | at December 31, | 1975 |
| 1948 | Holding | at December 31, | 1975 |
| 1949 | 16 | 229% | 3,664 |
| 1950 | Holding | at December 31, | 1975 |
| 1951 | Holding | at December 31, | 1975 |
| 1952 | Holding | at December 31, | 1975 |
| 1953 | 11 | 50% | 550 |
| 1954 | Holding | at December 31, | 1975 |
| 1955 | Holding | at December 31, | 1975 |
| 1956 | Holding | at December 31, | 1975 |
| 1957 | Holding | at December 31, | 1975 |
| 1958 | 7 | 54% | 378 |
| 1959 | Holding | at December 31, | 1975 |
| 1960 | Holding | at December 31, | 1975 |
| 1961 | Holding | at December 31, | 1975 |
| 1962 | Holding | at December 31, | 1975 |
| 1963 | Holding | at December 31, | 1975 |
| 1964 | Holding | at December 31, | 1975 |
| 1965 | Holding | at December 31, | 1975 |
| 1966 | Holding | at December 31, | 1975 |
| 1967 | Holding | at December 31, | 1975 |
| 1968 | Holding | at December 31, | 1975 |
| 1969 | Holding | at December 31, | 1975 |
| 1970 | Holding | at December 31, | 1975 |
| 1971 | Holding | at December 31, | 1975 |
| 1972 | Holding | at December 31, | 1975 |
| 1973 | Holding | at December 31, | 1975 |
| 1974 | Holding | at December 31, | 1975 |

# D Quarter

## Minimum AAPP Goal: 50%

| Year Minted | Number of Years Held | AAPP Realized | Total Profit for Each $100 Invested |
|---|---|---|---|
| 1935 | 30 | 155% | $ 4,650 |
| 1936 | 29 | 2,041% | 59,189 |
| 1937 | 28 | 87% | 2,436 |
| 1939 | 27 | 85% | 2,295 |
| 1940 | 26 | 435% | 11,310 |
| 1941 | 24 | 50% | 1,200 |
| 1942 | 33 | 89% | 2,937 |
| 1943 | 32 | 67% | 2,144 |
| 1944 | Holding | at December 31, | 1975 |
| 1945 | Holding | at December 31, | 1975 |
| 1946 | Holding | at December 31, | 1975 |
| 1947 | Holding | at December 31, | 1975 |
| 1948 | Holding | at December 31, | 1975 |
| 1949 | 26 | 55% | 1,430 |
| 1950 | Holding | at December 31, | 1975 |
| 1951 | Holding | at December 31, | 1975 |
| 1952 | Holding | at December 31, | 1975 |
| 1953 | Holding | at December 31, | 1975 |
| 1954 | Holding | at December 31, | 1975 |
| 1955 | 9 | 124% | 1,116 |
| 1956 | Holding | at December 31, | 1975 |
| 1957 | Holding | at December 31, | 1975 |
| 1958 | Holding | at December 31, | 1975 |
| 1959 | Holding | at December 31, | 1975 |
| 1960 | Holding | at December 31, | 1975 |
| 1961 | Holding | at December 31, | 1975 |
| 1962 | Holding | at December 31, | 1975 |
| 1963 | Holding | at December 31, | 1975 |
| 1964 | Holding | at December 31, | 1975 |
| 1968 | Holding | at December 31, | 1975 |
| 1969 | Holding | at December 31, | 1975 |
| 1970 | Holding | at December 31, | 1975 |
| 1971 | Holding | at December 31, | 1975 |
| 1972 | Holding | at December 31, | 1975 |
| 1973 | Holding | at December 31, | 1975 |
| 1974 | Holding | at December 31, | 1975 |

# P Half-Dollar

## Minimum AAPP Goal: 50%

| Year Minted | Number of Years Held | AAPP Realized | Total Profit for Each $100 Invested |
|---|---|---|---|
| 1935 | 40 | 78% | $3,120 |
| 1936 | 38 | 76% | 2,888 |
| 1937 | 38 | 79% | 3,002 |
| 1938 | 28 | 119% | 3,332 |
| 1939 | Holding at December 31, 1975 | | |
| 1940 | Holding at December 31, 1975 | | |
| 1941 | 34 | 64% | 2,176 |
| 1942 | 33 | 60% | 1,980 |
| 1943 | 32 | 60% | 1,920 |
| 1944 | Holding at December 31, 1975 | | |
| 1945 | 30 | 64% | 1,920 |
| 1946 | 29 | 80% | 2,320 |
| 1947 | 23 | 52% | 1,196 |
| 1948 | 17 | 77% | 1,309 |
| 1949 | 7 | 67% | 469 |
| 1950 | 15 | 125% | 1,875 |
| 1951 | 24 | 57% | 1,368 |
| 1952 | Holding at December 31, 1975 | | |
| 1953 | 12 | 134% | 1,608 |
| 1954 | Holding at December 31, 1975 | | |
| 1955 | 11 | 100% | 1,100 |
| 1956 | Holding at December 31, 1975 | | |
| 1957 | Holding at December 31, 1975 | | |
| 1958 | Holding at December 31, 1975 | | |
| 1959 | Holding at December 31, 1975 | | |
| 1960 | Holding at December 31, 1975 | | |
| 1961 | Holding at December 31, 1975 | | |
| 1962 | Holding at December 31, 1975 | | |
| 1963 | Holding at December 31, 1975 | | |
| 1964 | Holding at December 31, 1975 | | |
| 1965 | Holding at December 31, 1975 | | |
| 1966 | Holding at December 31, 1975 | | |
| 1967 | Holding at December 31, 1975 | | |
| 1971 | Holding at December 31, 1975 | | |
| 1972 | Holding at December 31, 1975 | | |
| 1973 | Holding at December 31, 1975 | | |
| 1974 | Holding at December 31, 1975 | | |

# D Half-Dollar

## Minimum AAPP Goal: 50%

| Year Minted | Number of Years Held | AAPP Realized | Total Profit for Each $100 Invested |
|---|---|---|---|
| 1935 | 25 | 105% | $2,625 |
| 1936 | 30 | 60% | 1,800 |
| 1937 | 23 | 95% | 2,185 |
| 1938 | 11 | 74% | 814 |
| 1939 | Holding | at December 31, | 1975 |
| | | | |
| 1941 | 25 | 63% | 1,575 |
| 1942 | 24 | 64% | 1,536 |
| 1943 | 27 | 55% | 1,485 |
| 1944 | Holding | at December 31, | 1975 |
| 1945 | 29 | 94% | 2,726 |
| | | | |
| 1946 | 20 | 71% | 1,420 |
| 1947 | 27 | 109% | 2,943 |
| 1948 | Holding | at December 31, | 1975 |
| 1949 | 16 | 86% | 1,376 |
| 1950 | 15 | 82% | 1,230 |
| | | | |
| 1951 | 14 | 80% | 1,120 |
| 1952 | Holding | at December 31, | 1975 |
| 1953 | Holding | at December 31, | 1975 |
| 1954 | Holding | at December 31, | 1975 |
| 1957 | Holding | at December 31, | 1975 |
| | | | |
| 1958 | Holding | at December 31, | 1975 |
| 1959 | Holding | at December 31, | 1975 |
| 1960 | Holding | at December 31, | 1975 |
| 1961 | Holding | at December 31, | 1975 |
| 1962 | Holding | at December 31, | 1975 |
| | | | |
| 1963 | Holding | at December 31, | 1975 |
| 1964 | Holding | at December 31, | 1975 |
| 1968 | Holding | at December 31, | 1975 |
| 1969 | Holding | at December 31, | 1975 |
| 1970 | 5 | 451% | 2,255 |
| | | | |
| 1971 | Holding | at December 31, | 1975 |
| 1972 | Holding | at December 31, | 1975 |
| 1973 | Holding | at December 31, | 1975 |
| 1974 | Holding | at December 31, | 1975 |

## Actual Profits Always Exceed AAPP Goal

These tables illustrate an important principle of the "Seven Rules": *The minimum AAPP goal is a tool to produce profits substantially higher than the minimum goal itself.* The tables show that minimum AAPP goals of 75% on cents and 50% on nickels, dimes, quarters, and half-dollars produced *median*[1] average annual profits of:

139% on *P* cents
114% on *D* cents
232% on *S* cents
72% on *P* nickels
120% on *D* nickels
59% on *P* dimes
72% on *D* dimes
66% on *P* quarters
88% on *D* quarters
77% on *P* half-dollars
81% on *D* half-dollars

## Cents and Nickels are Most Profitable

The tables also show *which* coins produced the most profits. If you had invested in rolls of all coins minted each year between 1935 and 1974 (except *S* nickels, *S* dimes, *S* quarters, and *S* half-dollars) and had followed the "Seven Rules", you would have sold your coin investments as follows:

---

[1]The median is the middle amount. For example, the median average annual profit realized on *D* nickels was 120%. That is, of the 21 different coin rolls analyzed, 10 produced average annual profits below 120% and 10 produced average annual profits above 120%.

| Coin | Number of Years in Which the Coins Were Minted | Number of Years' Mintage Sold | Years' Mintage Sold as a Percentage of Total |
|------|------|------|------|
| S cents | 28 | 21 | 75% |
| P cents | 40 | 22 | 55% |
| P nickels | 38 | 21 | 55% |
| D nickels | 38 | 21 | 55% |
| D cents | 37 | 20 | 54% |
| P half-dollars | 37 | 16 | 43% |
| D half-dollars | 34 | 14 | 41% |
| D dimes | 37 | 13 | 35% |
| P dimes | 40 | 12 | 30% |
| D quarters | 36 | 10 | 28% |
| P quarters | 40 | 9 | 23% |

Although you can, of course, invest in any denomination of uncirculated coin rolls, the two analyses shown above indicate that cents and nickels produce significantly higher profits than dimes, quarters, or half-dollars.

# Chapter 4

# Buying Uncirculated Coin Rolls

*The fact is, in my opinion, that we often*
*buy money very much too dear.*

WILLIAM M. THACKERAY: Barry Lyndon XIII

## Where to Buy

There are many places to "buy" uncirculated coin rolls. Coin dealers are always happy to sell them to you at a substantial premium over face value. If you are in a hurry — and want to gamble — you might consider buying rolls of older uncirculated coins. But if you do you will be speculating — not investing. And you could lose a large part of your investment because *prices of coins go down as well as up!*

Look at the Retail Price Tables in Appendix I. Suppose you had bought rolls of 1935 *P* cents or 1939 *D* cents or 1955 *P* nickels in 1963 (28, 24, and 8 years respectively after the year minted)? Or suppose you had bought rolls of 1939 *D* nickels or 1953 *S* cents or 1954 *P* cents in 1964 (25, 11, and 10 years respectively after the year minted)? Your investment would be worth substantially less than you paid for it!

However, if you are willing to hold your coin rolls over a long period of time and watch them increase in value, the best place to get them is from a bank. *This is the only way you can invest in coins with absolutely no risk.*

## How to Buy

Neither the Mint nor the Federal Reserve Banks will supply uncirculated coins to you. The only place you can get them at face value is from a commercial or savings bank — the same place where coin dealers get them. Banks sometimes consider coin collectors a nuisance and refuse to make coins available to them. But you can get all the current-year uncirculated coin rolls you want if you follow a few basic rules:

1. Open a checking or savings account in the main office of each of several banks. Be sure to use the largest banks in town and the main office of each because, when the Federal Reserve Bank cuts back on coin shipments (as they do from time to time), the largest banks get the uncirculated coins. And, although many branches of even the largest banks sometimes have difficulty getting uncirculated coins, customers of the main office are usually able to get all the uncirculated coins they want.

2. Become known to one teller at each bank. Go in at least once a week and transact some business with that teller.

3. After several weeks, ask the teller at each bank for the coin rolls that you want. If he doesn't have them, ask him to put them aside for you when he gets some (the bank usually gets coin shipments from the Federal Reserve Bank every week or so).

4. Remind each teller of your request when you come in each week.

5. If you develop a good relationship with the tellers they will usually go out of their way to make sure you get the coin rolls you want. They'll even ask other branches to send them rolls of uncirculated coins for you.

6. A small Christmas gift will show the teller you appreciate his efforts (and will assure you of getting all the uncirculated coins you want — even when other collectors are having trouble getting any).

7. Remember, if you are a borrower or depositor, your business is important to the bank, and the teller will go out of his way to keep you happy.

Coins are shipped to commercial and savings banks by the Federal Reserve Bank in convenient cartons. Twenty-five dollars worth of cents (50 rolls) are shipped in a carton measuring 10″ x 4″ x 4″. One hundred dollars worth of nickels (50 rolls) are shipped in a carton measuring 10″ x 4½″ x 4″. It's a good idea to buy your coins in these quantities because:

- it is easier for the teller to give you a sealed carton of coins than for him to gather loose rolls from various places (and it's easier for you to carry, too)

- you will have a carton that is useful later for shipping the coins

## When to Buy

You can buy coins any time, of course, but the best time to buy them is during late January and early February of each year because:

- Bank activity is usually slow after the hectic Christmas rush. Therefore, bank tellers are more likely to go out of their way to get uncirculated coins for you.

- Demand for coins is high during the Christmas season but, after the holidays, new shipments of coins come in to replace the Christmas drain. Since demand is slow in January and February, the banks are usually happy to "sell" the coins to you.

- You will be getting the first coins minted with the new year's date. Sometimes the Mints make errors at the beginning of a new year's production which they usually discover and correct in later production runs. These *special* coins always increase in value much more rapidly than the *ordinary* coins. And occasionally the Mint curtails production of a particular coin during the year, resulting in a smaller supply of that coin than coin collectors had anticipated. This always increases the demand for the coin and its value to collectors.

### How to Obtain Coins Produced by Other Mints

Your bank only receives uncirculated coins from the Mint that serves your area. How, then, do you get uncirculated coin rolls produced by the other Mints?

You could buy them from dealers — at a premium. Many dealers charge as much as two to three times face value for uncirculated coins of the *current* year.

Or you could get the coins you want by trading. Remember, there are thousands of people all over the country just like you who are unwilling to pay a dealer two or three times face value for current-year uncirculated coins. And, like you, the banks with which these people deal are only able to get uncirculated coins from the Mint that serves their area.

**Trading Coin Rolls**

Here are the three simple steps to successful coin trading:

1. Determine how many coin rolls you want that were produced by Mints other than the one serving your area.

2. Buy this quantity of coin rolls from your local banks.

3. Place an advertisement in the classified section of one of the coin newspapers offering to trade your uncirculated coin rolls for an equal quantity of uncirculated coin rolls that have the desired mint mark.

The two major coin newspapers are:

Coin World
911 Vandemark Road
P.O. Box 150
Sidney, Ohio 45365

and

Numismatic News Weekly
Krause Publications, Inc.
Iola, Wisconsin 54945

*Coin World* has a classified section called FOR TRADE and *Numismatic News Weekly* has a smaller classified section called U.S. FOR TRADE. On the date this book was written they each charged less than $4 to run an advertisement of 30 words or less in one weekly issue.

The following is a suggested form of advertisement that will bring you the results you want:

> TRADE up to 100 my BU rolls
> 1976 P cents for like quantity your
> BU rolls 1976 D cents. Pay own
> postage. Write first. Jones, 1234
> Cedar Street, Pittsburgh, PA. 89765

Be sure your advertisement says *write first* so that you won't be swamped with more coins than you can handle.

There's always a chance that someone will keep the coins you send him and not send you his coins in return. But since you're dealing with current-year coins which, even in the quantity that you will be sending, have a relatively low value, your chances of being "ripped off" are minimal. Also, remember that you are dealing with collectors like yourself — and most coin collectors (unlike *some* coin dealers) are scrupulously honest. Nevertheless, if you don't want to take *any* chances, you can insist that the person responding to your advertisement send his coins to you first.

After you've completed two or three successful trades, you will probably establish a continuing trading arrangement with several collectors in other parts of the country and, thereafter, you will be assured of a continuous supply of coins from other Mints.

# Chapter 5

# Selling Your Coins

*Selling can never be reduced to an exact*
*science any more than medicine can be*
*reduced to an exact science, but it is*
*amazing how many things about selling can*
*be measured and forecast.*

FRANK BETTGER

The age-old goal of all investors is to buy low and sell high. In Chapter 4, I showed you how to buy low (you can't buy 100 pennies for less than $1.00). How about selling high?

## Retail Prices of Uncirculated Coin Rolls

The two major coin newspapers, *Coin World* and *Numismatic News Weekly,* are your best source of information about the value of your coin rolls (see page 65 for addresses). Each issue contains advertisements by dealers offering to sell uncirculated coin rolls. The prices in these advertisements are retail prices. Since they include the dealer's costs and profit, he obviously won't *buy* them from you for these prices. But the dealer's prices are your guide to the wholesale value of your coin rolls — the price that you should be able to get when you sell them.

### How to Calculate the Wholesale Price of Your Coin Rolls

By comparing dealer retail prices with dealer wholesale prices over the years, I have developed the following *Wholesale Price Factors* which you can apply to advertised retail prices of uncirculated coin rolls to arrive at average wholesale prices:

| Coin Roll | Wholesale Price Factor |
|---|---|
| cents | 78% |
| nickels | 83% |
| dimes | 79% |
| quarters | 76% |
| half-dollars | 76% |

### Dealer Advertisements

Reproduced on the following pages are two dealer "sell" advertisements from the October 8, 1975 issue of *Coin World:*

# BRILLIANT UNCIRCULATED ROLLS

## CENTS

| | |
|---|---|
| 1936-P | 26.00 |
| 1936-D | 32.00 |
| 1936-S | 35.00 |
| 1937-P | 16.00 |
| 1937-D | WTD |
| 1937-S | 35.00 |
| 1938-P | 33.00 |
| 1938-D | 42.50 |
| 1938-S | 70.00 |
| 1939-P | 20.00 |
| 1939-D | WTD |
| 1939-S | 38.00 |
| 1940-P | 19.00 |
| 1940-D | WTD |
| 1940-S | 20.00 |
| 1941-P | 15.00 |
| 1941-D | 58.00 |
| 1941-S | 75.00 |
| 1942-P-D ea. | 9.75 |
| 1942-S | WTD |
| 1943-P | 15.00 |
| 1943-D | 27.00 |
| 1943-S | 56.00 |
| 1944-P | 6.00 |
| 1944-D | 7.50 |
| 1944-S | 10.00 |
| 1945-P | 7.00 |
| 1945-D | 12.00 |
| 1945-S | 11.00 |
| 1946-P | 7.00 |
| 1946-D | 5.50 |
| 1946-S | 18.00 |
| 1947-P | 14.50 |
| 1947-D | 8.75 |
| 1947-S | 15.50 |
| 1948-P | 10.00 |
| 1948-D | 7.50 |
| 1948-S | 16.00 |
| 1949-P | 16.00 |
| 1949-D | 16.00 |
| 1949-S | 36.00 |
| 1950-P | 11.00 |
| 1950-D | 6.00 |
| 1950-S | 13.00 |
| 1951-P | 42.00 |
| 1951-D | 4.75 |
| 1951-S | 24.00 |
| 1952-P | 19.00 |
| 1952-D | 3.50 |
| 1952-S | 23.00 |
| 1953-P | 3.75 |
| 1953-D | 3.50 |
| 1953-S | 11.50 |
| 1954-P | 11.00 |
| 1954-D | 4.25 |
| 1954-S | 5.50 |
| 1955-P | 3.00 |
| 1955-D | 2.75 |
| 1955-S | 12.75 |
| 1956-P | 3.75 |
| 1956-D | 3.00 |

## CENTS

| | |
|---|---|
| 1957-P | 2.50 |
| 1957-D | 2.00 |
| 1958-P | 2.00 |
| 1958-D | 1.75 |
| 1959-P-D ea. | 1.00 |
| 1960-P-D ea. | 1.00 |
| 1961-P-D ea. | 1.00 |
| 1962-P-D ea. | 1.00 |
| 1963-P-D ea. | 1.00 |
| 1964-P-D ea. | 1.00 |
| 1965-P-D ea. | 2.50 |
| 1967-8 ea. | 3.00 |
| 1968-D-S ea. | 1.25 |
| 1969-P | 5.00 |
| 1969-D-S ea. | 1.25 |
| 1970-P | 2.75 |
| 1970-D | 2.00 |
| 1971-P-D ea. | 1.60 |
| 1971-S | 2.00 |
| 1972-P-S ea. | 1.25 |
| 1973-P-D-S ea. | 1.00 |
| 1974-P-D ea. | 1.00 |
| 1974-S | 2.50 |

## NICKELS

| | |
|---|---|
| 1939-P | 33.00 |
| 1940-P | 24.00 |
| 1940-D | 38.00 |
| 1940-S | 43.00 |
| 1941-P | 20.00 |
| 1941-D | 30.00 |
| 1941-S | 38.00 |
| 1942-P | 53.00 |
| 1942-P Ty. 2 | WTD |
| 1942-D | WTD |
| 1942-S | 140.00 |
| 1943-P | 50.00 |
| 1943-D | 79.00 |
| 1943-S | 57.00 |
| 1944-P-D-S | WTD |
| 1945-P | 60.00 |
| 1945-D | 45.00 |
| 1945-S | 43.00 |
| 1946-P | 9.50 |
| 1946-D | 15.00 |
| 1946-S | 18.50 |
| 1947-P | 8.00 |
| 1947-D | 18.00 |
| 1947-S | 21.00 |
| 1948-P | 10.00 |
| 1948-D | 22.00 |
| 1948-S | 32.00 |
| 1949-P | 18.00 |
| 1949-D | 28.00 |
| 1949-S | 67.50 |
| 1950-P | 39.00 |
| 1950-D | WTD |
| 1951-P | 22.00 |
| 1951-S | 80.00 |
| 1952-P | 11.00 |
| 1952-D | 46.00 |
| 1952-S | 15.50 |

## NICKELS

| | |
|---|---|
| 1953-P | 5.50 |
| 1953-D | 7.50 |
| 1953-S | 10.50 |
| 1954-P | WTD |
| 1954-D | 5.25 |
| 1954-S | 5.75 |
| 1955-P | 21.00 |
| 1955-D | 6.25 |
| 1956-P-D | 4.00 |
| 1957-P-D | 4.50 |
| 1958-P | 6.00 |
| 1958-D | 4.50 |
| 1959-P-D ea. | 3.50 |
| 1960-P-D ea. | 3.50 |
| 1961-P-D ea. | 3.50 |
| 1962-P-D ea. | 3.50 |
| 1963-P-D ea. | 3.50 |
| 1964-P-D ea. | 3.50 |
| 1965-6 ea. | 4.00 |
| 1967 | 4.50 |
| 1968-D-S ea. | 4.00 |
| 1969-D-S ea. | 4.00 |
| 1970-D-S ea. | 4.00 |
| 1971-P | WTD |
| 1971-D | 4.00 |
| 1972-P | 4.50 |
| 1972-D | 4.00 |
| 1973-P-D | 4.00 |

## DIMES

| | |
|---|---|
| 1935-P | 400.00 |
| 1937-P | 225.00 |
| 1938-P | 350.00 |
| 1940-S | 240.00 |
| 1942-P | 119.00 |
| 1942-S | 250.00 |
| 1943-P | 119.00 |
| 1943-D | 125.00 |
| 1944-P | 119.00 |
| 1944-D | 130.00 |
| 1944-S | 135.00 |
| 1945-P | 119.00 |
| 1945-D | 130.00 |
| 1945-S | 130.00 |
| 1946-P | 28.00 |
| 1946-D | 32.00 |
| 1946-S | 39.00 |
| 1947-P | 32.50 |
| 1947-D | 49.00 |
| 1947-S | 39.00 |
| 1948-P | 79.00 |
| 1948-D | 48.00 |
| 1948-S | 56.00 |
| 1949-P | WTD |
| 1949-D | 230.00 |
| 1949-S | WTD |
| 1950-P | WTD |
| 1950-D | 49.00 |
| 1951-P | 48.00 |
| 1951-D | 34.00 |
| 1951-S | WTD |
| 1952-P | 29.50 |

## DIMES

| | |
|---|---|
| 1952-D | 35.00 |
| 1952-S | 95.00 |
| 1953-P | 31.00 |
| 1953-D | 24.50 |
| 1953-S | 28.00 |
| 1954-P-D ea. | 25.00 |
| 1954-S | 27.50 |
| 1955-P | 55.00 |
| 1955-D | 30.00 |
| 1955-S | 27.00 |
| 1956-P-D ea. | 21.00 |
| 1957-P | 21.00 |
| 1957-D | 23.00 |
| 1958-P | 25.00 |
| 1958-D | 20.00 |
| 1959-P-D ea. | 20.00 |
| 1960-P-S ea. | 20.00 |
| 1961-P-D ea. | 20.00 |
| 1962-P-D ea. | 20.00 |
| 1963-P-D ea. | 20.00 |
| 1964-P-D ea. | 20.00 |
| 1965-6-7 ea. | 10.00 |
| 1968-P-D ea. | 10.00 |
| 1969-P-D ea. | 10.00 |
| 1970-P-D ea. | 10.00 |
| 1971-P-D ea. | 10.00 |
| 1972-P-D ea. | 10.00 |
| 1973-P-D ea. | 8.00 |
| 1974-P-D ea. | 8.00 |

## QUARTERS

| | |
|---|---|
| 1935-P | 600.00 |
| 1939-P | 375.00 |
| 1941-P | 180.00 |
| 1942-P | 145.00 |
| 1943-P | 120.00 |
| 1944-P | 59.00 |
| 1944-D-S | WTD |
| 1945-P-D-S | WTD |
| 1946-P | 58.00 |
| 1946-D | WTD |
| 1946-S | 115.00 |
| 1947-P-D | WTD |
| 1947-S | 115.00 |
| 1948 | 64.00 |
| 1948-D | 80.00 |
| 1948-S | 72.00 |
| 1949-P | 490.00 |
| 1949-D | WTD |
| 1950-P | 85.00 |
| 1950-D | WTD |
| 1950-S | 195.00 |
| 1951-P | 65.00 |
| 1951-D | WTD |
| 1951-S | WTD |
| 1952-P | 70.00 |
| 1952-D | 48.00 |
| 1952-S | 115.00 |
| 1953-P | WTD |
| 1953-D | 47.00 |
| 1953-S | 87.00 |

## QUARTERS

| | |
|---|---|
| 1954-P | 44.00 |
| 1954-D | WTD |
| 1954-S | WTD |
| 1955-P | 46.00 |
| 1955-D | 119.00 |
| 1956-P-D ea. | 40.00 |
| 1957-P-D ea. | 40.00 |
| 1958-P | 50.00 |
| 1958-D | 40.00 |
| 1959-P-D ea. | 40.00 |
| 1960-P-D ea. | 40.00 |
| 1961-P-D ea. | 40.00 |
| 1962-P-D ea. | 40.00 |
| 1963-P-D ea. | 40.00 |
| 1964-P-D ea. | 40.00 |
| 1965-6-7 ea. | 18.00 |
| 1968-P | 17.00 |
| 1968-D | 21.00 |
| 1969-P | 17.00 |
| 1969-D | 24.00 |
| 1970-P-D ea. | 16.00 |
| 1971-P-D ea. | 16.00 |
| 1972-P-D ea. | 16.00 |
| 1973-D | 15.00 |

## HALF-DOLLARS

| | |
|---|---|
| 1936-P | 495.00 |
| 1940-P | 460.00 |
| 1942-P | 275.00 |
| 1948-D | 140.00 |
| 1949-P | 510.00 |
| 1950-D | 250.00 |
| 1951-P | 210.00 |
| 1951-D | 375.00 |
| 1951-S | 240.00 |
| 1952-PDS | WTD |
| 1953-P | WTD |
| 1953-D | 68.00 |
| 1953-S | 150.00 |
| 1954-P | 56.00 |
| 1954-D | 49.00 |
| 1954-S | 72.00 |
| 1955-P | 140.00 |
| 1956-P | 59.00 |
| 1957-P | 59.00 |
| 1957-D | 49.00 |
| 1958-P | 57.00 |
| 1958-D | 47.00 |
| 1959-P-D ea. | 48.00 |
| 1960-P-D ea. | 44.00 |
| 1961-P | 44.00 |
| 1961-D | WTD |
| 1962-P-D ea. | 43.00 |
| 1963-P-D ea. | 43.00 |
| 1964-P-D ea. | 40.00 |
| 1965-6 | 20.00 |
| 1967 | 19.00 |
| 1968-D | 18.00 |
| 1969-D | 18.00 |
| 1971-P | 18.00 |
| 1973-D | 15.00 |

M & S HIRSCHHORN Inc.

A.N.A. 17211 — MAIL ORDER ONLY
Telephone 516-LY3-3353

Hirschhorn Bldg., 255 Broadway          Lynbrook, L.I., N.Y. 11563

## CH. BU LINCOLN CENT ROLLS

| Year | Price | Year | Price |
|---|---|---|---|
| 1940 | 18.00 | 1962 | .90 |
| 1942-D | 8.25 | 1962-D | .90 |
| 1944-D | 7.50 | 1963 | .90 |
| 1947-S | 16.50 | 1963-D | .90 |
| 1950 | 11.50 | 1964 | .90 |
| 1950-D | 5.90 | 1964-D | .90 |
| 1951-D | 4.75 | 1965 | 2.50 |
| 1952 | 19.00 | 1966 | 2.60 |
| 1953-D | 3.50 | 1967 | 2.85 |
| 1953-S | 11.50 | 1968 | 2.85 |
| 1954 | 11.75 | 1968-D | 1.05 |
| 1954-D | 4.25 | 1968-S | 1.00 |
| 1954-S | 5.25 | 1969 | 5.25 |
| 1955 | 2.50 | 1969-D | .95 |
| 1955-D | 2.35 | 1969-S | 1.30 |
| 1955-S | 12.75 | 1970 | 2.65 |
| 1956 | 3.75 | 1970-D | 1.80 |
| 1956-D | 2.10 | 1970-S | 1.65 |
| 1957 | 2.50 | 1971 | 1.65 |
| 1957-D | 1.80 | 1971-D | 1.45 |
| 1958 | 1.95 | 1971-S | 1.90 |
| 1958-D | 1.55 | 1972 | .90 |
| 1959 | .90 | 1972-D | 1.30 |
| 1959-D | .90 | 1972-S | .95 |
| 1960 | .90 | 1973 | .90 |
| 1960 SD | 105.00 | 1973-D | .90 |
| 1960-D | .90 | 1973-S | .95 |
| 1960-D SD | 2.50 | 1974 | .90 |
| 1961 | .90 | 1974-D | .90 |
| 1961-D | .90 | 1974-S | 2.10 |
| | | 1975 | .90 |
| | | 1975-D | .90 |

## MORE CH. BU LINCOLN CENT ROLLS

| Year | Price | Year | Price |
|---|---|---|---|
| 1934 | 59.00 | 1941-S | 83.00 |
| 1934-D | 580.00 | 1942 | 11.00 |
| 1935 | 29.00 | 1942-S | 125.00 |
| 1935-D | 41.00 | 1943 | 15.50 |
| 1935-S | 167.00 | 1943-D | 25.00 |
| 1936 | 29.00 | 1943-S | 57.50 |
| 1936-D | 34.00 | 1944 | 6.90 |
| 1936-S | 40.00 | 1944-S | 11.00 |
| 1937 | 17.75 | 1945 | 7.90 |
| 1937-D | 35.00 | 1945-D | 14.00 |
| 1937-S | 37.00 | 1945-S | 11.50 |
| 1938 | 35.00 | 1946 | 7.75 |
| 1938-D | 43.00 | 1946-D | 6.90 |
| 1938-S | 70.00 | 1946-S | 13.00 |
| 1939 | 20.00 | 1947 | 16.00 |
| 1939-D | 90.00 | 1947-D | 9.00 |
| 1939-S | 43.00 | 1948 | 10.50 |
| 1940-D | 33.00 | 1948-D | 8.75 |
| 1940-S | 24.00 | 1948-S | 18.50 |
| 1941 | 16.50 | 1949 | 17.00 |
| 1941-D | 60.00 | 1950 | 11.75 |
| | | 1951 | 42.00 |

## CH. BU NICKEL ROLLS

| Year | Price | Year | Price |
|---|---|---|---|
| 38- D | 140.00 | 1954-S | 5.25 |
| 1939 | 33.00 | 1955 | 21.50 |
| 1940 | 24.00 | 1955-D | 6.00 |
| 1940-D | 38.00 | 1956 | 4.00 |
| 1940-S | 43.00 | 1956-D | 4.00 |
| 1941 | 18.50 | 1957 | 4.00 |
| 1941-D | 28.50 | 1957-D | 4.00 |
| 1941-S | 38.00 | 1958 | 5.80 |
| 42-S | 125.00 | 1958-D | 4.00 |
| 1943 | 50.00 | 1959 | 3.75 |
| 1943-D | 75.00 | 1959-D | 3.40 |
| 1943-S | 57.00 | 1960 | 3.25 |
| 1944-S | 60.00 | 1960-D | 3.25 |
| 1945-D | 45.00 | 1961 | 3.25 |
| 1945-S | 42.50 | 1961-D | 3.25 |
| 1946 | 9.75 | 1962 | 3.25 |
| 1946-D | 14.00 | 1962-D | 3.25 |
| 1946-S | 18.50 | 1963 | 3.25 |
| 1947 | 7.50 | 1963-D | 3.25 |
| 1947-D | 16.00 | 1964 | 3.25 |
| 1947-S | 18.00 | 1964-D | 3.25 |
| 1948 | 9.75 | 1965 | 4.00 |
| 1948-D | 20.75 | 1966 | 4.25 |
| 1948-S | 32.00 | 1967 | 4.75 |
| 1949-S | 65.00 | 1968-D | 4.00 |
| 50-D | 310.00 | 1968-S | 4.00 |
| 1951 | 19.00 | 1969-D | 4.00 |
| 1951-D | 33.00 | 1969-S | 4.00 |
| 1951-S | 78.00 | 1970-D | 4.00 |
| 1952 | 8.75 | 1970-D | 4.00 |
| 1952-D | 38.00 | 1971 | 5.25 |
| 1952-S | 15.00 | 1971-D | 4.00 |
| 1953 | 5.50 | 1972 | 4.95 |
| 1953-D | 6.25 | 1972-D | 4.00 |
| 1953-S | 10.50 | 1973 | 4.00 |
| 1954 | 4.50 | 1973-D | 4.00 |
| 1954-D | 5.25 | 1974 | 3.25 |
| | | 1974-D | 3.50 |

## CH. BU DIME ROLLS

| Year | Price | Year | Price |
|---|---|---|---|
| 1947 | 32.50 | 1959-D | 20.00 |
| 1948 | 79.00 | 1960 | 20.50 |
| 1951-D | 34.00 | 1960-D | 20.00 |
| 1953 | 31.00 | 1961 | 20.00 |
| 1953-D | 22.00 | 1961-D | 20.00 |
| 1953-S | 25.50 | 1962 | 20.00 |
| 1954 | 22.50 | 1962-D | 20.00 |
| 1954-D | 22.50 | 1963 | 20.00 |
| 1954-S | 25.50 | 1963-D | 19.00 |
| 1955 | 51.50 | 1964 | 19.50 |
| 1955-D | 28.50 | 1964-D | 19.50 |
| 1955-S | 25.00 | 1965 | 9.25 |
| 1956 | 20.00 | 1966 | 9.25 |
| 1956-D | 20.00 | 1967 | 9.25 |
| 1957 | 20.00 | 1968 | 10.50 |
| 1957-D | 22.00 | 1968-D | 10.00 |
| 1958 | 22.50 | 1969 | 13.00 |
| 1958-D | 20.00 | 1969-D | 10.00 |
| 1959 | 20.00 | 1970 | 9.50 |

## CH. BU DIME ROLLS

| Year | Price | Year | Price |
|---|---|---|---|
| 1950-D | 9.25 | 1973 | 9.25 |
| 1971 | 11.00 | 1973-D | 9.00 |
| 1971-D | 9.50 | 1974 | 7.75 |
| 1972 | 10.00 | 1974-D | 7.75 |
| 1972-D | 9.25 | 1975 | 7.25 |

## CH. BU QUARTER ROLLS

| Year | Price | Year | Price |
|---|---|---|---|
| 1944 | 55.00 | 1961 | 39.00 |
| 1945 | 63.00 | 1961-D | 39.00 |
| 1946 | 58.00 | 1962 | 39.00 |
| 1946- D | 140.00 | 1962-D | 39.00 |
| 1947 | 76.00 | 1963 | 39.00 |
| 1949 | 450.00 | 1963-D | 39.00 |
| 1951-D | 70.00 | 1964 | 39.00 |
| 1952-D | 45.00 | 1964-D | 39.00 |
| 1953-D | 44.00 | 1965 | 16.00 |
| 1953-S | 78.00 | 1966 | 18.00 |
| 1954 | 42.00 | 1967 | 17.00 |
| 1954-D | 42.00 | 1968-D | 21.00 |
| 1954-S | 43.00 | 1969 | 17.00 |
| 1955 | 43.00 | 1969-D | 24.00 |
| 55-D | 119.00 | 1970 | 15.00 |
| 1956 | 39.00 | 1970-D | 15.00 |
| 1956-D | 39.00 | 1971 | 16.00 |
| 1957 | 39.00 | 1971-D | 15.00 |
| 1957-D | 39.00 | 1972 | 16.00 |
| 1958 | 49.00 | 1972-D | 15.00 |
| 1958-D | 39.00 | 1973 | 15.00 |
| 1959 | 39.00 | 1973-D | 14.00 |
| 1959-D | 39.00 | 1974 | 14.00 |
| 1960 | 39.00 | 1974-D | 14.00 |
| 1960-D | 39.00 | 1976 | 13.50 |
| | | 1976-D | 13.50 |

## CH. BU HALF DOLLAR ROLLS

| Year | Price | Year | Price |
|---|---|---|---|
| 1943 | 265.00 | 1962-D | 43.00 |
| 1944 | 265.00 | 1963 | 43.00 |
| 1945 | 265.00 | 1963-D | 43.00 |
| 1951 | 195.00 | 1964 | 38.00 |
| 51-S | 235.00 | 1964-D | 38.00 |
| 1952-D | 58.00 | 1965 | 18.50 |
| 1954 | 56.00 | 1966 | 18.50 |
| 1954-D | 45.00 | 1967 | 18.50 |
| 1954-S | 68.00 | 1968-D | 18.00 |
| 1955 | 133.00 | 1969-D | 18.00 |
| 1956 | 57.00 | 70-D | 310.00 |
| 1957 | 57.00 | 1971 | 16.00 |
| 1957-D | 44.00 | 1971-D | 14.00 |
| 1958 | 55.00 | 1972 | 16.00 |
| 1958-D | 44.00 | 1972-D | 14.00 |
| 1959 | 46.00 | 1973 | 14.00 |
| 1959-D | 45.00 | 1973-D | 14.00 |
| 1960 | 44.00 | 1974 | 14.00 |
| 1960-D | 44.00 | 1974-D | 14.00 |
| 1961 | 44.00 | 1976 | 13.75 |
| 1961-D | 44.00 | 1976-D | 13.75 |
| 1962 | 43.00 | | |

5 day return privilege. Calif. Residents please add 6% sales tax. Orders under $50.00 please add $1.00 for postage and handling. All coins accurately graded. Personal checks must clear. 24 hour service on money orders.

# COIN-A-RAMA CITY

ANA — AMERICAN NUMISMATIC ASSOCIATION MEMBER

213-679-9151

13304 Inglewood Ave.                    Hawthorne, Calif. 90250

## All Dealer Prices Are Not the Same

In the two advertisements reproduced on the preceding pages, prices for rolls of cents (selected at random) varied as follows:

### CENT ROLLS

| Year and Mint | M&S Hirschhorn, Inc. | Coin-A-Rama City | Average |
|---|---|---|---|
| 1937 P | $16.00 | $ 17.75 | $ 16.88 |
| 1938 S | 70.00 | 70.00 | 70.00 |
| 1942 S | — | 125.00 | 125.00 |
| 1955 S | 12.75 | 12.75 | 12.75 |
| 1968 P | 3.00 | 2.85 | 2.93 |
| 1969 P | 5.00 | 5.25 | 5.13 |
| 1970 P | 2.75 | 2.65 | 2.70 |
| 1971 D | 1.60 | 1.45 | 1.53 |
| 1974 S | 2.50 | 2.10 | 2.30 |

Therefore, when developing a wholesale price for your coin rolls, you should begin with an *average* of the advertised dealer retail prices and multiply it by the appropriate Wholesale Price Factor from page 68.

## Selling to Dealers

The easiest way to sell your coin rolls is to a dealer. However, this is usually the least profitable way to sell them. Remember that dealers are in business to make a profit and, therefore, most dealers will offer you less than the wholesale price that you have calculated..

## Selling by Mail Bid

Another way to sell your coin rolls is by mail bid. Few large mail bid companies will handle coins less than 30 years old unless the coins are extremely rare. But there are some smaller companies and individuals who will handle recent date uncirculated rolls and singles. You can locate mail bid companies by going through the MAIL BID OFFERS column in the classified section of the coin newspapers.

## Selling Through Classified Advertisements

There *is* a way to get more for your coin rolls than by selling either to dealers or by mail bid. From the Wholesale Price Factors on page 68 you know that a fair wholesale price is from 17% below retail (for rolls of nickels) to 24% below retail (for rolls of quarters and half-dollars). Therefore, all you need to do is go through a recent issue of *Coin World* or *Numismatic News Weekly* and select the lowest advertised dealer "sell" price for the coin rolls that you want to sell. Reduce that price by 10% and run an advertisement like the one shown below in the classified section of one (or both) of the coin newspapers:

> BU CENT ROLLS. 1955 S—$11.50;
> 1969 P—$4.60. Any quantity up to
> 100 rolls. Ten rolls or more post-
> paid. Others please add postage.
> Jones, 1234 Cedar Street.
> Pittsburgh, PA 89765.

If you don't get a satisfactory response, reduce the price by a few percent more and rerun the advertisement.

This method should easily sell all the coin rolls you have for sale at prices higher than most dealers would pay you.

## Higher Profits From Selling Singles

If you are willing to put forth a little more effort you can increase your profits substantially. Instead of selling your coins in rolls, why not sell them as singles?

Let's compare several dealer advertisements from the October 8, 1975 issue of *Coin World* that offered single coins for sale with the two coin roll advertisements that we discussed earlier in this chapter.

## CENTS

| Year and Mint | Lyle Clark & Foothill Coins | Coin-A-Rama City | Plainfield Coins on Boca Ratan, Inc. | Average Retail Price of 50 Single Coins (equivalent of 1 roll) | Average Retail Price of One Coin Roll (from page 71) |
|---|---|---|---|---|---|
| 1937 P | $ .60 | $ .85 | $1.15 | $ 43.50 | $ 16.88 |
| 1938 S | 1.95 | 2.10 | 2.30 | 106.00 | 70.00 |
| 1942 S | 2.95 | 4.00 | 5.00 | 199.00 | 125.00 |
| 1955 S | .40 | .40 | .40 | 20.00 | 12.75 |
| 1968 P | — | .10 | .15 | 6.50 | 2.93 |
| 1969 P | — | .20 | .15 | 9.00 | 5.13 |
| 1970 P | — | .10 | .15 | 6.50 | 2.70 |
| 1971 D | — | .10 | .10 | 5.00 | 1.53 |
| 1974 S | — | .20 | .15 | 9.00 | 2.30 |

By selling single coins instead of rolls you would have increased your profits by anywhere from 51% for the 1938 S cents to 291% for the 1974 S cents. Furthermore, since there are many more collectors of single coins than of rolls, you will increase the number of potential buyers more than a thousandfold by selling your coins as singles. Incidentally, the advertisement on page 72 will work just as well for single coins as for coin rolls.

Selling single coins is obviously much more profitable than selling rolls. But it requires more time and effort to sell to several hundred buyers than to sell to just a few. Is it worth the effort? Only you can answer this question.,

# Chapter 6

# How to Preserve and Protect Your Coins

*Simple steps, promptly taken —*
*forestall the losses time would bring.*

## Factors That Affect the Condition of Coins

Condition is a function of various factors. Certainly, as coins pass from hand to hand in the normal course of commerce, infinitesimal amounts of metal wear away. After a few weeks these coins become worn and scratched. Even if you put your uncirculated coins in your dresser drawer and forget about them they will, over a period of time, become discolored, tarnished, and perhaps even pitted or corroded.

The enemies of coins are many:

- air, even dry air, causes coin metals to oxidize
- dampness causes corrosion of most coin metals

- direct sun causes coins to become dull and lusterless

- breathing on coins frequently causes black pit marks after the coins have aged

- industrial fumes, air-borne materials, high humidity, and other atmospheric conditions may affect your coins in various ways

- cellophane, polyurethane, polyvinyl chloride, acetate, butyrate, plexiglass, and materials that have been used for some other purpose, such as foil from cigarette packages, will cause copper coins to tarnish or spot

- rubber bands and certain types of adhesives and pressure-sensitive adhesive tapes give off chemical vapors that react with coin surfaces and cause discoloration, corrosion, and pitting

- cedar chests, cigar boxes, and most other wooden boxes and cabinets contain tannic acid and other chemicals that attack copper, iron, tin, zinc, and certain other metals

- the mere handling of coins stimulates corrosion from the oils, salts, and acids of your body

- most paper (except chemically treated paper) contains some sulphur which causes copper coins to tarnish or spot. *Even many bank wrappers have about five percent sulphur content and are, therefore, dangerous to coins over a period of time*

Your coins will retain their uncirculated condition (and, therefore, increase in value at the highest possible rate) only if they are protected against these hazards.

## Preserving Your Coins

A simple and inexpensive method of preserving your coins is as follows:

1. Always wear clean cotton gloves when handling coins. Never touch the coins with your bare hands (or any other part of your body). You can purchase cotton gloves at nominal cost in most drug stores, photo stores, and hobby shops.

2. Remove your coins from their bank wrappers as soon as you get them and wrap each roll-quantity of coins (50 cents, 40 nickels, etc.) in a sheet of VCI paper. Then wrap that roll in aluminum foil, making sure that the seam and both ends are tightly sealed.

   VCI paper is a special paper that has been treated with volatile corrosion inhibitors which emit vapors intended to maintain metals in a state of preservation. In order for these vapors to be effective, both the VCI paper and the coins must be sealed in an air-tight enclosure that can retain the vapors.

   I have been able to locate only two companies that manufacture VCI papers, but they have advised me that they are not interested in selling the quantities and sizes of their paper that would be appropriate for wrapping coin rolls. While you *can* preserve your coins without using VCI paper, the extra measure of protection that VCI paper provides is definitely worth the small additional cost. I have, therefore, purchased large quantities of VCI paper from the manufacturers and have had it cut into the proper size to wrap coin rolls. I will send you a Coin

Preservation Starter Pack which includes 100 sheets of VCI paper as well as other very useful coin preservation items for the nominal price of $8.00. All you have to do to receive your Coin Preservation Starter Pack is to fill in and mail the coupon that is provided in Appendix VI.

3. Fill an *unused* paint can (which you can purchase at your local paint or hardware store) with as many wrapped coin rolls as the can will hold. A one gallon can will hold 110 rolls of cents (or 86 rolls of nickels) and weigh approximately 35 pounds. A one quart can will hold 23 rolls of cents (or 16 rolls of nickels) and weigh approximately 7 pounds.

4. Put a 1/3 unit or larger bag of silica gel into each gallon can (or a 1/6 unit or larger bag in each quart can) and close the lid properly to obtain an air-tight seal.

Silica gel is a unique material that acts like a sponge by pulling water out of the air and holding it in its pores. Silica gel can absorb 40% of its own weight of water. Even when saturated with water it looks and feels dry. Since silica gel is chemically inert it will not cause coins to corrode, even if the silica gel physically comes into contact with the coins.

Silica gel is manufactured by more than a dozen companies, but none of those that I contacted were willing to sell in less than commercial quantities. I have, therefore, purchased a large quantity of silica gel from the manufacturers. I will send you enough to protect the contents of several gallon cans of coins as

part of the Coin Preservation Starter Pack
(see Appendix VI).

## Protection From Theft

The purpose of storing your coins in unused paint cans
is to protect them from air and moisture. But this method
of storage has another benefit — protection from theft.
What thief would expect to find anything of value in a
paint can in your (dry) basement or workshop? You can
identify the type, date, mintage, and quantity of the coins
that are in the can by using a simple code and marking
the can accordingly (or by affixing a small label to the
bottom of the can). This will eliminate the need to open
the cans and will, therefore, preserve the protective
environment in which your coins have been placed.

The above steps will give your coins maximum
protection and make sure that, when the time comes to
sell, the coins that you put away years before will still
command the high prices that only uncirculated coins
bring.

# Chapter 7

# Retirement Income

*O blest retirement! friend to life's decline—*
*Retreats from care, that never must be mine.*
*How blest is he who crowns, in shades like these,*
*A youth of labour with an age of ease!*

OLIVER GOLDSMITH: Deserted Village

The principles that I have explained in the preceding chapters can also be used to provide you with a high retirement income for the rest of your life and a sizeable estate after your death.

**Example No. One: $400 Annual Investment Produces $15,000 A Year for Life**

Let's assume you have thirty years until retirement and you want an income, beginning when you retire, of $15,000 a year (not counting social security) for the rest of your life. You can develop a good estimate of the amount of money that you should invest each year in order to produce this annual income by using the *Median Wholesale Values of $100 Face Value of Rolls of*

*Uncirculated Coins* table in Appendix V. This table shows the values of all coins that were minted between 1935 and 1974 (except S nickels, S dimes, S quarters, and S half-dollars). The prices are the median prices that dealers were *paying* for the coins.

Under column 30 (30 years after year minted) on the table you will find:

|  |  |
|---|---|
| $100 face value of |  |
| P cents | $2,184 |
| D cents | 5,110 |
| S cents | 6,084 |
| average cents | 4,459 |
| P nickels | 2,418 |
| D nickels | 5,084 |
| average nickels | 3,751 |
| P dimes | 1,343 |
| D dimes | 2,054 |
| average dimes | 1,699 |
| P quarters | 931 |
| D quarters | 2,109 |
| average quarters | 1,520 |
| P half-dollars | 1,102 |
| D half-dollars | 2,687 |
| average half-dollars | 1,895 |

Since *D* and *S* cent rolls and *D* nickel rolls were the most profitable, it follows that they are the coins you should buy. However, in order to be as conservative as possible, you should use the _lowest_ of the *average cents* and *average nickels* values to formulate your investment target. This amount ($3,751) represents the probable *minimum* value, thirty years from now, of a $100 investment in rolls of current-year uncirculated $D$ and $S$ cents and $D$ nickels. Or, to put it another way, if you invest $100 today in rolls of current-year uncirculated $D$ and $S$ cents and $D$ nickels, that investment will probably be worth a minimum of $3,751, thirty years from now. Although your investment might be worth as much as $6,084 — or even more, it is always a good idea to assume the "worst case" for the sake of conservatism.

To determine how much you will have to invest to produce a minimum of $15,000, thirty years from now, divide $3,751 into $15,000 and multiply the result by 100 ($15,000 ÷ $3,751 = 4; 4 x $100 = $400). Therefore, all you have to do is buy $133 face value of current-year uncirculated $D$ cent rolls, $133 of $S$ cent rolls, and $134 of $D$ nickel rolls (total investment of $400) this year and each year thereafter. When you retire thirty years from now, sell your first year's purchase (or as much as is necessary). Each year thereafter you should sell as many of your oldest coins as is necessary to provide the income you desire. Some years you may have to sell more than just one year's mintage and some years you may need to sell only a part of a year's mintage. But the highs and the lows will balance out and, on average, you will earn at least the amount of annual income that you had anticipated.

**Higher Profits**

Since you will have plenty of free time after you retire, you might wish to sell your coins singly rather than as rolls in order to earn even higher profits. (See Chapter 5).

**Example No. Two: Retirement Income Starting in Twenty Years**

Suppose you only have 20 years until retirement and you want $10,000 a year when you retire. Look under column

20 (20 years after year minted) on the *Median Wholesale Values of $100 Face Value of Rolls of Uncirculated Coins* table in Appendix V. There you will find:

| $100 face value of | |
|---|---:|
| P cents | $1,872 |
| D cents | 1,778 |
| S cents | 2,730 |
| average cents | 2,127 |
| P nickels | 695 |
| D nickels | 1,349 |
| average nickels | 1,022 |
| P dimes | 442 |
| D dimes | 474 |
| average dimes | 458 |
| P quarters | 342 |
| D quarters | 623 |
| average quarters | 483 |
| P half-dollars | 559 |
| D half-dollars | 570 |
| average half-dollars | 565 |

Since *P*, *D*, and *S* cent rolls were the most profitable, they are obviously the ones you will select. However, since *average cents* had a higher value than either the *P* cent rolls or the *D* cent rolls, that average does not represent the conservative figure you are seeking. In this case you should select the <u>lowest</u> of the cent rolls — the *D* cent — as your investment target. This amount ($1,778) represents the probable *minimum* value, twenty years from now, of a $100 investment today in rolls of current-year uncirculated *P*, *D*, and *S* cents. Your investment might be worth as much as $2,730 or even more but, as in the previous illustration, you should use the most conservative figure in your calculations.

If an investment of $100 will produce $1,778, twenty years from now, an investment of $560 will produce $10,000 ($10,000 ÷ $1,788 = 5.62; 5.62 x $100 = $562) (rounded to $560). Therefore, all you have to do is buy $186 face value of current-year uncirculated P cent rolls, $186 of D cent rolls, and $188 of S cent rolls (total investment of $560) this year and each year thereafter.

## Retirement Income That Continues After Your Death

Think of it. If you invest $400 each year starting now in rolls of current-year uncirculated D and S cents and D nickels you will have investments that you can sell, starting when you retire thirty years from now, which will produce $15,000 or more *every year for the rest of your life*. Of, if you invest $560 each year starting now in rolls of current-year uncirculated P, D, and S cents you will have investments that you can sell, starting twenty years from now, which will produce $10,000 or more *every year for the rest of your life*.

And that's not all. *After your death this momentum that you have built up will continue to produce the same income every year thereafter for anyone that you choose.* This small yearly investment will not only provide a retirement income for you but it will also take care of your wife (or husband) after your death, or give your son or daughter a supplementary income, or give your grandchild a tremendous financial assist.

# Chapter 8

# Money for College

*An investment in knowledge pays the best interest.*
BENJAMIN FRANKLIN, Poor Richard's Almanack

If you have a new baby and are wondering how you'll be able to pay the cost of college eighteen years from now, you have plenty of company. Every parent wonders the same thing. Unfortunately, most parents rationalize that eighteen years is a long time and that, by then, something will happen to provide the money. But eighteen years is not a long time — it passes before you know it. And there usually isn't any rich relative waiting to provide the money.

The only way to pay for your child's college education, marriage, start in business, etc. is to take the necessary steps *now*. Chapter 7 explains how you can create a retirement income for the rest of your life. That same method can also be used to provide the money to pay for your child's college education.

### Example: $5,000 Per Year

Let's assume that your child is now one year old and you want to have $5,000 each year of his or her four-year stay at college to help pay tuition costs. And let's assume that your child will enter college at age eighteen.

Look under column 17 (17 years after year minted) on the *Median Wholesale Values of $100 Face Value of Rolls of Uncirculated Coins* table in Appendix V.

There you will find:

$100 face value of

| | |
|---|---:|
| P cents | $1,248 |
| D cents | 976 |
| S cents | 1,814 |
| average cents | 1,346 |
| P nickels | 644 |
| D nickels | 706 |
| average nickels | 675 |
| P dimes | 292 |
| D dimes | 348 |
| average dimes | 320 |
| P quarters | 264 |
| D quarters | 285 |
| average quarters | 275 |
| P half-dollars | 302 |
| D half-dollars | 361 |
| average half-dollars | 332 |

Since *P*, *D*, and *S* cent rolls were the most profitable, they are the coins you should buy. However, since *average cents* had a higher value than either the *P* cent rolls or the *D* cent rolls, and since you should always use as conservative a figure as possible to formulate your investment target, you should select the *lowest* of the cent rolls — the *D* cent. This amount ($976) represents the probable *minimum* value, seventeen years from now, of a $100 investment in rolls of current-year uncirculated *P*, *D*, and *S* cents. Or, to put it another way, if you invest $100 today in rolls of current-year uncirculated *P*, *D*, and *S* cents, that investment will probably be worth a minimum of $976, seventeen years from now. Although your investment might be worth as much as $1,814 — or even more, you should always use the most conservative figure in your calculations.

If an investment of $100 will produce $976, seventeen years from now, an investment of $510 will produce $5,000 ($5,000 ÷ $976 = 5.12; 5.12 x $100 = $512) (rounded to $510). Therefore, all you have to do is buy $170 face value of current-year uncirculated *P* cent rolls, $170 of *D* cent rolls, and $170 of *S* cent rolls (total investment of $510) this year and each of the next three years (or longer if you want to provide money for graduate school, etc.)

When your child enters college, sell as many of your oldest coins as is necessary to provide $5,000 toward your child's tuition costs. Do the same thing each year thereafter during his or her college stay. (To maximize your profits when selling your coins, be sure to follow the advice in Chapter 5).

**Income After Graduation For You or Your Child**

*If you continue to make these annual investments, you will continue to receive the flow of income after your child finishes college.* Or, if you wish, you can give your child a financial assist after he or she finishes college by transferring your coin rolls to him or her. The child can continue the annual investment after graduation to provide himself with a lifetime income. And he can, if he wishes, increase the amount of the annual investment to increase the amount of income.

# Chapter 9

## Take the First Step Today

*It is a maxim universally agreed upon in agriculture,*
*that nothing must be done too late;*
*and again, that everything must be done at its proper season;*
*while there is a third precept which reminds us*
*that opportunities lost can never be regained.*

PLINY THE ELDER, *Historia Naturalis.*
Bk. xviii, sec. 44.

If you're like most people, you will put this book on the shelf and forget about it. And ten years from now (if you happen to look at it) you will probably ask yourself why you let those years go by without taking any action. *I want to do everything I can to prevent those ten years from being wasted.*

### The AAPP Calculator Chart

I've devised a chart that you can use to calculate the Average Annual Profit Percentage (AAPP) of your own coin investments. The chart is easy to use. Just follow these six steps:

1. Determine the *Average Retail Price* of one coin roll from dealer "sell" advertisements in the coin newspapers (see page 67).

2. Determine the *Wholesale Price Factor* for that denomination coin roll (see page 68).

3. Multiply the *Average Retail Price* times the *Wholesale Price Factor* to determine the *Average Wholesale Price*.

4. A—Divide the *Average Wholesale Price* by the *Face Value of One Coin Roll* (see page 37).

   B—Subtract 1.00 from the resulting figure (to eliminate the original cost of the coin roll) to arrive at the *Cumulative Profit Amount* (CPA).

5. Convert the *Cumulative Profit Amount* (CPA) to the *Cumulative Profit Percentage* (CPP) by moving the decimal point two places to the right and adding a "%" sign.

6. Divide the *Cumulative Profit Percentage* (CPP) by the *Number of Years Since Year Minted* to arrive at the *Average Annual Profit Percentage* (AAPP).

NOTE: Round all numbers to the nearest whole cent or percent.

## Calculation of AAPP: Example

CALCULATION OF AAPP FOR 1955 P NICKEL IN THE FOURTH YEAR AFTER THE YEAR MINTED:

*Basic Information:*

Face Value of One Coin Roll (from page 37): $2.00
Number of years since year minted: 4

## *The Six Steps:*

1. Determination of *Average Retail Price* of one roll:
   from dealer "sell" advertisements in coin newspapers:     $10.00

2. Determination of *Wholesale Price Factor* for that
   denomination coin roll:
   from page 68:                                             83%

3. Calculation of *Average Wholesale Price:*

| Average Retail Price | times | Wholesale Price Factor | equals | Average Wholesale Price |
|---|---|---|---|---|
| $10.00 | X | 83% | = | $8.30 |

4. Calculation of *Cumulative Profit Amount* (CPA):

A:

| Average Wholesale Price | divided by | Face Value of One Coin Roll | equals | Cumulative Dollar Amount |
|---|---|---|---|---|
| $8.30 | ÷ | $2.00 | = | 4.15 |

B:

| Cumulative Dollar Amount | minus | 1.00 | equals | Cumulative Profit Amount |
|---|---|---|---|---|
| 4.15 | – | 1.00 | = | 3.15 |

5. Calculation of *Cumulative Profit Percentage* (CPP):
   convert *Cumulative Profit Amount* to *Cumulative Profit Percentage* by moving the decimal point two places to the right and adding a "%" sign:

                                                    3.15 = 315%

. Calculation of *Average Annual Profit Percentage* (AAPP):

| Cumulative Profit Percentage | divided by | Number of Years Since Year Minted | equals | Average Annual Profit Percentage |
|---|---|---|---|---|
| 315% | ÷ | 4 | = | 79% |

You will find a blank AAPP Calculator Chart printed on the inside of the dust jacket of this book. You can make copies for your own use on any Xerox or similar copying machine. If you don't have a copier available to you, you can probably use the one at your public library.

(Ten Blank AAPP Calculator Charts are included with the Coin Preservation Starter Pack — see Appendix VI).

## Two Filled-In AAPP Calculator Charts

In order to illustrate how easy it is to use the AAPP Calculator Chart, I've included two filled-in Charts on the next two pages.

**AAPP CALCULATOR CHART**

Denomination and Mint Mark of Coin Roll __P Nickel__
Year Minted __1955__
Face Value of One Coin Roll $ __2.00__
Minimum AAPP Goal __50__ %

| Year | 1959 | 1960 | 1961 | | | |
|---|---|---|---|---|---|---|
| Number of Years Since Year Minted | 4 | 5 | 6 | | | |
| 1. Average Retail Price | $10.00 | $47.50 | $36.00 | $ | $ | $ |
| 2. Wholesale Price Factor | 83 % | 83 % | 83 % | % | % | % |
| 3. Average Wholesale Price [Average Retail Price times Wholesale Price Factor] | $8.30 | $39.43 | $29.88 | $ | $ | $ |
| 4. CPA — Cumulative Profit Amount [(Average Wholesale Price ÷ Face Value of One Coin Roll) minus 1.00] | 3.15 | 18.72 | 13.94 | | | |
| 5. CPP — Cumulative Profit Percentage [move decimal point in CPA two places to the right and add "%"] | 315 % | 1,872 % | 1,394 % | % | % | % |
| 6. AAPP — Average Annual Profit Percentage [CPP ÷ Number of Years Since Year Minted] | 79 % | 374 % | 232 % | % | % | % |

*Round all numbers to the nearest whole cent or percent.*

## AAPP CALCULATOR CHART

Denomination and Mint Mark of Coin Roll __5 Cent__
Year Minted __1955__
Face Value of One Coin Roll $ __.50__
Minimum AAPP Goal __75__ %

| Year | 1959 | 1960 | 1961 | 1962 | 1963 | 1964 | |
|---|---|---|---|---|---|---|---|
| Number of Years Since Year Minted | 4 | 5 | 6 | 7 | 8 | 9 | |
| 1. Average Retail Price | $7.25 | $10.00 | $13.25 | $35.00 | $42.50 | $38.00 | $ |
| 2. Wholesale Price Factor | 78 % | 78 % | 78 % | 78 % | 78 % | 78 % | % |
| 3. Average Wholesale Price [Average Retail Price times Wholesale Price Factor] | $5.66 | $7.80 | $10.34 | $27.30 | $33.15 | $29.64 | $ |
| 4. CPA — Cumulative Profit Amount [(Average Wholesale Price ÷ Face Value of One Coin Roll) minus 1.00] | 10.32 | 14.60 | 19.68 | 53.60 | 65.30 | 58.28 | |
| 5. CPP — Cumulative Profit Percentage [move decimal point in CPA two places to the right and add "%"] | 1,032 % | 1,460 % | 1,968 % | 5,360 % | 6,530 % | 5,828 % | % |
| 6. AAPP — Average Annual Profit Percentage [CPP ÷ Number of Years Since Year Minted] | 258 % | 292 % | 328 % | 766 % | 816 % | 648 % | % |

Round all numbers to the nearest whole cent or percent.

## The Rest is Up to You

Take your first step to high profits without risk *now*. Go to the bank today and make your first purchase of current-year uncirculated coin rolls. Follow the simple guidelines that this book has given you. Then watch your investment increase in value while the stock market takes its usual roller coaster ride.

# APPENDIX I

## Retail Price Tables

The following pages show the average retail prices, from one to forty years after the year minted, of uncirculated rolls of all coins that were minted between 1935 and 1974 (except S nickels, S dimes, S quarters, and S half-dollars which, on the date this book was written, were no longer minted for general circulation).

To determine the average retail price of one roll of uncirculated coins of any denomination and mintage at any number of years after the year minted, go to the table for that mintage coin, find the date of the coin under the *Year Minted* column and locate the retail price under the *Number of Years After Year Minted* column.

For example, if you want to know the retail price of a roll of uncirculated 1948 S cents, fifteen years after the year minted, go to the *Retail Prices — Uncirculated Rolls of S Cents* table on page 110 and find *1948* under the *Year Minted* column. Across the page under column 15 you will find $53.00 — the retail price of one roll of uncirculated 1948 S cents, fifteen years after the year the coins were minted.

## Retail Prices — Uncirculated Rolls of P Cents

Face Value of One Roll: $.50

| Year Minted | Number of Years After Year Minted | | | | | | | | | |
|---|---|---|---|---|---|---|---|---|---|---|
| | 1 | 2 | 3 | 4 | 5 | 6 | 7 | 8 | 9 | 10 |
| 1935 | $ 1.00 | $ 1.90 | $ 1.85 | $ 1.85 | $ 1.85 | $ 1.50 | $ 2.25 | $ 3.00 | $ 3.00 | $ 2.25 |
| 1936 | 1.75 | 1.75 | 1.75 | 1.75 | 1.50 | 1.35 | 2.00 | 2.00 | 2.10 | 2.35 |
| 1937 | .80 | 1.00 | 1.25 | 1.25 | 1.40 | 2.00 | 1.65 | 1.75 | 1.75 | 2.00 |
| 1938 | .90 | 1.00 | 1.25 | 1.25 | 1.85 | 2.00 | 2.50 | 2.75 | 3.00 | 3.10 |
| 1939 | .75 | 1.15 | 1.15 | 1.50 | 1.25 | 1.60 | 1.70 | 1.70 | 1.80 | 1.80 |
| 1940 | 1.00 | 1.00 | 1.25 | 1.25 | 1.25 | 1.25 | 1.40 | 1.50 | 1.75 | 1.40 |
| 1941 | .85 | 1.10 | 1.10 | 1.10 | 1.15 | 1.25 | 1.35 | 1.35 | 1.35 | 1.50 |
| 1942 | .90 | .90 | 1.00 | 1.00 | 1.00 | 1.10 | 1.00 | .90 | .90 | 1.00 |
| 1943 | .75 | .80 | 1.00 | 1.00 | 1.10 | 1.00 | 1.55 | 1.90 | 1.50 | 1.00 |
| 1944 | .75 | .80 | .80 | .90 | .90 | .85 | .90 | .90 | .90 | .90 |
| 1945 | .75 | .75 | .85 | .80 | .85 | .90 | .90 | .90 | .90 | .95 |
| 1946 | .70 | .85 | .80 | .75 | .75 | .80 | .80 | .90 | .85 | .90 |
| 1947 | .75 | .75 | .75 | .85 | .85 | 1.00 | 2.90 | 3.00 | 3.00 | 3.40 |
| 1948 | .70 | .75 | .85 | .90 | 1.00 | 2.25 | 2.50 | 2.70 | 3.20 | 5.00 |
| 1949 | .75 | .85 | .85 | 1.00 | 1.30 | 3.55 | 3.70 | 4.00 | 7.00 | 22.50 |
| 50 | .85 | .85 | .85 | 2.50 | 2.50 | 2.55 | 2.65 | 4.00 | 12.50 | 18.50 |
| 51 | .75 | .80 | .95 | 1.00 | 1.50 | 2.00 | 5.00 | 18.00 | 20.00 | 17.50 |
| 52 | .75 | .90 | 1.00 | 1.35 | 2.00 | 5.00 | 12.50 | 16.00 | 14.00 | 15.00 |
| 53 | .80 | .90 | .85 | 1.15 | 1.50 | 3.75 | 9.50 | 6.50 | 7.00 | 10.00 |
| 54 | .70 | 1.40 | 1.75 | 3.25 | 11.00 | 14.00 | 12.50 | 23.50 | 32.00 | 40.00 |
| 55 | .80 | 1.10 | 1.65 | 3.50 | 6.50 | 5.50 | 5.50 | 8.50 | 8.00 | 6.75 |
| 56 | .75 | .90 | 1.50 | 4.50 | 3.00 | 3.00 | 6.00 | 6.00 | 4.50 | 4.50 |
| 57 | .85 | 1.25 | 3.50 | 2.75 | 3.00 | 6.00 | 5.50 | 3.50 | 3.00 | 3.50 |
| 58 | .85 | 3.25 | 2.35 | 2.60 | 6.50 | 6.00 | 4.50 | 3.50 | 3.00 | 2.50 |
| 59 | 1.50 | 1.50 | 1.25 | 3.25 | 3.00 | 1.75 | 1.00 | 1.25 | 1.00 | 1.00 |
| 60 | 1.00 | 1.00 | 1.70 | 2.25 | 1.25 | 1.25 | 1.00 | 1.00 | .90 | 1.00 |
| 61 | .85 | 1.25 | 1.75 | 1.50 | 1.00 | 1.00 | 1.00 | 1.00 | 1.00 | 1.00 |
| 62 | 1.05 | 2.00 | 1.50 | 1.50 | 1.20 | 1.00 | 1.00 | 1.00 | 1.00 | 1.00 |
| 63 | .80 | .80 | 1.00 | 1.00 | 1.00 | 1.00 | 1.00 | 1.00 | 1.00 | 1.25 |
| 64 | .75 | .90 | 1.00 | 1.00 | 1.00 | 1.00 | 1.00 | 1.00 | 1.25 | 1.25 |
| 65 | .85 | .90 | 1.00 | 1.00 | 1.00 | 1.00 | 1.10 | 1.75 | 3.00 | 2.50 |
| 66 | .85 | .95 | 1.00 | 1.00 | 1.00 | 1.20 | 1.75 | 3.50 | 2.60 | |
| 67 | .95 | 1.00 | 1.00 | 1.00 | 1.25 | 1.75 | 3.50 | 2.95 | | |
| 68 | 1.00 | 1.00 | 1.00 | 1.00 | 2.50 | 3.50 | 2.95 | | | |
| 69 | .90 | 1.00 | 1.00 | 1.75 | 6.50 | 5.15 | | | | |
| | .85 | .90 | 1.50 | 3.50 | 2.70 | | | | | |
| | .85 | 1.75 | 2.25 | 1.65 | | | | | | |
| | 1.15 | 1.50 | 1.10 | | | | | | | |
| | 1.00 | .95 | | | | | | | | |
| | .95 | | | | | | | | | |

## Retail Prices — Uncirculated Rolls of P Cents

Face Value of One Roll: $.5

| Year Minted | 11 | 12 | 13 | 14 | 15 | 16 | 17 | 18 | 19 | 20 |
|---|---|---|---|---|---|---|---|---|---|---|
| | | | | Number of Years After Year Minted | | | | | | |
| 1935 | $ 2.35 | $ 2.50 | $ 2.65 | $ 2.75 | $ 2.75 | $ 2.85 | $ 3.00 | $ 3.25 | $ 4.00 | $ 6.6 |
| 1936 | 2.75 | 2.75 | 2.25 | 2.25 | 2.35 | 2.50 | 2.60 | 3.00 | 7.00 | 8.1 |
| 1937 | 2.25 | 1.75 | 1.75 | 1.75 | 1.75 | 1.80 | 1.90 | 5.00 | 4.50 | 9. |
| 1938 | 2.50 | 2.60 | 2.60 | 2.65 | 2.75 | 3.25 | 6.00 | 10.00 | 20.00 | 38. |
| 1939 | 1.75 | 1.75 | 1.75 | 1.75 | 2.00 | 4.50 | 5.00 | 5.00 | 11.00 | 14.5 |
| 1940 | 1.50 | 1.60 | 1.75 | 2.00 | 3.60 | 4.10 | 8.50 | 12.00 | 15.00 | 17. |
| 1941 | 1.50 | 1.65 | 1.85 | 3.60 | 3.95 | 7.00 | 8.00 | 12.50 | 13.50 | 16. |
| 1942 | 1.00 | 1.00 | 1.25 | 1.50 | 2.95 | 6.00 | 9.50 | 11.50 | 11.50 | 12. |
| 1943 | 1.00 | 1.25 | 2.50 | 4.00 | 6.50 | 9.50 | 10.50 | 8.50 | 8.75 | 12. |
| 1944 | .95 | .95 | 1.50 | 2.25 | 7.50 | 10.00 | 7.00 | 8.00 | 9.00 | 9. |
| 1945 | .95 | 1.40 | 2.00 | 7.50 | 17.00 | 11.00 | 11.00 | 12.00 | 16.00 | 10. |
| 1946 | 1.65 | 2.00 | 6.00 | 7.50 | 5.50 | 5.50 | 8.50 | 10.00 | 8.00 | 7 |
| 1947 | 5.50 | 19.50 | 27.50 | 23.00 | 24.00 | 29.00 | 35.00 | 24.00 | 19.50 | 17 |
| 1948 | 12.50 | 21.00 | 17.00 | 16.00 | 18.00 | 16.00 | 15.00 | 10.00 | 8.00 | 11 |
| 1949 | 25.50 | 19.00 | 24.00 | 30.00 | 32.00 | 20.00 | 15.00 | 13.50 | 15.50 | 14 |
| 1950 | 13.00 | 14.50 | 18.00 | 16.00 | 12.50 | 10.00 | 9.00 | 13.00 | 12.50 | 12 |
| 1951 | 22.00 | 26.00 | 32.00 | 22.00 | 18.50 | 16.00 | 17.75 | 17.75 | 13.75 | 15 |
| 1952 | 18.00 | 30.00 | 25.00 | 20.00 | 18.00 | 15.75 | 15.00 | 11.00 | 10.00 | 12 |
| 1953 | 11.00 | 9.00 | 7.00 | 6.00 | 6.75 | 6.25 | 4.00 | 3.50 | 4.75 | 5 |
| 1954 | 32.00 | 27.50 | 20.00 | 17.50 | 15.00 | 11.25 | 8.00 | 11.00 | 14.00 | 12 |
| 1955 | 5.00 | 4.50 | 4.50 | 4.50 | 3.50 | 2.00 | 3.00 | 4.75 | 5.00 | 2 |
| 1956 | 3.50 | 3.50 | 2.50 | 2.00 | 1.00 | 1.35 | 1.75 | 5.50 | 3.75 | |
| 1957 | 2.50 | 2.00 | 1.85 | 1.00 | 1.50 | 2.00 | 2.90 | 2.50 | | |
| 1958 | 2.00 | 1.75 | 1.00 | 1.75 | 2.25 | 3.00 | 2.00 | | | |
| 1959 | 1.00 | 1.00 | 1.00 | 1.50 | 1.25 | .95 | | | | |
| 1960 | 1.00 | 1.00 | 1.25 | 1.25 | .95 | | | | | |
| 1961 | 1.00 | 1.25 | 1.25 | .95 | | | | | | |
| 1962 | 1.25 | 1.25 | .95 | | | | | | | |
| 1963 | 1.25 | .95 | | | | | | | | |
| 1964 | .95 | | | | | | | | | |

## Retail Prices — Uncirculated Rolls of P Cents

*Face Value of One Roll: $.50*

| 'ear inted | Number of Years After Year Minted | | | | | | | | | |
|---|---|---|---|---|---|---|---|---|---|---|
| | 21 | 22 | 23 | 24 | 25 | 26 | 27 | 28 | 29 | 30 |
| 935 | $ 8.00 | $ 9.85 | $18.00 | $22.50 | $25.00 | $34.00 | $40.00 | $60.00 | $52.50 | $36.00 |
| 336 | 8.85 | 16.00 | 19.00 | 32.50 | 28.00 | 30.00 | 40.00 | 35.00 | 24.00 | 21.00 |
| 937 | 11.50 | 15.00 | 21.00 | 18.00 | 21.00 | 36.50 | 35.00 | 20.00 | 20.00 | 20.00 |
| 938 | 39.00 | 46.00 | 38.00 | 48.00 | 92.00 | 60.00 | 40.00 | 37.50 | 35.00 | 36.00 |
| 939 | 18.00 | 16.00 | 19.00 | 31.50 | 32.50 | 22.50 | 17.50 | 17.00 | 25.00 | 23.00 |
| 340 | 17.00 | 24.00 | 34.00 | 27.50 | 22.50 | 16.50 | 15.00 | 16.00 | 15.00 | 11.00 |
| 341 | 25.50 | 33.75 | 35.00 | 26.00 | 16.50 | 16.00 | 17.00 | 17.50 | 13.25 | 10.75 |
| 342 | 16.50 | 21.00 | 10.00 | 9.00 | 8.00 | 9.00 | 9.00 | 6.75 | 5.75 | 8.35 |
| 343 | 14.50 | 12.50 | 9.00 | 10.00 | 9.50 | 8.50 | 6.75 | 5.75 | 7.00 | 14.00 |
| 344 | 7.50 | 7.00 | 6.00 | 6.75 | 6.00 | 3.65 | 3.50 | 6.70 | 5.00 | 8.00 |
| 345 | 11.00 | 10.00 | 9.50 | 8.50 | 6.75 | 6.25 | 6.25 | 9.25 | 11.00 | 7.45 |
| 46 | 6.00 | 6.75 | 6.00 | 3.75 | 2.75 | 6.70 | 5.75 | 7.00 | 7.40 | |
| 47 | 17.50 | 17.00 | 12.00 | 11.00 | 11.70 | 17.50 | 21.00 | 15.25 | | |
| 48 | 11.50 | 9.75 | 8.00 | 11.50 | 14.00 | 17.00 | 10.25 | | | |
| 49 | 11.00 | 10.00 | 13.50 | 18.00 | 31.00 | 16.50 | | | | |
| 50 | 8.00 | 12.00 | 14.50 | 13.75 | 11.25 | | | | | |
| 51 | 28.00 | 40.00 | 60.50 | 42.00 | | | | | | |
| 52 | 14.50 | 21.00 | 19.00 | | | | | | | |
| 53 | 6.50 | 3.75 | | | | | | | | |
| 54 | 11.25 | | | | | | | | | |

## Retail Prices — Uncirculated Rolls of P Cents

*Face Value of One Roll: $.5*

| Year Minted | Number of Years After Year Minted ||||||||||
|---|---|---|---|---|---|---|---|---|---|---|
| | 31 | 32 | 33 | 34 | 35 | 36 | 37 | 38 | 39 | 40 |
| 1935 | $32.00 | $30.00 | $37.50 | $39.00 | $32.25 | $25.00 | $24.00 | $22.00 | $36.00 | $29. |
| 1936 | 21.00 | 32.00 | 31.00 | 22.25 | 18.00 | 16.50 | 15.00 | 36.00 | 27.50 | |
| 1937 | 27.50 | 30.00 | 22.25 | 17.50 | 16.50 | 14.50 | 45.00 | 16.90 | | |
| 1938 | 37.50 | 24.75 | 18.00 | 19.75 | 27.00 | 40.00 | 34.00 | | | |
| 1939 | 17.50 | 13.00 | 18.75 | 17.50 | 29.00 | 20.00 | | | | |
| 1940 | 9.00 | 10.00 | 14.00 | 29.00 | 18.50 | | | | | |
| 1941 | 15.00 | 14.50 | 23.00 | 15.75 | | | | | | |
| 1942 | 9.50 | 11.00 | 10.40 | | | | | | | |
| 1943 | 20.00 | 15.25 | | | | | | | | |
| 1944 | 6.45 | | | | | | | | | |

## Retail Prices — Uncirculated Rolls of D Cents

Face Value of One Roll: $.50

| Year Minted | Number of Years After Year Minted | | | | | | | | | |
|---|---|---|---|---|---|---|---|---|---|---|
| | 1 | 2 | 3 | 4 | 5 | 6 | 7 | 8 | 9 | 10 |
| 1935 | $ .95 | $1.60 | $1.50 | $1.65 | $2.00 | $2.25 | $2.25 | $3.00 | $3.00 | $2.50 |
| 1936 | 1.10 | 1.10 | 1.25 | 1.75 | 1.75 | 1.65 | 2.25 | 2.00 | 2.25 | 2.35 |
| 1937 | .80 | 1.00 | 1.25 | 1.45 | 1.40 | 1.75 | 1.75 | 1.75 | 1.75 | 1.95 |
| 1938 | .80 | 1.00 | .85 | 1.10 | 1.85 | 2.00 | 2.40 | 2.65 | 2.85 | 3.00 |
| 1939 | .75 | 1.10 | 1.10 | 1.75 | 2.50 | 3.00 | 3.60 | 3.50 | 4.00 | 3.75 |
| 1940 | 1.00 | .95 | 1.25 | 1.25 | 1.25 | 1.35 | 1.45 | 1.50 | 1.50 | 1.40 |
| 1941 | .85 | 1.10 | 1.10 | 1.10 | 1.35 | 1.35 | 1.35 | 1.35 | 1.25 | 1.25 |
| 1942 | .90 | .90 | .90 | 1.00 | 1.00 | 1.10 | 1.00 | .90 | .90 | 1.00 |
| 1943 | .75 | .80 | 1.00 | 1.00 | 1.10 | 1.00 | 1.00 | 1.10 | 1.10 | 1.00 |
| 1944 | .75 | .80 | .80 | .90 | .80 | .75 | .75 | .90 | .90 | .90 |
| 1945 | .75 | .75 | .85 | .80 | .75 | .75 | .85 | .85 | .90 | .90 |
| 1946 | .70 | .85 | .80 | .75 | .75 | .80 | .80 | .90 | .90 | .95 |
| 1947 | .75 | .75 | .75 | .75 | .80 | 1.00 | 1.00 | 1.75 | 1.60 | 2.25 |
| 1948 | .70 | .75 | .75 | .80 | 1.00 | 1.25 | 2.50 | 2.70 | 3.25 | 4.00 |
| 1949 | .75 | .75 | .85 | 1.00 | 3.75 | 3.75 | 3.50 | 3.60 | 5.00 | 9.50 |
| 1950 | .75 | .75 | .85 | .95 | 2.30 | 2.55 | 2.70 | 3.25 | 6.50 | 10.50 |
| 1951 | .80 | .80 | .95 | 1.00 | 1.25 | 1.55 | 2.50 | 5.00 | 9.50 | 6.00 |
| 1952 | .75 | .90 | 1.00 | 1.00 | 1.20 | 2.25 | 4.25 | 8.00 | 5.00 | 5.00 |
| 1953 | .80 | .90 | .85 | .90 | 1.50 | 3.50 | 7.00 | 5.00 | 5.00 | 7.50 |
| 1954 | .75 | .80 | .90 | 1.50 | 3.25 | 6.00 | 4.50 | 4.50 | 9.00 | 8.00 |
| 1955 | .75 | .80 | 1.25 | 2.50 | 6.50 | 4.75 | 4.50 | 8.50 | 7.50 | 6.00 |
| 1956 | .95 | .90 | 1.50 | 4.00 | 2.75 | 2.50 | 3.50 | 3.00 | 1.75 | 1.25 |
| 1957 | .85 | 1.25 | 3.00 | 1.75 | 1.75 | 3.25 | 2.50 | 1.50 | 1.25 | 1.25 |
| 1958 | .85 | 2.25 | 1.50 | 1.50 | 2.50 | 2.50 | 1.50 | 1.25 | 1.25 | 1.10 |
| 1959 | 1.00 | 1.00 | 1.15 | 2.00 | 2.25 | 1.25 | 1.00 | 1.00 | 1.00 | 1.00 |
| 1960 | .85 | 1.00 | 1.25 | 1.75 | 1.25 | 1.00 | 1.00 | 1.00 | .90 | 1.00 |
| 1961 | .85 | 1.15 | 1.15 | 1.00 | 1.00 | 1.00 | 1.00 | 1.00 | 1.00 | 1.00 |
| 1962 | 1.05 | 1.10 | 1.00 | 1.00 | 1.00 | 1.00 | 1.00 | 1.00 | 1.00 | 1.00 |
| 1963 | .75 | .75 | 1.00 | 1.00 | 1.00 | 1.00 | 1.00 | 1.00 | 1.00 | 1.25 |
| 1964 | .75 | .90 | 1.00 | 1.00 | 1.00 | 1.00 | 1.00 | 1.10 | 1.25 | 1.25 |
| 1968 | 1.00 | 1.00 | 1.00 | 1.00 | 2.25 | 2.25 | 1.15 | | | |
| 1969 | 1.00 | 1.00 | 1.00 | 1.75 | 1.60 | 1.10 | | | | |
| 1970 | .85 | .90 | 1.50 | 2.50 | 1.90 | | | | | |
| 1971 | .85 | 1.40 | 2.25 | 1.55 | | | | | | |
| 1972 | 1.00 | 1.50 | 1.30 | | | | | | | |
| 1973 | 1.00 | .95 | | | | | | | | |
| 1974 | .95 | | | | | | | | | |

## Retail Prices — Uncirculated Rolls of D Cents

*Face Value of One Roll: $.*

| Year Minted | Number of Years After Year Minted | | | | | | | | | |
|---|---|---|---|---|---|---|---|---|---|---|
| | 11 | 12 | 13 | 14 | 15 | 16 | 17 | 18 | 19 | 20 |
| 1935 | $ 2.50 | $ 3.00 | $ 4.00 | $ 4.00 | $ 3.00 | $ 4.00 | $ 4.65 | $ 5.25 | $ 7.00 | $11.40 |
| 1936 | 2.75 | 2.75 | 2.25 | 2.35 | 2.40 | 2.45 | 2.60 | 2.90 | 7.60 | 8.00 |
| 1937 | 2.15 | 1.75 | 1.75 | 1.75 | 1.80 | 1.80 | 2.75 | 4.60 | 4.60 | 12.50 |
| 1938 | 2.50 | 2.75 | 2.70 | 2.80 | 2.80 | 3.75 | 6.00 | 8.00 | 20.00 | 25.00 |
| 1939 | 3.95 | 3.95 | 4.00 | 4.50 | 6.75 | 9.00 | 21.50 | 45.00 | 65.00 | 95.00 |
| 1940 | 1.40 | 1.50 | 1.75 | 1.95 | 5.50 | 6.00 | 6.50 | 12.50 | 17.50 | 18.00 |
| 1941 | 1.35 | 1.65 | 1.75 | 3.60 | 4.30 | 7.50 | 8.50 | 15.00 | 15.50 | 16.50 |
| 1942 | 1.00 | 1.00 | 1.25 | 1.50 | 2.00 | 5.00 | 7.50 | 9.50 | 8.00 | 12.50 |
| 1943 | 1.00 | 1.25 | 3.00 | 3.75 | 7.00 | 12.50 | 13.50 | 10.50 | 11.00 | 25.00 |
| 1944 | .90 | .95 | 1.30 | 2.45 | 7.50 | 10.00 | 7.00 | 8.00 | 11.00 | 15.00 |
| 1945 | .95 | 1.30 | 2.00 | 6.50 | 12.00 | 8.00 | 8.00 | 20.00 | 20.00 | 15.00 |
| 1946 | 1.50 | 2.00 | 6.00 | 8.00 | 5.00 | 5.75 | 10.00 | 19.00 | 15.50 | 8.50 |
| 1947 | 3.00 | 10.50 | 10.50 | 7.00 | 9.50 | 12.00 | 16.00 | 10.00 | 7.50 | 7.00 |
| 1948 | 11.50 | 11.50 | 8.00 | 11.00 | 17.25 | 16.00 | 14.00 | 10.00 | 8.50 | 7.50 |
| 1949 | 11.50 | 9.00 | 13.00 | 34.00 | 27.50 | 19.00 | 14.00 | 13.50 | 13.00 | 12.00 |
| 1950 | 8.00 | 9.50 | 10.00 | 11.00 | 8.00 | 8.00 | 8.00 | 5.50 | 6.00 | 4.00 |
| 1951 | 6.00 | 8.00 | 7.50 | 6.00 | 5.00 | 4.00 | 4.75 | 5.00 | 3.00 | 2.00 |
| 1952 | 7.50 | 6.50 | 5.00 | 4.00 | 4.00 | 3.50 | 3.25 | 3.00 | 2.00 | 3.7 |
| 1953 | 6.00 | 4.50 | 3.75 | 3.25 | 2.75 | 2.75 | 2.50 | 2.00 | 3.50 | 4.5 |
| 1954 | 6.00 | 5.00 | 3.75 | 3.50 | 3.00 | 2.50 | 2.50 | 3.75 | 4.50 | 6.2 |
| 1955 | 5.00 | 4.00 | 2.50 | 2.50 | 1.25 | 1.00 | 2.25 | 3.25 | 4.00 | 2.5 |
| 1956 | 1.25 | 1.25 | 1.25 | 1.25 | 1.00 | 1.35 | 1.75 | 3.00 | 2.55 | |
| 1957 | 1.15 | 1.00 | 1.00 | 1.00 | 1.25 | 1.50 | 2.85 | 1.90 | | |
| 1958 | 1.00 | 1.00 | 1.00 | 1.25 | 1.50 | 2.00 | 1.65 | | | |
| 1959 | 1.00 | 1.00 | 1.00 | 1.50 | 1.25 | .95 | | | | |
| 1960 | 1.00 | 1.00 | 1.25 | 1.25 | .95 | | | | | |
| 1961 | 1.00 | 1.25 | 1.25 | .95 | | | | | | |
| 1962 | 1.25 | 1.25 | .95 | | | | | | | |
| 1963 | 1.25 | .95 | | | | | | | | |
| 1964 | .95 | | | | | | | | | |

## Retail Prices — Uncirculated Rolls of D Cents

Face Value of One Roll: $.50

| Year Minted | 21 | 22 | 23 | 24 | 25 | 26 | 27 | 28 | 29 | 30 |
|---|---|---|---|---|---|---|---|---|---|---|
| | | | | Number of Years After Year Minted | | | | | | |
| 1935 | $ 19.00 | $ 22.50 | $ 35.00 | $ 38.50 | $ 37.50 | $ 45.00 | $ 90.00 | $150.00 | $115.00 | $100.00 |
| 1936 | 8.85 | 22.00 | 25.00 | 30.00 | 28.00 | 40.00 | 125.00 | 85.00 | 75.00 | 60.00 |
| 1937 | 17.00 | 16.00 | 16.00 | 17.00 | 23.00 | 80.00 | 50.00 | 42.50 | 33.00 | 33.00 |
| 1938 | 29.50 | 32.00 | 35.00 | 52.00 | 155.00 | 135.00 | 105.00 | 90.00 | 85.00 | 58.50 |
| 1939 | 105.00 | 125.00 | 165.00 | 262.50 | 240.00 | 182.50 | 156.00 | 130.00 | 135.00 | 120.00 |
| 1940 | 20.00 | 25.00 | 49.50 | 52.50 | 37.50 | 28.00 | 22.50 | 24.50 | 22.50 | 16.75 |
| 1941 | 33.50 | 65.00 | 60.00 | 45.00 | 35.00 | 28.50 | 37.50 | 37.50 | 30.50 | 32.75 |
| 1942 | 19.50 | 22.50 | 15.00 | 11.00 | 10.00 | 9.00 | 9.00 | 6.50 | 6.00 | 12.50 |
| 1943 | 27.50 | 20.00 | 20.00 | 20.00 | 18.50 | 18.00 | 12.00 | 11.00 | 13.40 | 18.00 |
| 1944 | 10.00 | 7.00 | 6.00 | 6.75 | 5.50 | 3.50 | 3.25 | 4.75 | 6.50 | 8.00 |
| 1945 | 11.00 | 10.00 | 9.50 | 9.00 | 6.75 | 6.25 | 5.35 | 9.25 | 26.00 | 13.00 |
| 1946 | 7.00 | 7.75 | 6.00 | 3.75 | 3.00 | 5.35 | 6.50 | 7.00 | 6.20 | |
| 1947 | 7.50 | 6.50 | 4.75 | 5.00 | 5.50 | 7.50 | 9.00 | 8.90 | | |
| 1948 | 7.50 | 5.50 | 4.50 | 4.25 | 7.00 | 11.00 | 8.15 | | | |
| 1949 | 8.00 | 7.00 | 9.50 | 15.00 | 19.50 | 16.00 | | | | |
| 1950 | 3.50 | 5.75 | 6.50 | 7.00 | 5.95 | | | | | |
| 1951 | 3.75 | 4.50 | 6.50 | 4.75 | | | | | | |
| 1952 | 4.25 | 4.75 | 3.50 | | | | | | | |
| 1953 | 4.50 | 3.50 | | | | | | | | |
| 1954 | 4.25 | | | | | | | | | |

## Retail Prices — Uncirculated Rolls of D Cents

Face Value of One Roll: $.5

| Year Minted | Number of Years After Year Minted | | | | | | | | | |
|---|---|---|---|---|---|---|---|---|---|---|
| | 31 | 32 | 33 | 34 | 35 | 36 | 37 | 38 | 39 | 40 |
| 1935 | $70.00 | $67.50 | $50.00 | $47.50 | $ 34.25 | $25.00 | $25.00 | $34.00 | $56.00 | $41.00 |
| 1936 | 60.00 | 45.00 | 45.00 | 30.00 | 20.50 | 20.00 | 31.00 | 41.00 | 33.00 | |
| 1937 | 35.00 | 31.00 | 22.25 | 17.25 | 18.75 | 27.00 | 55.00 | 35.00 | | |
| 1938 | 52.50 | 39.50 | 33.25 | 26.80 | 61.50 | 76.00 | 42.75 | | | |
| 1939 | 82.50 | 65.00 | 92.50 | 68.00 | 130.00 | 90.00 | | | | |
| 1940 | 14.75 | 12.00 | 21.00 | 37.00 | 33.00 | | | | | |
| 1941 | 42.50 | 41.00 | 85.00 | 59.00 | | | | | | |
| 1942 | 10.50 | 15.00 | 9.00 | | | | | | | |
| 1943 | 25.00 | 26.00 | | | | | | | | |
| 1944 | 7.50 | | | | | | | | | |

## Retail Prices — Uncirculated Rolls of S Cents

Face Value of One Roll: $.50

| Year Minted | Number of Years After Year Minted | | | | | | | | | |
|---|---|---|---|---|---|---|---|---|---|---|
| | 1 | 2 | 3 | 4 | 5 | 6 | 7 | 8 | 9 | 10 |
| 1935 | $1.00 | $1.40 | $1.40 | $1.50 | $ 1.75 | $ 2.25 | $ 2.25 | $ 2.90 | $ 3.50 | $ 4.00 |
| 1936 | 1.35 | 1.35 | 1.35 | 1.75 | 2.00 | 1.75 | 2.25 | 2.00 | 2.25 | 2.40 |
| 1937 | .80 | 1.10 | 1.25 | 1.25 | 1.40 | 2.00 | 2.00 | 2.00 | 2.00 | 2.00 |
| 1938 | .95 | 1.00 | .90 | 1.10 | 1.85 | 2.00 | 2.25 | 2.75 | 2.85 | 3.00 |
| 1939 | .75 | .75 | 1.00 | 1.50 | 1.50 | 1.85 | 2.00 | 2.00 | 2.10 | 1.80 |
| 1940 | 1.00 | .95 | 1.25 | 1.25 | 1.25 | 1.35 | 1.45 | 1.50 | 1.50 | 1.40 |
| 1941 | .85 | 1.10 | 1.10 | 1.25 | 1.50 | 1.40 | 1.50 | 1.50 | 1.25 | 1.85 |
| 1942 | 1.15 | 1.50 | 3.25 | 5.50 | 5.75 | 6.00 | 6.00 | 5.75 | 4.25 | 4.00 |
| 1943 | .80 | 1.60 | 2.50 | 2.25 | 2.35 | 2.35 | 2.25 | 3.00 | 2.75 | 2.50 |
| 1944 | .75 | .80 | .80 | .90 | .90 | .85 | .80 | .90 | .90 | .90 |
| 1945 | .75 | .75 | .85 | .80 | .75 | .75 | .85 | .85 | .90 | .85 |
| 1946 | .70 | .80 | .80 | .75 | .75 | .80 | .80 | .90 | .90 | .95 |
| 1947 | .75 | .75 | .75 | .85 | .85 | 1.00 | 1.00 | 1.75 | 1.70 | 3.00 |
| 1948 | .70 | .75 | .85 | .85 | .85 | 1.25 | 1.15 | 2.70 | 4.25 | 6.00 |
| 1949 | .75 | .85 | .85 | 1.00 | 3.00 | 3.00 | 4.25 | 6.00 | 11.50 | 25.50 |
| 1950 | .85 | .85 | .85 | .95 | 2.30 | 2.55 | 2.30 | 7.50 | 11.45 | 25.00 |
| 1951 | .80 | 1.00 | .95 | 3.60 | 3.00 | 4.50 | 8.95 | 22.50 | 30.00 | 30.00 |
| 1952 | 1.00 | 1.50 | 2.50 | 2.75 | 3.50 | 5.50 | 15.00 | 19.00 | 19.00 | 27.50 |
| 1953 | .80 | .90 | 1.85 | 2.50 | 4.00 | 9.50 | 12.50 | 11.50 | 19.25 | 27.00 |
| 1954 | .90 | 1.20 | 1.25 | 2.25 | 4.25 | 7.00 | 7.00 | 19.00 | 26.00 | 22.50 |
| 1955 | 1.60 | 1.65 | 1.90 | 7.25 | 10.00 | 13.25 | 35.00 | 42.50 | 38.00 | 28.00 |
| 1968 | 1.25 | 1.00 | 1.00 | 1.00 | 1.50 | 1.75 | 1.15 | | | |
| 1969 | 1.00 | 1.00 | 1.00 | 1.75 | 1.75 | 1.30 | | | | |
| 1970 | .85 | .90 | 1.50 | 2.20 | 1.65 | | | | | |
| 1971 | 1.50 | 2.25 | 2.35 | 1.95 | | | | | | |
| 1972 | 1.00 | 1.50 | 1.10 | | | | | | | |
| 1973 | 1.50 | 1.00 | | | | | | | | |
| 1974 | 2.30 | | | | | | | | | |

## Retail Prices — Uncirculated Rolls of S Cents

Face Value of One Roll: $.5

| Year Minted | Number of Years After Year Minted | | | | | | | | | |
|---|---|---|---|---|---|---|---|---|---|---|
| | 11 | 12 | 13 | 14 | 15 | 16 | 17 | 18 | 19 | 20 |
| 1935 | $ 4.85 | $ 5.00 | $ 5.00 | $ 5.00 | $ 5.00 | $ 5.00 | $ 5.10 | $ 5.25 | $ 7.00 | $14.15 |
| 1936 | 3.50 | 3.50 | 3.00 | 2.50 | 2.65 | 2.65 | 2.80 | 3.95 | 8.00 | 7.75 |
| 1937 | 2.25 | 1.75 | 1.75 | 1.75 | 1.80 | 1.80 | 2.75 | 5.00 | 6.00 | 17.50 |
| 1938 | 2.75 | 2.55 | 2.75 | 2.75 | 2.75 | 4.50 | 5.60 | 12.00 | 24.00 | 38.00 |
| 1939 | 1.75 | 2.25 | 2.55 | 3.00 | 3.75 | 7.50 | 9.00 | 10.00 | 20.00 | 22.50 |
| 1940 | 1.75 | 1.75 | 1.75 | 1.95 | 5.50 | 5.25 | 7.00 | 12.00 | 15.00 | 17.00 |
| 1941 | 2.00 | 2.35 | 2.50 | 4.60 | 5.75 | 9.00 | 11.75 | 15.00 | 17.00 | 20.00 |
| 1942 | 4.65 | 5.00 | 5.00 | 8.00 | 15.00 | 29.00 | 39.50 | 42.00 | 63.00 | 125.00 |
| 1943 | 3.50 | 7.60 | 8.00 | 13.00 | 30.00 | 35.00 | 35.00 | 35.00 | 39.00 | 52.00 |
| 1944 | .90 | .95 | 1.75 | 3.00 | 8.50 | 10.25 | 8.00 | 12.00 | 20.50 | 22.50 |
| 1945 | .95 | 2.10 | 3.00 | 7.50 | 10.00 | 9.00 | 12.50 | 20.00 | 23.00 | 19.00 |
| 1946 | 2.00 | 3.00 | 7.00 | 8.00 | 6.00 | 11.75 | 18.00 | 20.00 | 12.50 | 8.00 |
| 1947 | 5.75 | 12.50 | 13.00 | 9.00 | 24.00 | 45.50 | 48.00 | 30.00 | 20.00 | 12.50 |
| 1948 | 12.50 | 24.00 | 20.00 | 27.00 | 53.00 | 77.50 | 55.00 | 39.00 | 30.00 | 31.50 |
| 1949 | 39.00 | 32.50 | 45.00 | 76.00 | 87.50 | 70.00 | 50.00 | 45.00 | 40.00 | 40.00 |
| 1950 | 18.00 | 25.00 | 31.00 | 37.50 | 35.00 | 27.00 | 22.50 | 15.50 | 14.00 | 12.00 |
| 1951 | 42.00 | 55.00 | 60.00 | 48.00 | 27.50 | 22.50 | 27.50 | 26.50 | 17.00 | 15.00 |
| 1952 | 30.00 | 37.50 | 27.00 | 20.00 | 16.00 | 15.00 | 15.00 | 12.00 | 11.00 | 11.50 |
| 1953 | 27.50 | 21.00 | 15.00 | 12.00 | 8.00 | 8.00 | 5.50 | 6.00 | 7.00 | 8.00 |
| 1954 | 16.00 | 12.50 | 10.00 | 7.50 | 7.50 | 4.25 | 4.00 | 5.25 | 6.00 | 10.25 |
| 1955 | 23.00 | 18.00 | 17.00 | 15.75 | 11.00 | 10.00 | 11.75 | 12.00 | 16.50 | 12.75 |

## Retail Prices — Uncirculated Rolls of S Cents

Face Value of One Roll: $.50

| Year Minted | Number of Years After Year Minted | | | | | | | | | |
|---|---|---|---|---|---|---|---|---|---|---|
| | 21 | 22 | 23 | 24 | 25 | 26 | 27 | 28 | 29 | 30 |
| 1935 | $ 19.00 | $ 21.00 | $ 35.00 | $ 50.00 | $ 65.00 | $ 77.00 | $150.00 | $255.00 | $200.00 | $170.00 |
| 1936 | 8.85 | 25.00 | 29.50 | 40.00 | 40.00 | 54.00 | 160.00 | 120.00 | 95.00 | 83.00 |
| 1937 | 20.00 | 22.50 | 24.50 | 24.50 | 36.00 | 115.00 | 85.00 | 70.00 | 53.00 | 50.00 |
| 1938 | 40.00 | 47.00 | 58.00 | 120.00 | 211.50 | 180.00 | 115.00 | 100.00 | 90.00 | 73.00 |
| 1939 | 24.00 | 22.50 | 35.00 | 75.00 | 67.50 | 52.50 | 31.00 | 30.00 | 28.00 | 26.50 |
| 1940 | 19.00 | 23.00 | 42.50 | 40.00 | 24.00 | 20.00 | 16.50 | 16.00 | 15.00 | 11.00 |
| 1941 | 44.00 | 65.00 | 60.00 | 40.00 | 35.00 | 30.00 | 37.50 | 37.50 | 37.00 | 35.50 |
| 1942 | 220.00 | 220.00 | 185.00 | 140.00 | 120.00 | 128.00 | 120.00 | 85.00 | 78.00 | 139.50 |
| 1943 | 60.00 | 45.00 | 35.00 | 35.00 | 33.00 | 30.00 | 25.00 | 23.75 | 34.00 | 39.00 |
| 1944 | 17.50 | 11.00 | 9.00 | 9.50 | 8.50 | 6.75 | 5.75 | 8.00 | 8.00 | 13.00 |
| 1945 | 13.50 | 10.00 | 9.50 | 9.50 | 6.75 | 6.00 | 11.50 | 9.25 | 18.00 | 11.25 |
| 1946 | 7.25 | 7.75 | 7.00 | 3.75 | 3.50 | 10.00 | 19.50 | 18.00 | 15.50 | |
| 1947 | 16.50 | 16.00 | 16.25 | 17.50 | 20.00 | 23.00 | 26.00 | 16.00 | | |
| 1948 | 28.50 | 19.50 | 17.00 | 19.00 | 22.00 | 31.50 | 17.25 | | | |
| 1949 | 26.00 | 24.00 | 30.00 | 31.00 | 54.00 | 36.00 | | | | |
| 1950 | 9.50 | 14.00 | 18.00 | 14.75 | 13.00 | | | | | |
| 1951 | 25.00 | 23.50 | 32.00 | 24.00 | | | | | | |
| 1952 | 12.00 | 24.00 | 23.00 | | | | | | | |
| 1953 | 14.00 | 11.50 | | | | | | | | |
| 1954 | 5.40 | | | | | | | | | |

## Retail Prices — Uncirculated Rolls of S Cents

Face Value of One Roll: $.5

| Year Minted | Number of Years After Year Minted | | | | | | | | | |
|---|---|---|---|---|---|---|---|---|---|---|
| | 31 | 32 | 33 | 34 | 35 | 36 | 37 | 38 | 39 | 40 |
| 1935 | $160.00 | $157.50 | $102.50 | $105.00 | $70.00 | $57.50 | $92.00 | $97.00 | $195.00 | $167.00 |
| 1936 | 80.00 | 67.00 | 57.50 | 32.75 | 25.75 | 46.00 | 39.00 | 52.00 | 37.50 | |
| 1937 | 37.50 | 37.50 | 25.50 | 17.25 | 24.50 | 28.50 | 55.00 | 36.00 | | |
| 1938 | 70.00 | 50.00 | 41.75 | 79.50 | 82.00 | 100.00 | 70.00 | | | |
| 1939 | 20.25 | 16.50 | 25.00 | 34.00 | 64.00 | 40.50 | | | | |
| 1940 | 10.50 | 18.50 | 17.50 | 25.00 | 22.00 | | | | | |
| 1941 | 69.50 | 73.00 | 120.00 | 79.00 | | | | | | |
| 1942 | 127.50 | 210.00 | 125.00 | | | | | | | |
| 1943 | 62.00 | 56.75 | | | | | | | | |
| 1944 | 10.50 | | | | | | | | | |

## Retail Prices — Uncirculated Rolls of P Nickels

*Face Value of One Roll: $2.00*

| Year Minted | Number of Years After Year Minted | | | | | | | | | |
|---|---|---|---|---|---|---|---|---|---|---|
| | 1 | 2 | 3 | 4 | 5 | 6 | 7 | 8 | 9 | 10 |
| 1935 | $ 2.60 | $ 2.75 | $ 2.75 | $ 3.00 | $ 3.50 | $ 4.25 | $ 5.50 | $ 6.00 | $ 6.00 | $ 7.75 |
| 1936 | 2.65 | 2.95 | 3.00 | 4.00 | 4.00 | 4.00 | 4.00 | 5.50 | 5.50 | 5.50 |
| 1937 | 2.40 | 2.50 | 3.00 | 3.00 | 3.50 | 3.60 | 5.00 | 5.00 | 5.00 | 5.00 |
| 1938 | 2.50 | 2.90 | 3.00 | 3.10 | 4.50 | 5.00 | 5.75 | 6.00 | 6.00 | 6.00 |
| 1939 | 3.50 | 3.50 | 6.25 | 6.35 | 8.00 | 8.40 | 9.00 | 10.50 | 10.00 | 10.00 |
| 1940 | 2.75 | 3.00 | 3.20 | 4.00 | 4.15 | 4.40 | 4.50 | 4.75 | 4.50 | 4.50 |
| 1941 | 2.75 | 3.50 | 3.75 | 3.90 | 4.00 | 4.00 | 4.00 | 3.75 | 4.10 | 4.50 |
| *1942 | 7.25 | 7.00 | 9.00 | 9.00 | 7.50 | 7.50 | 6.50 | 6.95 | 6.95 | 5.95 |
| **1942 | 2.75 | 2.50 | 2.75 | 3.00 | 3.00 | 3.00 | 3.00 | 3.00 | 2.90 | 2.85 |
| 1943 | 2.35 | 2.50 | 2.75 | 3.00 | 3.00 | 2.75 | 2.95 | 3.00 | 2.75 | 2.95 |
| 1944 | 2.40 | 2.50 | 2.75 | 2.75 | 3.00 | 2.75 | 2.75 | 2.85 | 2.65 | 3.00 |
| 1945 | 2.45 | 2.75 | 2.75 | 2.60 | 2.75 | 2.75 | 2.75 | 2.75 | 2.75 | 2.85 |
| 1946 | 2.75 | 2.75 | 2.65 | 2.60 | 2.85 | 2.80 | 2.80 | 2.75 | 2.85 | 3.00 |
| 1947 | 2.75 | 2.60 | 2.50 | 2.75 | 2.75 | 2.75 | 2.75 | 2.75 | 2.75 | 3.50 |
| 1948 | 2.50 | 2.50 | 2.65 | 2.65 | 2.75 | 3.60 | 3.60 | 3.50 | 3.75 | 4.50 |
| 1949 | 2.45 | 2.45 | 2.50 | 2.75 | 4.00 | 4.30 | 4.00 | 4.95 | 5.50 | 5.50 |
| 1950 | 3.25 | 3.25 | 6.85 | 11.50 | 11.50 | 11.50 | 14.00 | 17.00 | 25.00 | 75.00 |
| 1951 | 2.60 | 2.75 | 2.60 | 2.60 | 6.00 | 6.50 | 6.50 | 9.00 | 25.00 | 16.00 |
| 1952 | 2.50 | 2.50 | 2.65 | 2.85 | 3.00 | 6.00 | 6.00 | 16.00 | 14.00 | 14.00 |
| 1953 | 2.50 | 2.60 | 2.65 | 3.00 | 3.75 | 4.00 | 12.00 | 10.00 | 9.00 | 18.00 |
| 1954 | 2.50 | 2.65 | 2.75 | 3.45 | 5.00 | 11.00 | 9.00 | 8.00 | 14.00 | 15.00 |
| 1955 | 9.00 | 9.50 | 9.50 | 10.00 | 47.50 | 36.00 | 50.00 | 147.00 | 135.00 | 90.00 |
| 1956 | 3.00 | 3.00 | 3.25 | 8.00 | 6.50 | 6.00 | 16.00 | 13.00 | 8.50 | 7.00 |
| 1957 | 2.85 | 3.50 | 7.00 | 6.75 | 5.75 | 14.00 | 14.50 | 12.00 | 8.00 | 4.75 |
| 1958 | 4.50 | 13.50 | 8.50 | 12.00 | 33.00 | 37.00 | 30.00 | 20.00 | 10.75 | 12.50 |
| 1959 | 8.00 | 4.75 | 5.00 | 16.00 | 14.00 | 12.00 | 8.00 | 5.50 | 6.00 | 5.50 |
| 1960 | 3.50 | 3.00 | 6.00 | 6.50 | 4.00 | 3.25 | 3.25 | 3.25 | 3.00 | 3.00 |
| 1961 | 2.75 | 3.50 | 4.50 | 4.00 | 3.00 | 3.00 | 3.25 | 3.50 | 3.00 | 3.00 |
| 1962 | 3.15 | 3.75 | 3.25 | 3.00 | 2.75 | 3.00 | 3.00 | 3.00 | 3.00 | 3.00 |
| 1963 | 2.50 | 2.75 | 2.75 | 2.75 | 3.00 | 3.00 | 3.00 | 3.00 | 3.00 | 3.15 |
| 1964 | 2.60 | 3.00 | 2.75 | 2.80 | 3.00 | 3.00 | 3.00 | 3.00 | 3.75 | 4.00 |
| 1965 | 3.25 | 2.65 | 2.75 | 3.00 | 2.85 | 2.80 | 3.00 | 3.90 | 4.00 | 4.00 |
| 1966 | 2.65 | 2.75 | 3.00 | 2.85 | 2.80 | 3.00 | 3.90 | 4.00 | 4.15 | |
| 1967 | 2.75 | 3.00 | 2.85 | 2.80 | 3.00 | 3.90 | 4.00 | 4.65 | | |
| 1971 | 2.80 | 3.50 | 4.00 | 5.25 | | | | | | |
| 1972 | 3.50 | 4.00 | 4.75 | | | | | | | |
| 1973 | 4.00 | 4.00 | | | | | | | | |
| 1974 | 3.25 | | | | | | | | | |

*e-War (made of nickel)
*artime Alloy

## Retail Prices — Uncirculated Rolls of P Nickels

*Face Value of One Roll: $2.00*

| Year Minted | 11 | 12 | 13 | 14 | 15 | 16 | 17 | 18 | 19 | 20 |
|---|---|---|---|---|---|---|---|---|---|---|
| | | | | Number of Years After Year Minted | | | | | | |
| 1935 | $10.25 | $12.50 | $11.40 | $11.25 | $10.00 | $10.00 | $10.30 | $10.75 | $12.00 | $13.00 |
| 1936 | 5.50 | 5.50 | 5.50 | 5.50 | 5.50 | 6.00 | 6.00 | 6.00 | 11.00 | 15.00 |
| 1937 | 5.00 | 5.00 | 5.00 | 5.00 | 5.00 | 5.00 | 6.00 | 7.00 | 9.25 | 15.00 |
| 1938 | 6.00 | 6.00 | 6.00 | 5.55 | 5.50 | 5.50 | 7.00 | 8.00 | 13.50 | 15.00 |
| 1939 | 10.00 | 11.00 | 10.25 | 9.75 | 9.50 | 16.50 | 29.00 | 30.00 | 40.00 | 80.00 |
| 1940 | 4.50 | 4.50 | 4.50 | 5.00 | 7.00 | 8.00 | 9.00 | 12.00 | 20.00 | 22.00 |
| 1941 | 4.00 | 4.00 | 5.00 | 7.00 | 6.00 | 7.00 | 8.00 | 12.00 | 17.50 | 21.00 |
| *1942 | 6.00 | 5.50 | 5.50 | 8.00 | 9.00 | 10.00 | 15.00 | 28.00 | 30.00 | 30.00 |
| **1942 | 3.00 | 3.00 | 3.50 | 4.00 | 4.00 | 15.50 | 65.00 | 110.00 | 88.00 | 110.50 |
| 1943 | 3.00 | 3.30 | 3.00 | 3.25 | 5.00 | 33.00 | 35.00 | 23.00 | 25.00 | 75.00 |
| 1944 | 3.00 | 3.00 | 4.00 | 5.00 | 33.00 | 35.00 | 28.00 | 26.00 | 85.00 | 120.00 |
| 1945 | 3.00 | 3.45 | 4.50 | 27.00 | 29.50 | 21.00 | 25.00 | 77.50 | 155.00 | 100.00 |
| 1946 | 3.50 | 4.00 | 4.50 | 10.50 | 10.00 | 10.00 | 16.00 | 22.50 | 15.00 | 8.50 |
| 1947 | 4.50 | 4.50 | 9.50 | 9.50 | 9.50 | 17.00 | 25.00 | 19.00 | 8.00 | 7.50 |
| 1948 | 7.00 | 10.00 | 11.00 | 10.00 | 18.00 | 24.00 | 18.00 | 10.00 | 7.00 | 13.50 |
| 1949 | 35.00 | 24.00 | 24.00 | 30.00 | 53.00 | 50.00 | 30.00 | 17.50 | 19.50 | 17.50 |
| 1950 | 52.50 | 65.00 | 220.00 | 190.00 | 140.00 | 85.00 | 60.00 | 85.00 | 70.00 | 51.50 |
| 1951 | 15.00 | 72.00 | 70.00 | 45.00 | 35.00 | 21.50 | 26.00 | 28.00 | 21.50 | 16.00 |
| 1952 | 15.00 | 24.00 | 20.00 | 10.00 | 8.00 | 16.50 | 15.50 | 13.00 | 8.50 | 9.00 |
| 1953 | 19.00 | 12.50 | 8.00 | 6.00 | 7.00 | 6.50 | 6.00 | 4.00 | 4.50 | 11.00 |
| 1954 | 12.50 | 6.50 | 4.75 | 6.50 | 6.50 | 5.00 | 5.00 | 3.75 | 5.25 | 6.00 |
| 1955 | 67.50 | 50.00 | 52.00 | 50.00 | 35.50 | 27.50 | 32.50 | 35.00 | 40.00 | 21.25 |
| 1956 | 4.25 | 6.00 | 5.00 | 4.50 | 4.00 | 3.50 | 4.00 | 4.00 | 4.00 | |
| 1957 | 6.00 | 5.50 | 4.50 | 4.00 | 3.50 | 4.00 | 4.00 | 4.25 | | |
| 1958 | 12.00 | 11.75 | 7.50 | 5.50 | 7.00 | 11.50 | 5.90 | | | |
| 1959 | 4.75 | 4.00 | 3.50 | 4.75 | 4.00 | 3.65 | | | | |
| 1960 | 3.00 | 3.00 | 3.50 | 4.00 | 3.40 | | | | | |
| 1961 | 3.00 | 3.25 | 4.00 | 3.40 | | | | | | |
| 1962 | 3.25 | 4.00 | 3.40 | | | | | | | |
| 1963 | 4.00 | 3.40 | | | | | | | | |
| 1964 | 3.40 | | | | | | | | | |

*Pre-War (made of nickel)
**Wartime Alloy

## Retail Prices — Uncirculated Rolls of P Nickels

*Face Value of One Roll: $2.00*

| Year Minted | Number of Years After Year Minted | | | | | | | | | |
|---|---|---|---|---|---|---|---|---|---|---|
| | 21 | 22 | 23 | 24 | 25 | 26 | 27 | 28 | 29 | 30 |
| 1935 | $ 15.00 | $ 20.00 | $ 27.00 | $ 40.00 | $ 35.00 | $ 43.00 | $ 80.00 | $120.00 | $135.00 | $125.00 |
| 1936 | 20.00 | 27.00 | 35.00 | 35.00 | 38.00 | 62.50 | 85.00 | 125.00 | 125.00 | 125.00 |
| 1937 | 17.50 | 20.00 | 32.50 | 43.00 | 57.50 | 100.00 | 145.00 | 145.00 | 145.00 | 95.00 |
| 1938 | 35.00 | 60.00 | 45.00 | 45.00 | 100.00 | 125.00 | 100.00 | 65.00 | 47.50 | 50.00 |
| 1939 | 75.00 | 75.00 | 75.00 | 70.00 | 65.00 | 35.00 | 34.00 | 30.00 | 42.50 | 44.00 |
| 1940 | 25.00 | 30.00 | 31.00 | 37.50 | 30.00 | 28.00 | 21.50 | 27.50 | 25.00 | 18.50 |
| 1941 | 21.00 | 25.00 | 35.00 | 27.50 | 26.00 | 21.00 | 24.00 | 24.00 | 18.50 | 14.00 |
| *1942 | 105.00 | 83.00 | 55.00 | 35.00 | 32.50 | 42.50 | 45.00 | 37.75 | 29.00 | 28.00 |
| *1942 | 365.00 | 400.00 | 275.00 | 235.00 | 160.00 | 270.00 | 257.00 | 156.50 | 144.75 | 183.00 |
| 1943 | 80.00 | 67.50 | 55.00 | 38.50 | 47.50 | 42.50 | 35.00 | 30.00 | 42.50 | 56.50 |
| 1944 | 110.00 | 92.50 | 60.00 | 70.00 | 67.50 | 46.75 | 37.75 | 47.50 | 71.50 | 70.00 |
| 1945 | 98.00 | 65.00 | 100.00 | 98.00 | 70.00 | 52.50 | 60.00 | 80.00 | 72.00 | 60.00 |
| 1946 | 6.50 | 10.00 | 8.00 | 6.75 | 5.00 | 6.00 | 11.00 | 12.00 | 9.65 | |
| 1947 | 15.00 | 11.00 | 7.00 | 5.00 | 6.00 | 9.00 | 9.00 | 7.75 | | |
| 1948 | 11.00 | 9.00 | 5.00 | 7.25 | 12.00 | 16.50 | 9.90 | | | |
| 1949 | 15.00 | 11.50 | 11.50 | 14.50 | 17.00 | 18.00 | | | | |
| 1950 | 46.50 | 49.00 | 57.00 | 70.75 | 39.00 | | | | | |
| 1951 | 30.00 | 23.00 | 32.00 | 20.50 | | | | | | |
| 1952 | 11.00 | 17.75 | 9.90 | | | | | | | |
| 1953 | 8.75 | 5.50 | | | | | | | | |
| 1954 | 4.50 | | | | | | | | | |

Pre-War (made of nickel)
Wartime Alloy

### Retail Prices — Uncirculated Rolls of P Nickels

*Face Value of One Roll: $2.00*

| Year Minted | 31 | 32 | 33 | 34 | 35 | 36 | 37 | 38 | 39 | 40 |
|---|---|---|---|---|---|---|---|---|---|---|
| | | | | Number of Years After Year Minted | | | | | | |
| 1935 | $125.00 | $125.00 | $125.00 | $135.00 | $ 90.00 | $115.00 | $127.00 | $245.00 | $395.00 | $306.00 |
| 1936 | 125.00 | 115.00 | 110.00 | 84.50 | 86.00 | 98.75 | 200.00 | 360.00 | 253.00 | |
| 1937 | 110.00 | 110.00 | 86.00 | 106.00 | 119.85 | 215.50 | 340.00 | 262.00 | | |
| 1938 | 47.00 | 33.00 | 25.00 | 32.50 | 36.00 | 43.00 | 33.25 | | | |
| 1939 | 27.00 | 25.00 | 22.75 | 24.00 | 42.00 | 33.00 | | | | |
| 1940 | 13.50 | 13.50 | 19.00 | 25.00 | 24.00 | | | | | |
| 1941 | 13.50 | 18.00 | 23.00 | 19.25 | | | | | | |
| *1942 | 36.00 | 57.00 | 53.00 | | | | | | | |
| **1942 | 300.00 | 400.00 | 314.00 | | | | | | | |
| 1943 | 67.00 | 50.00 | | | | | | | | |
| 1944 | 55.00 | | | | | | | | | |

*Pre-War (made of nickel)
**Wartime Alloy

## Retail Prices — Uncirculated Rolls of D Nickels

*Face Value of One Roll: $2.00*

| Year Minted | Number of Years After Year Minted | | | | | | | | | |
|---|---|---|---|---|---|---|---|---|---|---|
| | 1 | 2 | 3 | 4 | 5 | 6 | 7 | 8 | 9 | 10 |
| 1935 | $ 2.50 | $ 2.75 | $ 2.75 | $ 3.00 | $ 5.50 | $ 5.25 | $ 5.50 | $ 6.00 | $ 6.00 | $ 8.00 |
| 1936 | 2.65 | 2.75 | 3.10 | 4.00 | 4.00 | 4.00 | 4.95 | 5.50 | 5.50 | 9.00 |
| 1937 | 2.40 | 2.55 | 3.00 | 3.00 | 3.00 | 4.85 | 5.00 | 5.50 | 8.00 | 8.75 |
| *1938 | 2.75 | 2.85 | 3.00 | 3.00 | 4.75 | 3.75 | 4.00 | 3.75 | 4.00 | 4.00 |
| *1938 | 2.55 | 2.65 | 2.85 | 3.50 | 4.75 | 5.00 | 6.50 | 8.00 | 11.50 | 11.00 |
| 1939 | 4.00 | 15.00 | 16.75 | 20.00 | 20.00 | 36.00 | 50.00 | 75.00 | 50.00 | 61.50 |
| 1940 | 2.65 | 2.95 | 3.15 | 4.25 | 4.70 | 5.00 | 5.50 | 5.75 | 5.50 | 5.50 |
| 1941 | 2.75 | 3.25 | 3.75 | 3.90 | 4.00 | 4.00 | 4.00 | 4.00 | 4.50 | 4.50 |
| 1942 | 10.70 | 10.50 | 20.50 | 27.00 | 37.50 | 40.00 | 32.50 | 30.00 | 27.50 | 30.00 |
| 1943 | 2.35 | 2.75 | 2.95 | 3.00 | 3.00 | 3.00 | 2.95 | 3.50 | 3.00 | 2.95 |
| 1944 | 2.75 | 2.75 | 2.75 | 2.75 | 2.60 | 2.75 | 2.75 | 2.85 | 2.85 | 3.00 |
| 1945 | 2.45 | 2.75 | 2.75 | 2.60 | 2.75 | 2.75 | 2.75 | 2.85 | 2.75 | 3.00 |
| 1946 | 2.75 | 2.75 | 2.50 | 2.50 | 2.70 | 2.75 | 2.75 | 2.75 | 2.85 | 3.00 |
| 1947 | 2.65 | 2.65 | 2.45 | 2.70 | 2.75 | 2.60 | 2.75 | 2.85 | 3.00 | 3.50 |
| 1948 | 2.50 | 2.25 | 2.75 | 2.75 | 2.75 | 3.75 | 3.60 | 3.00 | 3.75 | 4.00 |
| 1949 | 2.45 | 2.45 | 2.55 | 2.75 | 4.00 | 4.30 | 4.00 | 4.00 | 4.75 | 5.25 |
| 1950 | 5.50 | 5.50 | 5.75 | 5.25 | 9.25 | 13.00 | 24.50 | 33.00 | 75.00 | 190.00 |
| 1951 | 2.65 | 2.75 | 2.70 | 7.60 | 7.00 | 7.00 | 7.50 | 12.00 | 65.00 | 35.00 |
| 1952 | 2.65 | 2.60 | 5.00 | 5.00 | 6.50 | 7.00 | 50.00 | 120.00 | 75.00 | 110.00 |
| 1953 | 2.50 | 2.55 | 2.65 | 2.75 | 3.75 | 5.00 | 16.00 | 10.00 | 10.00 | 23.00 |
| 1954 | 2.40 | 2.50 | 2.65 | 3.50 | 4.25 | 11.00 | 9.00 | 7.50 | 14.00 | 10.00 |
| 1955 | 2.60 | 2.75 | 2.75 | 3.00 | 13.00 | 8.75 | 8.00 | 28.00 | 20.00 | 14.00 |
| 1956 | 2.50 | 2.75 | 3.25 | 8.00 | 6.50 | 6.00 | 13.00 | 9.00 | 4.50 | 4.00 |
| 1957 | 2.85 | 3.25 | 6.50 | 6.50 | 5.00 | 8.00 | 5.00 | 3.50 | 3.00 | 3.50 |
| 1958 | 3.00 | 4.00 | 4.00 | 4.00 | 7.00 | 4.50 | 4.00 | 3.25 | 3.00 | 3.25 |
| 1959 | 2.75 | 3.25 | 3.25 | 4.50 | 4.00 | 3.00 | 3.00 | 3.00 | 3.00 | 3.00 |
| 1960 | 2.75 | 3.00 | 3.50 | 3.50 | 3.00 | 3.00 | 3.00 | 3.00 | 3.00 | 3.00 |
| 1961 | 2.75 | 3.35 | 3.50 | 3.00 | 3.00 | 2.75 | 3.00 | 3.00 | 3.00 | 3.00 |
| 1962 | 3.15 | 3.25 | 3.00 | 3.00 | 2.75 | 3.00 | 3.00 | 3.00 | 3.00 | 3.00 |
| 1963 | 2.35 | 2.50 | 2.50 | 2.75 | 3.00 | 3.00 | 3.00 | 3.00 | 3.00 | 3.15 |
| 1964 | 2.50 | 3.00 | 2.75 | 2.80 | 3.00 | 3.00 | 3.00 | 3.25 | 3.75 | 4.00 |
| 1968 | 2.85 | 2.70 | 2.75 | 3.00 | 3.75 | 4.00 | 4.00 | | | |
| 1969 | 2.70 | 2.75 | 2.80 | 3.60 | 4.00 | 4.00 | | | | |
| 1970 | 2.75 | 2.80 | 3.50 | 4.00 | 4.00 | | | | | |
| 1971 | 2.80 | 3.50 | 4.00 | 4.00 | | | | | | |
| 1972 | 3.50 | 4.00 | 4.00 | | | | | | | |
| 1973 | 4.00 | 4.00 | | | | | | | | |
| 1974 | 3.50 | | | | | | | | | |

———
*ffalo nickel
**fferson nickel

## Retail Prices — Uncirculated Rolls of D Nickels

*Face Value of One Roll: $2.0(*

| Year Minted | \| Number of Years After Year Minted | | | | | | | | | |
|---|---|---|---|---|---|---|---|---|---|---|
| | 11 | 12 | 13 | 14 | 15 | 16 | 17 | 18 | 19 | 20 |
| 1935 | $ 10.00 | $ 12.00 | $ 11.00 | $ 11.00 | $ 12.00 | $ 15.00 | $ 15.00 | $ 15.00 | $ 20.00 | $ 22.00 |
| 1936 | 12.00 | 9.00 | 9.00 | 8.75 | 8.50 | 8.75 | 8.75 | 16.75 | 17.50 | 18.00 |
| 1937 | 8.75 | 8.75 | 8.75 | 8.75 | 8.75 | 8.75 | 8.50 | 9.00 | 9.25 | 17.50 |
| *1938 | 4.00 | 3.95 | 3.95 | 3.85 | 4.00 | 3.75 | 4.00 | 5.50 | 15.00 | 17.50 |
| **1938 | 10.50 | 9.00 | 12.00 | 9.00 | 8.50 | 8.50 | 17.00 | 19.00 | 16.00 | 16.50 |
| 1939 | 62.75 | 62.50 | 70.00 | 70.00 | 85.00 | 90.00 | 145.00 | 225.00 | 320.00 | 700.00 |
| 1940 | 5.25 | 5.50 | 7.00 | 10.00 | 15.00 | 14.50 | 14.50 | 14.50 | 27.00 | 37.50 |
| 1941 | 4.00 | 4.00 | 5.75 | 7.00 | 6.00 | 7.00 | 8.00 | 15.00 | 25.00 | 33.00 |
| 1942 | 33.00 | 35.00 | 42.75 | 53.00 | 90.00 | 150.00 | 300.00 | 500.00 | 350.00 | 390.00 |
| 1943 | 3.00 | 3.30 | 6.00 | 7.00 | 12.00 | 35.00 | 45.00 | 38.00 | 45.00 | 160.00 |
| 1944 | 3.00 | 3.00 | 3.15 | 6.00 | 25.00 | 35.00 | 28.00 | 31.00 | 80.00 | 82.50 |
| 1945 | 3.00 | 3.50 | 4.50 | 10.00 | 27.00 | 20.00 | 22.00 | 62.00 | 70.00 | 60.00 |
| 1946 | 3.00 | 4.50 | 8.00 | 11.50 | 10.00 | 10.00 | 24.00 | 38.00 | 40.00 | 32.50 |
| 1947 | 4.50 | 4.50 | 10.00 | 10.00 | 10.00 | 38.00 | 44.00 | 35.00 | 23.00 | 19.00 |
| 1948 | 4.50 | 18.00 | 20.00 | 19.00 | 60.00 | 82.50 | 52.50 | 33.00 | 36.75 | 47.50 |
| 1949 | 19.00 | 21.00 | 22.00 | 44.00 | 67.50 | 52.50 | 35.00 | 32.00 | 39.00 | 32.50 |
| 1950 | 220.00 | 420.00 | 825.00 | 950.00 | 695.00 | 580.00 | 427.50 | 500.00 | 485.00 | 340.00 |
| 1951 | 45.00 | 85.00 | 90.00 | 72.50 | 45.00 | 25.00 | 37.50 | 32.00 | 35.00 | 30.00 |
| 1952 | 147.50 | 185.00 | 165.00 | 112.50 | 75.00 | 80.00 | 70.00 | 49.00 | 41.50 | 42.50 |
| 1953 | 19.00 | 15.00 | 9.00 | 5.75 | 6.00 | 8.00 | 9.00 | 6.50 | 6.50 | 12.00 |
| 1954 | 7.00 | 7.00 | 4.50 | 5.50 | 5.50 | 4.50 | 3.00 | 3.25 | 5.25 | 7.75 |
| 1955 | 10.00 | 5.75 | 6.75 | 7.50 | 4.50 | 4.00 | 4.75 | 4.00 | 5.75 | 6.1 |
| 1956 | 3.50 | 4.00 | 3.75 | 3.50 | 4.00 | 3.50 | 4.00 | 4.00 | 4.00 | |
| 1957 | 4.00 | 3.50 | 3.75 | 4.00 | 3.50 | 4.00 | 4.00 | 4.25 | | |
| 1958 | 3.00 | 2.75 | 3.00 | 3.25 | 3.50 | 4.00 | 4.25 | | | |
| 1959 | 3.00 | 3.50 | 3.00 | 3.50 | 4.00 | 3.45 | | | | |
| 1960 | 3.00 | 3.00 | 3.50 | 4.00 | 3.40 | | | | | |
| 1961 | 3.00 | 3.25 | 4.00 | 3.40 | | | | | | |
| 1962 | 3.25 | 4.00 | 3.40 | | | | | | | |
| 1963 | 4.00 | 3.40 | | | | | | | | |
| 1964 | 3.40 | | | | | | | | | |

*Buffalo nickel
**Jefferson nickel

## Retail Prices — Uncirculated Rolls of D Nickels

*Face Value of One Roll: $2.00*

| Year Minted | Number of Years After Year Minted | | | | | | | | | |
|---|---|---|---|---|---|---|---|---|---|---|
| | 21 | 22 | 23 | 24 | 25 | 26 | 27 | 28 | 29 | 30 |
| 1935 | $ 40.75 | $ 50.00 | $ 50.00 | $ 60.00 | $ 92.50 | $120.00 | $210.00 | $275.00 | $300.00 | $280.00 |
| 1936 | 25.00 | 30.00 | 45.00 | 50.00 | 56.00 | 72.50 | 100.00 | 135.00 | 125.00 | 125.00 |
| 1937 | 20.00 | 35.00 | 40.00 | 53.00 | 68.00 | 85.00 | 140.00 | 125.00 | 125.00 | 125.00 |
| *1938 | 25.00 | 25.00 | 28.00 | 67.00 | 100.00 | 125.00 | 115.00 | 110.00 | 110.00 | 105.00 |
| **1938 | 35.00 | 90.00 | 85.00 | 125.00 | 355.00 | 340.00 | 235.00 | 185.00 | 135.00 | 150.00 |
| 1939 | 1,600.00 | 1,200.00 | 1,400.00 | 2,250.00 | 2,500.00 | 2,050.00 | 1,575.00 | 1,000.00 | 1,400.00 | 1,300.00 |
| 1940 | 37.50 | 37.50 | 50.00 | 55.00 | 47.50 | 45.00 | 32.50 | 37.50 | 35.00 | 29.50 |
| 1941 | 33.00 | 35.00 | 45.00 | 47.50 | 34.00 | 26.00 | 27.50 | 30.00 | 26.50 | 19.00 |
| 1942 | 680.00 | 550.00 | 460.00 | 370.00 | 265.00 | 285.00 | 270.00 | 229.50 | 194.75 | 180.50 |
| 1943 | 185.00 | 145.00 | 115.00 | 77.50 | 160.00 | 155.00 | 87.50 | 60.25 | 99.50 | 120.00 |
| 1944 | 90.00 | 79.00 | 60.00 | 90.00 | 84.00 | 67.50 | 58.00 | 62.50 | 88.50 | 88.00 |
| 1945 | 47.50 | 34.50 | 52.00 | 49.00 | 41.00 | 35.75 | 38.50 | 54.50 | 56.00 | 45.00 |
| 1946 | 18.50 | 21.00 | 18.50 | 17.75 | 24.50 | 18.00 | 17.00 | 24.00 | 14.50 | |
| 1947 | 25.00 | 22.50 | 20.00 | 15.50 | 20.00 | 25.50 | 24.00 | 17.00 | | |
| 1948 | 40.00 | 29.00 | 32.50 | 37.00 | 32.00 | 34.50 | 21.40 | | | |
| 1949 | 35.00 | 23.50 | 22.50 | 17.00 | 30.50 | 28.00 | | | | |
| 1950 | 320.00 | 319.00 | 400.00 | 375.00 | 310.00 | | | | | |
| 1951 | 32.00 | 48.00 | 58.50 | 33.00 | | | | | | |
| 1952 | 68.00 | 59.00 | 42.00 | | | | | | | |
| 1953 | 11.00 | 6.90 | | | | | | | | |
| 1954 | 5.25 | | | | | | | | | |

*Buffalo nickel
Jefferson nickel

### Retail Prices — Uncirculated Rolls of D Nickels

*Face Value of One Roll: $2.00*

| Year Minted | Number of Years After Year Minted | | | | | | | | | |
|---|---|---|---|---|---|---|---|---|---|---|
| | 31 | 32 | 33 | 34 | 35 | 36 | 37 | 38 | 39 | 40 |
| 1935 | $280.00 | $280.00 | $295.00 | $295.00 | $255.00 | $280.00 | $271.00 | $430.00 | $650.00 | $644.00 |
| 1936 | 125.00 | 125.00 | 110.00 | 86.00 | 88.00 | 101.65 | 195.00 | 400.00 | 284.00 | |
| 1937 | 110.00 | 110.00 | 86.50 | 100.00 | 94.85 | 220.00 | 395.00 | 258.00 | | |
| *1938 | 105.00 | 79.50 | 90.00 | 94.85 | 220.00 | 195.00 | 140.00 | | | |
| **1938 | 185.00 | 147.25 | 110.75 | 101.65 | 195.00 | 195.00 | 116.00 | | | |
| 1939 | 965.00 | 810.00 | 745.25 | 1,795.00 | 1,750.00 | 1,135.00 | | | | |
| 1940 | 19.00 | 17.00 | 24.00 | 50.00 | 38.00 | | | | | |
| 1941 | 20.00 | 25.00 | 34.00 | 29.25 | | | | | | |
| 1942 | 285.00 | 400.00 | 273.00 | | | | | | | |
| 1943 | 105.00 | 77.00 | | | | | | | | |
| 1944 | 52.00 | | | | | | | | | |

*Buffalo nickel
**Jefferson nickel

## Retail Prices — Uncirculated Rolls of P Dimes

*Face Value of One Roll: $5.00*

| Year Minted | Number of Years After Year Minted | | | | | | | | | |
|---|---|---|---|---|---|---|---|---|---|---|
| | 1 | 2 | 3 | 4 | 5 | 6 | 7 | 8 | 9 | 10 |
| 1935 | $ 5.55 | $ 6.00 | $ 6.00 | $ 6.00 | $ 5.90 | $ 7.15 | $ 9.00 | $ 9.00 | $ 9.00 | $10.25 |
| 1936 | 5.50 | 5.80 | 5.80 | 5.85 | 7.45 | 9.00 | 10.50 | 9.50 | 10.75 | 11.25 |
| 1937 | 5.50 | 5.65 | 5.75 | 6.75 | 8.00 | 9.00 | 8.00 | 8.50 | 10.25 | 9.00 |
| 1938 | 5.95 | 6.75 | 6.95 | 8.00 | 9.25 | 8.00 | 9.00 | 9.80 | 10.50 | 9.00 |
| 1939 | 5.75 | 6.35 | 7.50 | 8.00 | 7.75 | 8.00 | 8.40 | 9.00 | 9.00 | 8.00 |
| 1940 | 6.25 | 7.00 | 7.50 | 7.00 | 7.25 | 7.00 | 7.00 | 7.75 | 8.00 | 8.00 |
| 1941 | 6.50 | 7.00 | 6.75 | 7.15 | 7.25 | 7.25 | 7.50 | 7.50 | 7.50 | 7.50 |
| 1942 | 6.50 | 6.50 | 6.75 | 7.50 | 7.25 | 7.25 | 7.25 | 7.25 | 7.50 | 7.50 |
| 1943 | 5.70 | 6.50 | 7.00 | 6.00 | 6.50 | 6.50 | 6.75 | 7.00 | 7.00 | 6.75 |
| 1944 | 5.75 | 6.00 | 6.00 | 6.25 | 6.00 | 6.25 | 6.60 | 6.75 | 6.50 | 7.00 |
| 1945 | 5.65 | 6.00 | 6.00 | 6.10 | 6.25 | 6.35 | 6.35 | 6.10 | 6.50 | 7.30 |
| 1946 | 5.75 | 6.15 | 6.00 | 6.00 | 6.50 | 6.15 | 6.00 | 7.00 | 11.25 | 11.75 |
| 1947 | 6.00 | 6.00 | 6.00 | 6.00 | 6.00 | 6.00 | 10.00 | 22.00 | 24.00 | 24.25 |
| 1948 | 5.95 | 6.00 | 6.00 | 6.00 | 6.50 | 10.00 | 22.25 | 29.00 | 29.00 | 29.00 |
| 1949 | 5.85 | 6.00 | 6.10 | 7.00 | 10.00 | 28.00 | 29.00 | 29.25 | 29.25 | 30.00 |
| 1950 | 5.75 | 5.85 | 6.00 | 11.00 | 26.50 | 28.00 | 29.00 | 29.00 | 30.00 | 95.00 |
| 1951 | 5.75 | 5.90 | 6.50 | 9.60 | 9.00 | 9.25 | 9.50 | 10.00 | 21.00 | 18.00 |
| 1952 | 5.75 | 6.00 | 6.40 | 7.65 | 8.00 | 8.00 | 9.00 | 17.50 | 14.00 | 15.00 |
| 1953 | 6.00 | 6.35 | 6.25 | 6.50 | 6.60 | 7.00 | 15.00 | 12.00 | 14.00 | 60.00 |
| 1954 | 5.85 | 5.50 | 6.00 | 6.60 | 7.00 | 10.50 | 9.00 | 9.00 | 15.75 | 15.00 |
| 1955 | 6.35 | 6.50 | 9.00 | 10.75 | 38.00 | 26.00 | 35.00 | 75.00 | 135.00 | 95.00 |
| 1956 | 5.75 | 5.85 | 6.25 | 7.50 | 8.00 | 8.00 | 11.00 | 15.00 | 10.50 | 8.50 |
| 1957 | 5.75 | 6.00 | 7.25 | 7.25 | 7.50 | 10.00 | 10.00 | 8.00 | 8.00 | 7.75 |
| 1958 | 6.00 | 18.00 | 12.00 | 12.00 | 31.00 | 45.00 | 37.50 | 30.00 | 18.50 | 35.00 |
| 1959 | 6.00 | 6.00 | 6.25 | 7.50 | 10.00 | 8.00 | 8.00 | 7.50 | 11.00 | 10.00 |
| 1960 | 6.00 | 6.25 | 10.00 | 11.00 | 9.00 | 8.25 | 7.50 | 10.00 | 10.00 | 8.50 |
| 1961 | 5.70 | 18.00 | 14.00 | 12.00 | 10.00 | 7.50 | 10.00 | 11.50 | 8.25 | 7.50 |
| 1962 | 6.25 | 10.00 | 8.00 | 8.00 | 7.00 | 9.00 | 10.00 | 8.00 | 7.00 | 8.00 |
| 1963 | 6.50 | 7.00 | 7.00 | 6.50 | 9.00 | 9.00 | 7.75 | 7.25 | 7.75 | 13.00 |
| 1964 | 5.60 | 6.25 | 6.50 | 8.00 | 6.75 | 7.50 | 7.75 | 7.75 | 13.00 | 22.00 |
| 1965 | 5.60 | 5.85 | 7.00 | 6.00 | 6.25 | 7.00 | 7.00 | 8.00 | 9.00 | 9.65 |
| 1966 | 5.80 | 6.25 | 6.00 | 6.25 | 7.00 | 7.00 | 7.50 | 9.00 | 9.65 | |
| 1967 | 6.00 | 6.00 | 6.25 | 7.00 | 7.00 | 7.50 | 9.00 | 9.65 | | |
| 1968 | 5.75 | 6.00 | 7.00 | 7.25 | 7.50 | 9.00 | 10.25 | | | |
| 1969 | 5.75 | 6.75 | 7.00 | 7.50 | 9.00 | 11.50 | | | | |
| 1970 | 6.25 | 6.75 | 7.00 | 9.00 | 9.75 | | | | | |
| 1971 | 6.50 | 7.50 | 9.00 | 10.50 | | | | | | |
| 1972 | 7.00 | 9.00 | 10.00 | | | | | | | |
| 1973 | 9.00 | 8.65 | | | | | | | | |
| 1974 | 7.90 | | | | | | | | | |

## Retail Prices — Uncirculated Rolls of P Dimes

*Face Value of One Roll: $5.00*

| Year Minted | Number of Years After Year Minted | | | | | | | | | |
|---|---|---|---|---|---|---|---|---|---|---|
| | 11 | 12 | 13 | 14 | 15 | 16 | 17 | 18 | 19 | 20 |
| 1935 | $ 11.25 | $ 11.25 | $ 11.50 | $ 11.50 | $ 11.75 | $ 12.00 | $ 12.75 | $ 15.00 | $ 21.00 | $ 25.00 |
| 1936 | 11.00 | 11.00 | 10.75 | 10.75 | 10.75 | 10.50 | 12.00 | 13.00 | 17.00 | 18.00 |
| 1937 | 9.00 | 9.00 | 9.00 | 8.50 | 8.75 | 8.75 | 12.50 | 13.00 | 15.00 | 17.25 |
| 1938 | 9.00 | 9.10 | 9.75 | 10.00 | 10.50 | 12.50 | 12.50 | 17.00 | 17.50 | 25.00 |
| 1939 | 8.10 | 8.25 | 9.00 | 11.00 | 10.50 | 11.25 | 13.00 | 16.00 | 20.85 | 28.00 |
| 1940 | 8.25 | 8.75 | 9.00 | 9.50 | 15.00 | 15.00 | 19.00 | 21.25 | 32.50 | 32.50 |
| 1941 | 7.50 | 7.50 | 7.50 | 11.00 | 16.00 | 19.00 | 21.00 | 22.00 | 22.50 | 31.50 |
| 1942 | 7.25 | 7.50 | 8.50 | 8.00 | 12.00 | 12.00 | 13.00 | 17.50 | 17.50 | 17.50 |
| 1943 | 7.50 | 8.50 | 8.00 | 8.00 | 10.50 | 11.00 | 15.00 | 16.00 | 18.00 | 21.00 |
| 1944 | 8.00 | 8.00 | 7.50 | 7.25 | 8.00 | 15.00 | 16.00 | 19.00 | 21.75 | 35.00 |
| 1945 | 7.50 | 7.50 | 7.60 | 8.00 | 15.00 | 16.00 | 17.00 | 19.50 | 35.00 | 57.50 |
| 1946 | 11.25 | 11.00 | 12.00 | 18.50 | 13.00 | 14.50 | 20.00 | 21.00 | 16.50 | 15.00 |
| 1947 | 24.00 | 25.00 | 85.00 | 41.00 | 44.00 | 85.00 | 70.00 | 45.00 | 28.00 | 28.00 |
| 1948 | 30.00 | 125.00 | 60.00 | 70.00 | 195.00 | 150.00 | 100.00 | 80.00 | 50.00 | 75.00 |
| 1949 | 360.00 | 235.00 | 225.00 | 475.00 | 435.00 | 400.00 | 317.50 | 230.00 | 285.00 | 320.00 |
| 1950 | 75.00 | 80.00 | 125.00 | 90.00 | 65.00 | 37.50 | 35.00 | 55.00 | 60.00 | 69.50 |
| 1951 | 18.00 | 110.00 | 80.00 | 55.00 | 45.00 | 27.50 | 37.50 | 30.00 | 28.00 | 29.50 |
| 1952 | 22.00 | 28.00 | 22.50 | 18.75 | 14.50 | 35.00 | 25.00 | 19.00 | 17.00 | 15.00 |
| 1953 | 55.00 | 44.00 | 27.50 | 19.50 | 28.00 | 30.00 | 18.00 | 19.00 | 25.00 | 48.00 |
| 1954 | 12.00 | 10.00 | 8.50 | 16.00 | 14.00 | 10.00 | 9.00 | 9.00 | 15.50 | 24.00 |
| 1955 | 73.50 | 57.50 | 69.00 | 62.50 | 42.00 | 32.00 | 32.50 | 42.00 | 42.00 | 30.00 |
| 1956 | 7.50 | 11.00 | 12.00 | 9.25 | 8.50 | 13.00 | 18.00 | 23.00 | 20.50 | |
| 1957 | 10.00 | 10.00 | 9.00 | 8.00 | 8.00 | 15.00 | 23.00 | 22.75 | | |
| 1958 | 26.00 | 17.50 | 12.00 | 17.00 | 19.00 | 26.50 | 22.75 | | | |
| 1959 | 8.75 | 7.50 | 8.00 | 13.75 | 22.00 | 20.00 | | | | |
| 1960 | 7.50 | 8.00 | 13.50 | 22.00 | 20.25 | | | | | |
| 1961 | 9.00 | 13.50 | 22.00 | 20.00 | | | | | | |
| 1962 | 13.00 | 22.00 | 20.00 | | | | | | | |
| 1963 | 22.00 | 20.00 | | | | | | | | |
| 1964 | 19.75 | | | | | | | | | |

## Retail Prices — Uncirculated Rolls of P Dimes

*Face Value of One Roll: $5.00*

| Year Minted | Number of Years After Year Minted | | | | | | | | | |
|---|---|---|---|---|---|---|---|---|---|---|
| | 21 | 22 | 23 | 24 | 25 | 26 | 27 | 28 | 29 | 30 |
| 1935 | $ 29.50 | $ 33.00 | $ 50.00 | $ 50.00 | $ 45.00 | $ 70.00 | $ 85.00 | $100.00 | $115.00 | $115.00 |
| 1936 | 17.50 | 30.00 | 40.00 | 38.00 | 42.50 | 42.50 | 50.00 | 52.50 | 82.50 | 82.50 |
| 1937 | 18.00 | 32.50 | 32.50 | 30.00 | 35.00 | 50.00 | 55.00 | 95.00 | 95.00 | 97.50 |
| 1938 | 32.50 | 30.00 | 41.00 | 50.00 | 75.00 | 90.00 | 85.00 | 85.00 | 85.00 | 140.00 |
| 1939 | 25.00 | 40.00 | 40.00 | 45.00 | 65.00 | 90.00 | 95.00 | 90.00 | 90.00 | 85.00 |
| 1940 | 35.00 | 41.00 | 41.00 | 50.00 | 90.00 | 86.50 | 75.00 | 80.00 | 77.50 | 69.00 |
| 1941 | 33.50 | 33.50 | 45.00 | 57.50 | 50.00 | 40.00 | 47.50 | 47.50 | 38.00 | 32.00 |
| 1942 | 21.00 | 40.00 | 52.50 | 55.00 | 40.00 | 45.00 | 45.00 | 38.00 | 32.00 | 35.00 |
| 1943 | 35.00 | 52.50 | 52.50 | 33.00 | 42.50 | 45.00 | 38.00 | 31.50 | 35.00 | 75.25 |
| 1944 | 45.00 | 45.00 | 33.00 | 42.50 | 45.00 | 38.00 | 30.00 | 35.00 | 75.25 | 125.00 |
| 1945 | 57.50 | 33.00 | 42.50 | 45.00 | 38.00 | 32.00 | 35.00 | 75.25 | 125.00 | 119.00 |
| 1946 | 10.50 | 16.50 | 16.00 | 12.75 | 12.75 | 12.50 | 21.75 | 24.00 | 28.00 | |
| 1947 | 40.00 | 34.00 | 26.00 | 19.25 | 19.50 | 49.00 | 34.00 | 32.50 | | |
| 1948 | 96.00 | 63.50 | 40.50 | 44.00 | 94.00 | 86.50 | 79.00 | | | |
| 1949 | 235.00 | 217.50 | 300.00 | 490.00 | 507.50 | 410.00 | | | | |
| 1950 | 59.50 | 70.00 | 95.00 | 84.00 | 64.00 | | | | | |
| 1951 | 42.50 | 82.00 | 66.00 | 48.00 | | | | | | |
| 1952 | 39.00 | 27.00 | 29.50 | | | | | | | |
| 1953 | 31.00 | 31.00 | | | | | | | | |
| 1954 | 23.75 | | | | | | | | | |

## Retail Prices — Uncirculated Rolls of P Dimes

*Face Value of One Roll: $5.0*

| Year Minted | Number of Years After Year Minted | | | | | | | | | |
|---|---|---|---|---|---|---|---|---|---|---|
| | 31 | 32 | 33 | 34 | 35 | 36 | 37 | 38 | 39 | 40 |
| 1935 | $115.00 | $115.00 | $120.00 | $122.50 | $109.50 | $105.00 | $113.75 | $148.75 | $275.00 | $400.00 |
| 1936 | 82.50 | 100.00 | 90.00 | 62.00 | 70.00 | 78.75 | 131.25 | 225.00 | 205.00 | |
| 1937 | 80.00 | 75.00 | 62.00 | 52.50 | 61.25 | 105.00 | 195.00 | 205.00 | | |
| 1938 | 145.00 | 107.00 | 105.00 | 105.00 | 148.75 | 270.00 | 312.50 | | | |
| 1939 | 70.00 | 61.25 | 61.25 | 87.50 | 160.00 | 170.00 | | | | |
| 1940 | 61.25 | 61.25 | 105.00 | 140.00 | 135.00 | | | | | |
| 1941 | 32.00 | 78.75 | 140.00 | 135.00 | | | | | | |
| 1942 | 75.25 | 125.00 | 117.00 | | | | | | | |
| 1943 | 125.00 | 119.00 | | | | | | | | |
| 1944 | 117.00 | | | | | | | | | |

## Retail Prices — Uncirculated Rolls of D Dimes

*Face Value of One Roll: $5.00*

| Year Minted | Number of Years After Year Minted | | | | | | | | | |
|---|---|---|---|---|---|---|---|---|---|---|
| | 1 | 2 | 3 | 4 | 5 | 6 | 7 | 8 | 9 | 10 |
| 1935 | $ 5.55 | $ 6.00 | $ 6.50 | $ 6.75 | $ 6.75 | $ 7.50 | $ 9.00 | $10.00 | $11.50 | $12.50 |
| 1936 | 5.50 | 5.85 | 6.00 | 6.50 | 7.50 | 9.00 | 10.00 | 10.00 | 10.00 | 10.50 |
| 1937 | 5.70 | 6.00 | 6.70 | 7.50 | 8.00 | 8.00 | 8.00 | 9.25 | 10.00 | 10.50 |
| 1938 | 6.35 | 6.75 | 7.55 | 8.00 | 8.00 | 8.00 | 8.50 | 8.50 | 9.00 | 9.00 |
| 1939 | 5.75 | 6.00 | 7.50 | 9.00 | 7.90 | 8.00 | 9.00 | 8.50 | 9.00 | 8.50 |
| 1940 | 6.00 | 7.00 | 7.50 | 7.00 | 7.00 | 7.00 | 7.00 | 7.75 | 8.00 | 8.00 |
| 1941 | 6.25 | 7.00 | 6.75 | 7.00 | 7.50 | 6.50 | 7.50 | 7.45 | 7.45 | 7.40 |
| 1942 | 7.00 | 6.50 | 6.75 | 7.00 | 6.25 | 7.25 | 6.25 | 6.95 | 7.35 | 7.35 |
| 1943 | 5.70 | 6.75 | 7.00 | 6.00 | 6.50 | 6.00 | 6.25 | 6.15 | 6.25 | 6.50 |
| 1944 | 5.65 | 6.00 | 6.00 | 6.25 | 6.00 | 6.10 | 6.25 | 6.25 | 6.50 | 7.00 |
| 1945 | 5.65 | 5.75 | 6.00 | 6.00 | 6.10 | 6.10 | 6.25 | 6.10 | 6.50 | 7.30 |
| 1946 | 5.75 | 6.15 | 6.55 | 6.75 | 6.75 | 6.25 | 6.00 | 7.00 | 12.60 | 12.60 |
| 1947 | 6.00 | 5.75 | 5.95 | 6.00 | 6.25 | 6.00 | 7.00 | 22.50 | 24.00 | 24.00 |
| 1948 | 5.60 | 5.50 | 6.10 | 6.10 | 6.50 | 7.00 | 24.00 | 24.00 | 24.00 | 26.00 |
| 1949 | 5.45 | 6.00 | 5.85 | 6.50 | 7.50 | 15.10 | 14.00 | 14.00 | 14.00 | 15.00 |
| 1950 | 5.75 | 5.85 | 6.00 | 6.50 | 13.00 | 12.00 | 12.00 | 13.75 | 15.00 | 25.00 |
| 1951 | 5.75 | 5.90 | 6.50 | 9.60 | 9.00 | 9.00 | 9.00 | 10.00 | 21.00 | 21.00 |
| 1952 | 5.75 | 6.00 | 7.40 | 7.75 | 8.00 | 8.50 | 9.00 | 18.50 | 16.00 | 16.00 |
| 1953 | 6.00 | 6.35 | 6.40 | 6.50 | 6.60 | 7.00 | 11.00 | 11.00 | 11.00 | 20.00 |
| 1954 | 5.85 | 6.00 | 6.00 | 6.25 | 7.00 | 10.50 | 9.00 | 9.00 | 15.00 | 15.00 |
| 1955 | 6.00 | 6.25 | 6.00 | 7.25 | 37.00 | 20.00 | 25.00 | 60.00 | 75.00 | 65.00 |
| 1956 | 5.75 | 5.75 | 6.00 | 7.50 | 7.50 | 7.50 | 9.00 | 10.00 | 7.50 | 7.50 |
| 1957 | 5.70 | 6.00 | 7.25 | 7.25 | 7.50 | 9.00 | 9.50 | 10.00 | 10.00 | 9.50 |
| 1958 | 6.00 | 6.50 | 6.50 | 6.50 | 7.00 | 9.50 | 8.00 | 8.00 | 7.50 | 11.00 |
| 1959 | 6.00 | 6.00 | 6.25 | 6.50 | 7.00 | 6.75 | 7.50 | 7.50 | 9.50 | 9.00 |
| 1960 | 5.50 | 5.75 | 8.50 | 7.00 | 6.50 | 6.50 | 7.00 | 9.00 | 9.00 | 8.50 |
| 1961 | 5.65 | 7.50 | 6.50 | 6.00 | 7.00 | 7.00 | 9.50 | 9.00 | 8.25 | 7.50 |
| 1962 | 6.00 | 6.00 | 6.25 | 7.75 | 6.50 | 9.00 | 9.00 | 8.00 | 7.25 | 8.00 |
| 1963 | 5.90 | 6.00 | 6.00 | 6.50 | 9.00 | 9.00 | 7.75 | 7.25 | 7.75 | 13.00 |
| 1964 | 5.50 | 6.25 | 6.50 | 7.00 | 6.75 | 7.50 | 7.75 | 7.75 | 13.00 | 22.00 |
| 1968 | 5.75 | 6.00 | 7.00 | 7.25 | 7.50 | 9.00 | 10.00 | | | |
| 1969 | 5.75 | 6.75 | 7.00 | 7.50 | 9.00 | 10.00 | | | | |
| 1970 | 6.25 | 6.75 | 7.00 | 9.00 | 9.65 | | | | | |
| 1971 | 6.50 | 7.00 | 9.00 | 9.75 | | | | | | |
| 1972 | 7.00 | 9.00 | 9.65 | | | | | | | |
| 1973 | 9.00 | 8.50 | | | | | | | | |
| 1974 | 7.90 | | | | | | | | | |

## Retail Prices — Uncirculated Rolls of D Dimes

*Face Value of One Roll: $5.0*

| Year Minted | \multicolumn{10}{c}{Number of Years After Year Minted} | | | | | | | | | |
|---|---|---|---|---|---|---|---|---|---|---|
| | 11 | 12 | 13 | 14 | 15 | 16 | 17 | 18 | 19 | 20 |
| 1935 | $ 15.95 | $ 16.00 | $ 22.50 | $ 22.50 | $ 24.00 | $ 24.50 | $ 30.00 | $ 36.00 | $ 56.00 | $106.25 |
| 1936 | 14.00 | 17.25 | 20.25 | 22.95 | 24.00 | 24.50 | 35.00 | 50.00 | 55.00 | 60.00 |
| 1937 | 12.00 | 14.10 | 15.95 | 16.50 | 17.00 | 19.00 | 22.00 | 31.25 | 42.00 | 50.00 |
| 1938 | 9.00 | 9.40 | 9.00 | 9.75 | 10.00 | 12.00 | 18.75 | 35.00 | 45.00 | 46.00 |
| 1939 | 8.50 | 8.00 | 8.00 | 8.75 | 9.25 | 13.00 | 15.75 | 22.00 | 30.00 | 30.00 |
| 1940 | 8.40 | 8.40 | 9.00 | 9.50 | 20.00 | 20.00 | 22.00 | 24.50 | 32.50 | 30.00 |
| 1941 | 7.50 | 7.50 | 13.50 | 12.75 | 16.00 | 19.00 | 24.00 | 27.00 | 25.00 | 37.00 |
| 1942 | 7.35 | 7.50 | 8.50 | 8.00 | 9.50 | 13.00 | 14.00 | 18.00 | 27.00 | 27.00 |
| 1943 | 7.50 | 8.50 | 8.00 | 8.50 | 10.00 | 11.00 | 17.50 | 24.00 | 25.00 | 30.00 |
| 1944 | 8.00 | 8.00 | 7.75 | 7.50 | 8.50 | 16.00 | 19.25 | 19.25 | 23.00 | 40.00 |
| 1945 | 7.75 | 7.85 | 8.00 | 9.00 | 16.00 | 16.00 | 17.00 | 21.50 | 35.00 | 45.00 |
| 1946 | 12.00 | 11.00 | 12.00 | 20.00 | 13.00 | 18.00 | 25.00 | 55.00 | 37.50 | 24.00 |
| 1947 | 24.00 | 25.00 | 40.00 | 26.00 | 27.00 | 50.00 | 57.50 | 47.50 | 26.50 | 28.00 |
| 1948 | 26.00 | 42.50 | 30.00 | 31.50 | 44.00 | 65.00 | 60.00 | 35.00 | 28.00 | 49.00 |
| 1949 | 50.00 | 65.00 | 55.00 | 120.00 | 150.00 | 115.00 | 110.00 | 90.00 | 110.00 | 105.00 |
| 1950 | 21.00 | 23.00 | 42.00 | 65.00 | 70.00 | 38.00 | 30.00 | 41.00 | 55.00 | 99.5 |
| 1951 | 20.00 | 45.00 | 60.00 | 40.00 | 28.00 | 18.50 | 26.00 | 35.00 | 25.50 | 23.5 |
| 1952 | 23.00 | 25.00 | 30.00 | 37.00 | 22.50 | 28.00 | 22.50 | 22.50 | 23.00 | 22.5 |
| 1953 | 21.00 | 14.00 | 12.50 | 8.75 | 16.50 | 11.00 | 9.75 | 12.00 | 13.00 | 27.0 |
| 1954 | 12.00 | 9.00 | 8.50 | 17.50 | 15.00 | 10.00 | 9.00 | 9.00 | 15.50 | 23.0 |
| 1955 | 48.50 | 44.50 | 52.50 | 45.00 | 23.75 | 18.50 | 20.00 | 26.00 | 28.50 | 29.2 |
| 1956 | 7.00 | 11.00 | 13.50 | 13.00 | 9.00 | 9.75 | 16.00 | 23.00 | 20.50 | |
| 1957 | 30.00 | 16.00 | 17.00 | 19.00 | 19.50 | 21.00 | 25.00 | 23.00 | | |
| 1958 | 13.00 | 9.50 | 7.75 | 11.00 | 13.75 | 22.00 | 20.00 | | | |
| 1959 | 8.75 | 7.50 | 8.00 | 13.75 | 22.00 | 20.00 | | | | |
| 1960 | 7.50 | 8.00 | 13.50 | 22.00 | 20.00 | | | | | |
| 1961 | 9.00 | 13.50 | 22.00 | 20.00 | | | | | | |
| 1962 | 13.00 | 22.00 | 20.00 | | | | | | | |
| 1963 | 22.00 | 19.50 | | | | | | | | |
| 1964 | 19.75 | | | | | | | | | |

## Retail Prices — Uncirculated Rolls of D Dimes

*Face Value of One Roll: $5.00*

| Year Minted | Number of Years After Year Minted | | | | | | | | | |
|---|---|---|---|---|---|---|---|---|---|---|
| | 21 | 22 | 23 | 24 | 25 | 26 | 27 | 28 | 29 | 30 |
| 1935 | $115.00 | $140.00 | $192.00 | $230.00 | $240.00 | $250.00 | $335.00 | $475.00 | $750.00 | $1,075.00 |
| 1936 | 75.00 | 132.00 | 200.00 | 220.00 | 230.00 | 250.00 | 325.00 | 500.00 | 575.00 | 575.00 |
| 1937 | 65.50 | 80.00 | 91.00 | 135.00 | 135.00 | 165.00 | 205.00 | 225.00 | 225.00 | 225.00 |
| 1938 | 45.00 | 55.00 | 65.00 | 85.00 | 165.00 | 315.00 | 450.00 | 425.00 | 400.00 | 410.00 |
| 1939 | 35.00 | 30.00 | 41.00 | 69.00 | 65.00 | 80.00 | 90.00 | 90.00 | 80.00 | 80.00 |
| 1940 | 40.00 | 45.00 | 53.00 | 65.00 | 80.00 | 77.00 | 75.00 | 82.00 | 82.50 | 68.75 |
| 1941 | 39.00 | 52.00 | 75.00 | 120.00 | 120.00 | 80.00 | 82.00 | 75.00 | 68.00 | 34.00 |
| 1942 | 27.00 | 50.00 | 62.50 | 52.50 | 40.00 | 45.00 | 55.00 | 40.00 | 35.00 | 35.00 |
| 1943 | 40.00 | 55.00 | 55.00 | 36.00 | 45.00 | 45.00 | 40.00 | 35.00 | 35.00 | 87.50 |
| 1944 | 42.50 | 42.50 | 33.00 | 45.00 | 45.00 | 39.75 | 35.00 | 35.00 | 87.50 | 130.00 |
| 1945 | 47.50 | 35.00 | 45.00 | 50.00 | 40.00 | 35.00 | 35.00 | 87.50 | 155.00 | 130.00 |
| 1946 | 20.00 | 25.00 | 22.50 | 18.00 | 16.50 | 23.75 | 55.00 | 31.00 | 32.00 | |
| 1947 | 52.50 | 50.00 | 39.75 | 35.00 | 38.00 | 72.00 | 56.00 | 49.00 | | |
| 1948 | 49.00 | 34.00 | 33.00 | 35.00 | 65.00 | 57.25 | 48.00 | | | |
| 1949 | 95.00 | 85.00 | 125.00 | 275.00 | 240.00 | 230.00 | | | | |
| 1950 | 89.00 | 75.00 | 86.00 | 76.00 | 49.00 | | | | | |
| 1951 | 24.00 | 52.00 | 50.00 | 34.00 | | | | | | |
| 1952 | 50.00 | 37.00 | 34.75 | | | | | | | |
| 1953 | 28.00 | 23.25 | | | | | | | | |
| 1954 | 23.75 | | | | | | | | | |

## Retail Prices — Uncirculated Rolls of D Dimes

*Face Value of One Roll: $5*

| Year Minted | Number of Years After Year Minted | | | | | | | | | |
|---|---|---|---|---|---|---|---|---|---|---|
| | 31 | 32 | 33 | 34 | 35 | 36 | 37 | 38 | 39 | 40 |
| 1935 | $1,075.00 | $1,075.00 | $1,075.00 | $1,075.00 | $800.00 | $647.50 | $787.50 | $1,115.00 | $1,789.00 | $3,490.00 |
| 1936 | 575.00 | 700.00 | 750.00 | 595.00 | 507.50 | 612.50 | 980.00 | 1,268.00 | 1,681.00 | |
| 1937 | 250.00 | 250.00 | 209.50 | 175.00 | 192.50 | 332.50 | 660.00 | 830.00 | | |
| 1938 | 410.00 | 290.00 | 262.50 | 262.50 | 358.75 | 575.00 | 575.00 | | | |
| 1939 | 66.50 | 65.00 | 65.00 | 157.50 | 230.00 | 275.00 | | | | |
| 1940 | 61.25 | 61.25 | 262.50 | 360.00 | 305.00 | | | | | |
| 1941 | 61.25 | 119.00 | 215.00 | 213.50 | | | | | | |
| 1942 | 87.50 | 149.00 | 165.00 | | | | | | | |
| 1943 | 145.00 | 128.50 | | | | | | | | |
| 1944 | 128.50 | | | | | | | | | |

## Retail Prices — Uncirculated Rolls of P Quarters

Face Value of One Roll: $10.00

| Year minted | | | | | | | | | | |
|---|---|---|---|---|---|---|---|---|---|---|

| Year minted | Number of Years After Year Minted | | | | | | | | | |
|---|---|---|---|---|---|---|---|---|---|---|
|  | 1 | 2 | 3 | 4 | 5 | 6 | 7 | 8 | 9 | 10 |
| 935 | $11.50 | $12.00 | $12.00 | $11.90 | $13.95 | $16.00 | $21.00 | $21.00 | $24.50 | $27.00 |
| 936 | 11.85 | 12.50 | 13.15 | 13.20 | 14.25 | 19.00 | 20.00 | 20.00 | 20.00 | 25.00 |
| 937 | 11.50 | 12.25 | 12.25 | 14.75 | 16.50 | 17.00 | 17.50 | 20.00 | 22.50 | 22.50 |
| 938 | 11.75 | 13.25 | 13.75 | 15.50 | 17.00 | 17.00 | 23.25 | 27.00 | 34.75 | 40.00 |
| 939 | 11.75 | 12.75 | 14.50 | 16.00 | 16.00 | 17.25 | 18.75 | 20.00 | 24.75 | 26.00 |
| 940 | 12.00 | 13.00 | 15.50 | 15.50 | 16.00 | 24.00 | 36.75 | 50.00 | 45.00 | 42.00 |
| 941 | 12.50 | 15.00 | 13.00 | 14.50 | 15.00 | 15.00 | 16.00 | 15.00 | 15.00 | 14.25 |
| 942 | 13.00 | 13.00 | 13.50 | 14.75 | 14.75 | 15.00 | 14.50 | 14.50 | 14.50 | 14.50 |
| 943 | 11.50 | 12.00 | 12.65 | 14.00 | 14.50 | 14.25 | 14.25 | 14.25 | 14.25 | 14.25 |
| 944 | 11.25 | 11.25 | 11.50 | 13.00 | 12.00 | 12.00 | 12.45 | 12.50 | 13.00 | 13.00 |
| 945 | 11.00 | 11.25 | 11.75 | 12.00 | 12.00 | 12.10 | 12.25 | 13.00 | 13.00 | 13.00 |
| 946 | 11.00 | 11.25 | 11.50 | 11.75 | 12.00 | 12.00 | 13.00 | 13.00 | 14.00 | 13.95 |
| 947 | 11.75 | 11.50 | 11.85 | 12.00 | 12.25 | 13.00 | 13.00 | 13.00 | 14.75 | 14.00 |
| 948 | 11.50 | 11.75 | 12.00 | 12.35 | 12.50 | 12.00 | 13.00 | 13.75 | 13.00 | 13.50 |
| 949 | 11.35 | 11.45 | 11.95 | 13.00 | 14.50 | 15.00 | 15.00 | 17.00 | 23.00 | 27.00 |
| 50 | 11.25 | 11.75 | 12.50 | 14.00 | 16.00 | 17.00 | 17.75 | 18.75 | 20.00 | 21.00 |
| 51 | 11.50 | 12.00 | 12.00 | 12.85 | 12.85 | 16.50 | 16.50 | 17.50 | 17.50 | 20.00 |
| 52 | 12.00 | 12.00 | 12.65 | 13.00 | 12.85 | 20.00 | 24.50 | 20.00 | 19.50 | 19.50 |
| 53 | 11.50 | 12.00 | 12.00 | 12.00 | 12.00 | 13.00 | 17.50 | 18.00 | 22.00 | 95.00 |
| 54 | 11.25 | 11.50 | 11.50 | 11.50 | 12.50 | 15.50 | 15.50 | 15.00 | 15.00 | 20.00 |
| 55 | 11.25 | 12.00 | 12.75 | 13.25 | 22.00 | 25.00 | 25.00 | 50.00 | 55.00 | 47.50 |
| 56 | 11.00 | 10.85 | 12.00 | 14.00 | 14.00 | 15.50 | 17.00 | 20.00 | 15.50 | 16.50 |
| 57 | 10.85 | 11.50 | 13.00 | 13.00 | 13.50 | 15.00 | 15.00 | 14.00 | 15.00 | 14.00 |
| 58 | 13.50 | 18.00 | 15.00 | 17.00 | 40.00 | 75.00 | 62.50 | 65.00 | 42.50 | 60.00 |
| 59 | 12.50 | 13.00 | 13.50 | 14.00 | 20.00 | 16.00 | 16.00 | 14.50 | 19.00 | 22.00 |
| 60 | 12.00 | 12.00 | 12.50 | 14.00 | 15.00 | 15.00 | 14.50 | 19.50 | 19.00 | 16.75 |
| 61 | 11.50 | 12.00 | 13.50 | 13.50 | 15.00 | 13.50 | 20.00 | 20.00 | 17.50 | 15.00 |
| 62 | 12.00 | 12.50 | 14.00 | 16.00 | 14.75 | 16.50 | 17.00 | 17.00 | 14.75 | 15.50 |
| 63 | 12.00 | 12.50 | 14.00 | 12.75 | 18.00 | 17.00 | 15.00 | 14.50 | 15.00 | 28.00 |
| 64 | 11.00 | 12.50 | 13.75 | 14.75 | 14.50 | 15.00 | 15.50 | 15.00 | 27.00 | 44.00 |
| 65 | 11.00 | 11.50 | 12.25 | 13.75 | 13.00 | 13.50 | 13.00 | 15.00 | 18.00 | 17.00 |
| 66 | 11.25 | 11.50 | 13.00 | 13.00 | 13.50 | 14.00 | 18.00 | 18.00 | 18.00 | |
| 67 | 12.00 | 12.50 | 13.00 | 13.50 | 14.00 | 15.00 | 18.00 | 17.50 | | |
| 68 | 11.75 | 13.00 | 13.50 | 14.50 | 15.00 | 18.00 | 17.00 | | | |
| 69 | 11.75 | 13.00 | 12.75 | 15.00 | 18.00 | 17.00 | | | | |
| 70 | 11.75 | 12.00 | 14.00 | 16.00 | 15.50 | | | | | |
| 71 | 11.50 | 15.00 | 16.00 | 16.00 | | | | | | |
| 72 | 13.00 | 16.00 | 16.00 | | | | | | | |
| 73 | 16.00 | 15.00 | | | | | | | | |
| 74 | 14.00 | | | | | | | | | |

## Retail Prices — Uncirculated Rolls of P Quarters

Face Value of One Roll: $10.0

| Year Minted | 11 | 12 | 13 | 14 | 15 | 16 | 17 | 18 | 19 | 20 |
|---|---|---|---|---|---|---|---|---|---|---|
| | | | | Number of Years After Year Minted | | | | | | |
| 1935 | $ 30.25 | $ 33.75 | $ 36.00 | $ 48.00 | $ 46.00 | $ 42.50 | $ 42.50 | $ 45.00 | $ 46.00 | $ 50.00 |
| 1936 | 25.00 | 25.00 | 32.75 | 32.00 | 33.00 | 40.00 | 40.00 | 40.00 | 45.00 | 60.00 |
| 1937 | 37.45 | 42.50 | 37.00 | 37.50 | 37.00 | 39.00 | 37.00 | 40.00 | 60.00 | 80.00 |
| 1938 | 42.50 | 40.00 | 42.00 | 40.00 | 46.00 | 50.00 | 85.00 | 135.00 | 192.00 | 340.00 |
| 1939 | 26.00 | 26.50 | 28.00 | 30.00 | 34.00 | 55.00 | 76.00 | 85.00 | 90.00 | 140.00 |
| 1940 | 40.00 | 40.00 | 45.00 | 55.00 | 75.00 | 100.00 | 110.00 | 120.00 | 150.00 | 135.00 |
| 1941 | 14.50 | 17.00 | 14.50 | 16.00 | 19.50 | 20.00 | 20.00 | 21.00 | 40.00 | 45.00 |
| 1942 | 14.50 | 14.50 | 14.00 | 15.25 | 30.00 | 45.00 | 45.00 | 45.00 | 57.00 | 50.00 |
| 1943 | 14.50 | 14.00 | 14.50 | 16.00 | 18.00 | 20.00 | 30.00 | 30.00 | 35.00 | 39.00 |
| 1944 | 13.00 | 13.00 | 13.00 | 14.00 | 14.00 | 25.00 | 20.00 | 33.50 | 35.50 | 45.00 |
| 1945 | 13.75 | 13.75 | 13.00 | 14.00 | 25.00 | 20.00 | 22.00 | 25.00 | 40.00 | 30.0 |
| 1946 | 13.75 | 13.75 | 13.75 | 17.50 | 17.50 | 21.00 | 22.75 | 45.00 | 37.50 | 30.00 |
| 1947 | 13.60 | 13.50 | 18.00 | 18.25 | 20.00 | 30.00 | 70.00 | 65.00 | 57.00 | 42.5 |
| 1948 | 13.50 | 16.00 | 19.00 | 19.00 | 25.00 | 40.00 | 32.50 | 25.00 | 25.00 | 32.0 |
| 1949 | 90.00 | 160.00 | 175.00 | 190.00 | 525.00 | 495.00 | 420.00 | 340.00 | 300.00 | 280.0 |
| 1950 | 28.00 | 31.50 | 90.00 | 65.00 | 50.00 | 35.00 | 32.50 | 45.00 | 40.00 | 29.0 |
| 1951 | 21.00 | 25.00 | 40.00 | 32.50 | 26.00 | 24.00 | 30.00 | 30.00 | 24.00 | 30.0 |
| 1952 | 19.50 | 35.00 | 30.00 | 23.00 | 23.00 | 27.50 | 30.00 | 21.00 | 30.00 | 31.0 |
| 1953 | 85.00 | 70.00 | 50.00 | 39.00 | 53.00 | 55.00 | 37.00 | 47.50 | 47.50 | 89.0 |
| 1954 | 15.00 | 16.00 | 15.00 | 27.50 | 23.00 | 17.25 | 16.00 | 17.00 | 32.00 | 44.7 |
| 1955 | 35.00 | 22.50 | 50.00 | 46.00 | 27.50 | 25.00 | 31.50 | 52.00 | 50.00 | 44.5 |
| 1956 | 16.00 | 27.50 | 20.00 | 18.00 | 16.00 | 17.00 | 30.00 | 45.00 | 39.50 | |
| 1957 | 21.00 | 21.00 | 22.00 | 15.50 | 16.50 | 29.00 | 45.00 | 39.50 | | |
| 1958 | 50.00 | 42.50 | 35.00 | 45.00 | 45.00 | 55.00 | 49.50 | | | |
| 1959 | 18.00 | 16.50 | 15.75 | 29.00 | 44.00 | 39.50 | | | | |
| 1960 | 15.50 | 15.75 | 29.00 | 44.00 | 39.50 | | | | | |
| 1961 | 15.50 | 28.00 | 44.00 | 39.50 | | | | | | |
| 1962 | 28.00 | 44.00 | 39.50 | | | | | | | |
| 1963 | 44.00 | 39.50 | | | | | | | | |
| 1964 | 39.50 | | | | | | | | | |

## Retail Prices — Uncirculated Rolls of P Quarters

*Face Value of One Roll: $10.00*

| Year Minted | Number of Years After Year Minted | | | | | | | | | |
|---|---|---|---|---|---|---|---|---|---|---|
| | 21 | 22 | 23 | 24 | 25 | 26 | 27 | 28 | 29 | 30 |
| 1935 | $ 66.00 | $ 75.00 | $125.00 | $125.00 | $130.00 | $185.00 | $210.00 | $225.00 | $250.00 | $250.00 |
| 1936 | 66.00 | 90.00 | 85.00 | 85.00 | 135.00 | 180.00 | 190.00 | 250.00 | 275.00 | 275.00 |
| 1937 | 100.00 | 150.00 | 215.00 | 175.00 | 215.00 | 240.00 | 225.00 | 225.00 | 225.00 | 225.00 |
| 1938 | 520.00 | 540.00 | 1,000.00 | 1,200.00 | 1,600.00 | 1,500.00 | 1,650.00 | 1,650.00 | 1,250.00 | 1,400.00 |
| 1939 | 140.00 | 175.00 | 210.00 | 235.00 | 230.00 | 215.00 | 215.00 | 200.00 | 165.00 | 140.00 |
| 1940 | 190.00 | 250.00 | 300.00 | 400.00 | 270.00 | 265.00 | 240.00 | 235.00 | 195.00 | 122.50 |
| 1941 | 43.00 | 50.00 | 80.00 | 75.00 | 75.00 | 50.00 | 55.00 | 52.50 | 42.75 | 38.90 |
| 1942 | 65.00 | 95.00 | 80.00 | 80.00 | 50.00 | 52.00 | 50.00 | 38.00 | 35.00 | 41.75 |
| 1943 | 47.50 | 45.00 | 45.00 | 40.00 | 79.50 | 70.00 | 52.00 | 62.00 | 62.50 | 115.00 |
| 1944 | 45.00 | 40.00 | 27.50 | 37.50 | 40.00 | 31.50 | 38.50 | 41.75 | 64.00 | 64.00 |
| 1945 | 30.00 | 27.50 | 35.00 | 35.00 | 28.00 | 27.50 | 27.50 | 60.00 | 90.00 | 63.00 |
| 1946 | 25.00 | 32.50 | 33.00 | 28.00 | 27.80 | 37.50 | 59.00 | 60.00 | 58.00 | |
| 1947 | 50.00 | 57.50 | 44.25 | 40.00 | 42.50 | 75.00 | 90.00 | 76.00 | | |
| 1948 | 32.50 | 28.00 | 29.50 | 27.50 | 58.00 | 56.50 | 64.00 | | | |
| 1949 | 246.50 | 237.50 | 250.00 | 435.00 | 530.00 | 470.00 | | | | |
| 1950 | 30.00 | 32.00 | 60.00 | 60.00 | 85.00 | | | | | |
| 1951 | 36.50 | 53.00 | 61.00 | 65.00 | | | | | | |
| 1952 | 50.00 | 65.00 | 70.00 | | | | | | | |
| 1953 | 72.50 | 69.00 | | | | | | | | |
| 1954 | 43.00 | | | | | | | | | |

## Retail Prices — Uncirculated Rolls of P Quarters

*Face Value of One Roll: $10.*

| Year Minted | Number of Years After Year Minted | | | | | | | | | |
|---|---|---|---|---|---|---|---|---|---|---|
| | 31 | 32 | 33 | 34 | 35 | 36 | 37 | 38 | 39 | 40 |
| 1935 | $250.00 | $300.00 | $250.00 | $250.00 | $179.50 | $166.80 | $180.70 | $243.25 | $485.00 | $600.00 |
| 1936 | 290.00 | 250.00 | 230.00 | 182.50 | 166.80 | 193.20 | 271.00 | 475.00 | 497.00 | |
| 1937 | 220.00 | 220.00 | 169.50 | 180.70 | 208.50 | 326.50 | 675.00 | 585.00 | | |
| 1938 | 1,400.00 | 995.00 | 973.00 | 820.00 | 1,105.00 | 1,470.00 | 1,400.00 | | | |
| 1939 | 109.50 | 139.00 | 146.00 | 201.50 | 325.00 | 375.00 | | | | |
| 1940 | 139.00 | 153.00 | 152.90 | 350.00 | 388.00 | | | | | |
| 1941 | 46.00 | 135.00 | 195.00 | 180.00 | | | | | | |
| 1942 | 100.00 | 129.00 | 145.00 | | | | | | | |
| 1943 | 125.00 | 120.00 | | | | | | | | |
| 1944 | 57.00 | | | | | | | | | |

## Retail Prices — Uncirculated Rolls of D Quarters

*Face Value of One Roll: $10.00*

| Year Minted | \#1 | 2 | 3 | 4 | 5 | 6 | 7 | 8 | 9 | 10 |
|---|---|---|---|---|---|---|---|---|---|---|
| 1935 | $11.50 | $12.00 | $12.00 | $12.75 | $14.00 | $14.35 | $21.00 | $23.00 | $24.50 | $26.25 |
| 1936 | 11.85 | 12.00 | 12.00 | 12.95 | 14.00 | 19.00 | 20.00 | 25.00 | 30.00 | 50.00 |
| 1937 | 11.50 | 12.00 | 12.00 | 14.00 | 16.50 | 17.50 | 17.00 | 22.00 | 22.50 | 27.50 |
| 1939 | 11.75 | 12.50 | 14.50 | 15.00 | 16.00 | 18.00 | 18.00 | 18.00 | 20.00 | 21.75 |
| 1940 | 12.00 | 13.00 | 15.50 | 15.50 | 16.00 | 17.25 | 30.00 | 50.00 | 55.00 | 55.00 |
| 1941 | 12.50 | 15.00 | 14.00 | 14.50 | 15.00 | 16.00 | 15.00 | 15.00 | 15.00 | 15.75 |
| 1942 | 13.00 | 12.00 | 12.50 | 15.00 | 15.00 | 15.00 | 14.55 | 14.50 | 14.55 | 14.50 |
| 1943 | 11.50 | 12.50 | 12.65 | 14.00 | 14.50 | 14.25 | 14.25 | 14.25 | 14.25 | 14.25 |
| 1944 | 11.25 | 11.25 | 11.75 | 13.00 | 12.50 | 12.45 | 12.45 | 12.50 | 12.50 | 13.00 |
| 1945 | 11.00 | 11.25 | 11.75 | 11.50 | 11.50 | 11.65 | 12.00 | 12.50 | 13.00 | 13.00 |
| 1946 | 11.25 | 11.25 | 11.50 | 11.65 | 11.85 | 12.00 | 12.50 | 13.00 | 13.00 | 13.95 |
| 1947 | 11.75 | 11.50 | 11.90 | 12.00 | 11.80 | 12.00 | 13.00 | 13.00 | 14.75 | 14.00 |
| 1948 | 11.00 | 11.25 | 12.00 | 11.75 | 12.00 | 13.00 | 13.00 | 13.50 | 13.00 | 13.75 |
| 1949 | 11.85 | 12.50 | 11.80 | 12.25 | 13.00 | 13.00 | 14.00 | 13.00 | 12.80 | 13.60 |
| 1950 | 12.00 | 11.75 | 12.50 | 14.00 | 13.50 | 13.75 | 12.75 | 12.75 | 14.00 | 17.00 |
| 1951 | 11.50 | 12.00 | 12.00 | 13.00 | 12.85 | 12.85 | 12.80 | 13.50 | 17.50 | 17.25 |
| 1952 | 12.00 | 12.00 | 12.65 | 13.00 | 13.00 | 12.75 | 13.00 | 16.50 | 17.00 | 18.00 |
| 1953 | 11.50 | 12.00 | 12.50 | 12.35 | 12.00 | 12.75 | 17.00 | 16.00 | 17.00 | 19.00 |
| 1954 | 11.25 | 12.00 | 11.85 | 11.50 | 13.00 | 16.00 | 15.50 | 15.50 | 50.00 | 36.00 |
| 1955 | 15.00 | 14.00 | 13.50 | 15.00 | 40.00 | 31.00 | 45.00 | 145.00 | 160.00 | 145.00 |
| 1956 | 11.00 | 10.85 | 12.00 | 14.00 | 15.75 | 18.50 | 17.00 | 20.00 | 19.50 | 16.50 |
| 1957 | 10.75 | 11.50 | 13.00 | 13.00 | 13.50 | 15.00 | 14.00 | 13.50 | 15.00 | 14.00 |
| 1958 | 11.50 | 15.00 | 13.50 | 14.00 | 13.50 | 15.00 | 13.00 | 14.00 | 13.50 | 19.00 |
| 1959 | 12.00 | 11.75 | 12.50 | 15.00 | 15.00 | 13.00 | 13.00 | 13.00 | 19.00 | 18.00 |
| 1960 | 11.75 | 11.75 | 12.50 | 12.50 | 12.50 | 15.00 | 14.00 | 19.50 | 16.00 | 16.75 |
| 1961 | 11.50 | 12.00 | 12.00 | 13.00 | 14.50 | 14.00 | 18.00 | 17.00 | 17.50 | 15.00 |
| 1962 | 12.00 | 12.50 | 12.50 | 14.00 | 13.50 | 18.50 | 17.00 | 17.00 | 14.75 | 15.50 |
| 1963 | 12.00 | 12.50 | 14.00 | 12.00 | 17.50 | 16.00 | 15.00 | 14.50 | 15.00 | 28.00 |
| 1964 | 10.75 | 12.50 | 13.75 | 13.50 | 14.00 | 15.00 | 15.50 | 16.00 | 27.00 | 44.00 |
| 1968 | 11.75 | 13.00 | 15.00 | 20.00 | 22.00 | 24.00 | 21.00 | | | |
| 1969 | 11.75 | 13.00 | 20.00 | 28.00 | 25.00 | 24.00 | | | | |
| 1970 | 11.75 | 12.00 | 14.00 | 16.00 | 15.50 | | | | | |
| 1971 | 11.50 | 13.00 | 16.00 | 15.50 | | | | | | |
| 1972 | 13.00 | 16.00 | 15.50 | | | | | | | |
| 1973 | 16.00 | 14.50 | | | | | | | | |
| 1974 | 14.00 | | | | | | | | | |

*Number of Years After Year Minted*

## Retail Prices — Uncirculated Rolls of D Quarters

*Face Value of One Roll: $10.0*

| Year Minted | Number of Years After Year Minted | | | | | | | | | |
|---|---|---|---|---|---|---|---|---|---|---|
| | 11 | 12 | 13 | 14 | 15 | 16 | 17 | 18 | 19 | 20 |
| 1935 | $ 28.00 | $ 30.00 | $ 40.00 | $ 40.00 | $ 45.00 | $ 45.00 | $ 45.00 | $ 50.00 | $ 99.00 | $100.00 |
| 1936 | 85.00 | 100.00 | 120.00 | 150.00 | 200.00 | 240.00 | 350.00 | 540.00 | 800.00 | 1,000.00 |
| 1937 | 30.00 | 27.00 | 27.25 | 27.35 | 30.00 | 34.00 | 34.00 | 55.00 | 75.00 | 79.00 |
| 1939 | 25.00 | 25.00 | 24.50 | 27.50 | 25.00 | 40.00 | 60.00 | 75.00 | 90.00 | 100.00 |
| 1940 | 58.00 | 67.00 | 67.50 | 67.50 | 90.00 | 120.00 | 127.50 | 170.00 | 250.00 | 330.00 |
| 1941 | 15.75 | 16.50 | 16.50 | 16.50 | 40.00 | 39.00 | 45.00 | 55.00 | 60.00 | 85.00 |
| 1942 | 14.50 | 14.50 | 14.00 | 15.25 | 16.00 | 17.50 | 35.00 | 45.00 | 41.00 | 47.00 |
| 1943 | 14.50 | 15.50 | 16.00 | 16.25 | 16.00 | 20.00 | 37.50 | 36.00 | 36.00 | 45.00 |
| 1944 | 13.00 | 13.95 | 13.00 | 13.00 | 14.00 | 30.00 | 25.00 | 34.00 | 38.00 | 140.00 |
| 1945 | 14.00 | 13.75 | 13.75 | 14.00 | 22.50 | 21.50 | 21.50 | 30.00 | 80.00 | 90.00 |
| 1946 | 13.50 | 13.75 | 13.75 | 18.00 | 20.00 | 23.50 | 30.00 | 130.00 | 95.00 | 100.00 |
| 1947 | 13.00 | 14.00 | 16.50 | 19.00 | 20.00 | 25.00 | 75.00 | 65.00 | 46.75 | 40.00 |
| 1948 | 14.00 | 17.50 | 19.00 | 20.00 | 22.75 | 70.00 | 60.00 | 45.00 | 38.50 | 55.00 |
| 1949 | 18.50 | 49.50 | 66.00 | 80.00 | 120.00 | 140.00 | 122.00 | 80.00 | 147.50 | 160.00 |
| 1950 | 17.00 | 22.00 | 30.00 | 55.00 | 50.00 | 32.00 | 32.50 | 50.00 | 47.50 | 36.50 |
| 1951 | 19.50 | 21.00 | 45.00 | 30.00 | 22.00 | 22.00 | 27.50 | 32.50 | 27.00 | 35.00 |
| 1952 | 20.00 | 35.00 | 22.50 | 21.00 | 19.00 | 30.00 | 28.00 | 22.00 | 23.50 | 24.50 |
| 1953 | 26.00 | 20.00 | 16.50 | 16.50 | 26.00 | 25.00 | 17.00 | 19.75 | 19.75 | 38.00 |
| 1954 | 25.00 | 17.50 | 15.75 | 30.00 | 25.00 | 17.00 | 16.00 | 17.00 | 33.00 | 43.50 |
| 1955 | 126.00 | 115.00 | 150.00 | 150.00 | 95.00 | 95.00 | 82.50 | 100.00 | 126.00 | 119.00 |
| 1956 | 15.75 | 25.00 | 21.00 | 18.00 | 16.00 | 17.00 | 30.00 | 45.00 | 39.50 | |
| 1957 | 20.00 | 16.50 | 17.50 | 15.50 | 16.50 | 29.00 | 45.00 | 39.50 | | |
| 1958 | 18.00 | 14.50 | 16.00 | 15.75 | 29.00 | 44.00 | 39.50 | | | |
| 1959 | 14.75 | 16.00 | 15.75 | 29.00 | 44.00 | 39.50 | | | | |
| 1960 | 15.50 | 15.75 | 29.00 | 44.00 | 39.50 | | | | | |
| 1961 | 15.50 | 28.00 | 44.00 | 39.50 | | | | | | |
| 1962 | 28.00 | 44.00 | 39.50 | | | | | | | |
| 1963 | 44.00 | 39.50 | | | | | | | | |
| 1964 | 39.50 | | | | | | | | | |

## Retail Prices — Uncirculated Rolls of D Quarters

*Face Value of One Roll: $10.00*

| Year Minted | Number of Years After Year Minted | | | | | | | | | |
|---|---|---|---|---|---|---|---|---|---|---|
| | 21 | 22 | 23 | 24 | 25 | 26 | 27 | 28 | 29 | 30 |
| 1935 | $120.00 | $160.00 | $250.00 | $380.00 | $395.00 | $700.00 | $750.00 | $950.00 | $1,000.00 | $625.00 |
| 1936 | 1,130.00 | 1,650.00 | 2,200.00 | 2,300.00 | 3,500.00 | 4,400.00 | 5,400.00 | 7,800.00 | 7,800.00 | 7,600.00 |
| 1937 | 80.00 | 90.00 | 80.00 | 200.00 | 225.00 | 300.00 | 335.00 | 335.00 | 335.00 | 335.00 |
| 1939 | 110.00 | 160.00 | 180.00 | 250.00 | 280.00 | 315.00 | 315.00 | 285.00 | 310.00 | 290.00 |
| 1940 | 590.00 | 740.00 | 1,000.00 | 1,200.00 | 1,500.00 | 1,500.00 | 1,250.00 | 1,300.00 | 1,275.00 | 995.00 |
| 1941 | 95.00 | 95.00 | 195.00 | 170.00 | 170.00 | 105.00 | 110.00 | 165.00 | 199.00 | 153.00 |
| 1942 | 47.00 | 90.00 | 137.50 | 137.50 | 50.00 | 97.50 | 95.00 | 86.50 | 76.50 | 97.25 |
| 1943 | 125.00 | 115.00 | 115.00 | 75.00 | 100.00 | 92.50 | 84.50 | 83.50 | 104.25 | 265.00 |
| 1944 | 125.00 | 110.00 | 50.00 | 95.00 | 91.00 | 76.50 | 69.50 | 97.25 | 111.00 | 175.00 |
| 1945 | 90.00 | 75.00 | 90.00 | 88.00 | 69.50 | 69.50 | 90.25 | 140.00 | 145.00 | 102.00 |
| 1946 | 80.00 | 115.00 | 95.00 | 73.75 | 60.00 | 69.50 | 94.00 | 270.00 | 140.00 | |
| 1947 | 50.00 | 52.50 | 40.00 | 34.75 | 48.75 | 82.00 | 86.00 | 84.00 | | |
| 1948 | 80.00 | 60.00 | 89.50 | 83.25 | 94.00 | 83.50 | 80.00 | | | |
| 1949 | 100.00 | 90.00 | 96.00 | 245.00 | 267.50 | 200.00 | | | | |
| 1950 | 33.50 | 35.00 | 85.00 | 133.50 | 112.00 | | | | | |
| 1951 | 43.00 | 53.00 | 82.00 | 70.00 | | | | | | |
| 1952 | 40.00 | 53.00 | 46.50 | | | | | | | |
| 1953 | 47.00 | 45.50 | | | | | | | | |
| 1954 | 42.00 | | | | | | | | | |

## Retail Prices — Uncirculated Rolls of D Quarters

*Face Value of One Roll: $10.0*

| Year Minted | Number of Years After Year Minted | | | | | | | | | |
|---|---|---|---|---|---|---|---|---|---|---|
| | 31 | 32 | 33 | 34 | 35 | 36 | 37 | 38 | 39 | 40 |
| 1935 | $675.00 | $625.00 | $1,600.00 | $1,600.00 | $1,850.00 | $1,807.00 | $2,210.00 | $1,918.00 | $2,564.00 | $2,723.00 |
| 1936 | 7,800.00 | 7,000.00 | 7,000.00 | 7,000.00 | 6,533.00 | 6,533.00 | 7,228.00 | 8,546.00 | 8,295.00 | |
| 1937 | 375.00 | 400.00 | 300.00 | 264.00 | 271.00 | 660.00 | 781.00 | 829.00 | | |
| 1939 | 200.00 | 180.75 | 193.25 | 221.00 | 680.00 | 603.00 | | | | |
| 1940 | 903.50 | 1,042.50 | 1,306.00 | 1,545.00 | 1,471.00 | | | | | |
| 1941 | 208.50 | 368.00 | 600.00 | 516.00 | | | | | | |
| 1942 | 420.00 | 650.00 | 400.00 | | | | | | | |
| 1943 | 340.00 | 297.00 | | | | | | | | |
| 1944 | 155.00 | | | | | | | | | |

## Retail Prices — Uncirculated Rolls of P Half-Dollars

*Face Value of One Roll: $10.00*

| Year Minted | Number of Years After Year Minted | | | | | | | | | |
|---|---|---|---|---|---|---|---|---|---|---|
| | 1 | 2 | 3 | 4 | 5 | 6 | 7 | 8 | 9 | 10 |
| 1935 | $10.95 | $11.25 | $11.25 | $12.40 | $12.50 | $15.25 | $16.00 | $16.00 | $16.00 | $20.00 |
| 1936 | 11.00 | 11.25 | 12.50 | 13.00 | 15.00 | 16.00 | 18.00 | 18.00 | 20.00 | 22.25 |
| 1937 | 11.00 | 11.50 | 12.50 | 14.00 | 15.00 | 17.00 | 16.00 | 18.00 | 19.65 | 21.75 |
| 1938 | 11.55 | 12.95 | 14.00 | 14.00 | 16.50 | 16.00 | 16.75 | 16.00 | 18.25 | 20.00 |
| 1939 | 12.00 | 13.50 | 14.00 | 16.50 | 16.50 | 17.65 | 19.25 | 20.75 | 25.45 | 30.00 |
| 1940 | 11.85 | 12.50 | 15.00 | 14.00 | 15.00 | 16.50 | 16.50 | 16.50 | 16.25 | 16.00 |
| 1941 | 12.00 | 15.00 | 12.50 | 13.00 | 13.50 | 14.50 | 15.00 | 14.25 | 14.10 | 13.75 |
| 1942 | 13.00 | 13.00 | 13.50 | 13.75 | 14.00 | 15.00 | 14.00 | 14.75 | 15.00 | 15.00 |
| 1943 | 11.25 | 12.50 | 12.00 | 13.00 | 14.00 | 12.00 | 12.00 | 12.75 | 12.75 | 13.00 |
| 1944 | 11.25 | 11.35 | 12.00 | 13.00 | 11.10 | 11.50 | 13.00 | 13.00 | 13.00 | 14.00 |
| 1945 | 11.00 | 11.50 | 12.00 | 12.00 | 12.15 | 12.15 | 12.50 | 13.00 | 13.00 | 13.00 |
| 1946 | 11.50 | 11.50 | 10.95 | 11.50 | 11.95 | 12.00 | 13.25 | 14.00 | 13.00 | 13.50 |
| 1947 | 11.00 | 11.25 | 11.45 | 13.20 | 15.75 | 19.85 | 25.00 | 22.25 | 22.25 | 22.50 |
| 1948 | 11.15 | 11.45 | 12.50 | 15.00 | 17.20 | 30.00 | 45.00 | 40.50 | 45.00 | 42.00 |
| 1949 | 11.25 | 14.75 | 28.85 | 35.00 | 46.70 | 75.00 | 75.00 | 80.00 | 120.00 | 160.00 |
| 1950 | 11.25 | 11.90 | 12.50 | 22.50 | 22.50 | 23.00 | 22.00 | 45.00 | 80.00 | 115.00 |
| 1951 | 11.75 | 11.75 | 12.00 | 12.00 | 17.50 | 18.00 | 17.00 | 18.00 | 25.00 | 31.00 |
| 1952 | 11.75 | 12.00 | 12.25 | 13.80 | 13.50 | 13.00 | 13.75 | 21.50 | 20.00 | 21.00 |
| 1953 | 12.50 | 15.00 | 15.25 | 19.00 | 24.00 | 40.00 | 42.50 | 40.00 | 50.00 | 75.00 |
| 1954 | 12.00 | 11.50 | 11.85 | 11.75 | 12.75 | 16.00 | 16.00 | 16.00 | 15.00 | 28.00 |
| 955 | 13.00 | 13.00 | 13.00 | 13.75 | 27.00 | 21.00 | 25.00 | 45.00 | 140.00 | 165.00 |
| 956 | 11.00 | 11.25 | 12.00 | 16.00 | 14.50 | 17.00 | 21.00 | 55.00 | 75.00 | 60.00 |
| 957 | 11.00 | 11.75 | 13.50 | 13.00 | 14.00 | 18.00 | 37.50 | 42.50 | 38.50 | 32.50 |
| 958 | 11.75 | 15.00 | 15.00 | 15.00 | 24.00 | 50.00 | 60.00 | 47.50 | 38.50 | 57.50 |
| 959 | 12.50 | 13.00 | 13.50 | 16.00 | 24.00 | 40.00 | 35.00 | 25.50 | 42.50 | 35.00 |
| 960 | 12.00 | 12.00 | 15.00 | 24.00 | 37.50 | 35.00 | 24.50 | 35.00 | 32.50 | 22.50 |
| 961 | 11.00 | 13.30 | 20.00 | 25.00 | 25.00 | 20.00 | 33.50 | 25.00 | 21.00 | 22.00 |
| 962 | 13.00 | 21.50 | 22.00 | 26.00 | 18.75 | 32.00 | 26.00 | 21.00 | 20.00 | 20.00 |
| 963 | 14.00 | 13.50 | 16.00 | 14.75 | 19.00 | 17.00 | 15.00 | 15.00 | 15.50 | 28.00 |
| 964 | 13.00 | 12.50 | 13.50 | 16.00 | 13.50 | 15.00 | 15.50 | 15.00 | 26.00 | 38.50 |
| 965 | 12.00 | 12.00 | 20.00 | 22.50 | 15.00 | 14.00 | 14.00 | 15.00 | 20.00 | 19.25 |
| 966 | 11.50 | 15.00 | 13.00 | 12.50 | 12.50 | 12.75 | 16.00 | 20.00 | 19.25 | |
| 967 | 14.00 | 12.50 | 12.00 | 12.50 | 12.50 | 15.00 | 20.00 | 18.75 | | |
| 971 | 11.00 | 15.00 | 17.50 | 17.00 | | | | | | |
| 972 | 14.00 | 15.00 | 16.00 | | | | | | | |
| 73 | 14.00 | 14.00 | | | | | | | | |
| 74 | 14.00 | | | | | | | | | |

## Retail Prices — Uncirculated Rolls of P Half-Dollars

*Face Value of One Roll: $10.00*

| Year Minted | Number of Years After Year Minted | | | | | | | | | |
|---|---|---|---|---|---|---|---|---|---|---|
| | 11 | 12 | 13 | 14 | 15 | 16 | 17 | 18 | 19 | 20 |
| 1935 | $ 23.85 | $ 27.50 | $ 25.00 | $ 24.00 | $ 23.75 | $ 23.00 | $ 22.50 | $ 23.50 | $ 26.00 | $ 30.00 |
| 1936 | 23.00 | 25.00 | 21.00 | 22.00 | 22.25 | 22.00 | 23.00 | 22.00 | 20.00 | 27.00 |
| 1937 | 21.75 | 21.00 | 21.50 | 21.50 | 23.85 | 25.00 | 25.00 | 39.50 | 40.00 | 40.00 |
| 1938 | 22.50 | 23.00 | 25.75 | 28.00 | 29.85 | 40.00 | 39.50 | 40.00 | 42.00 | 73.50 |
| 1939 | 25.00 | 24.50 | 24.50 | 26.00 | 26.00 | 33.00 | 40.00 | 57.50 | 75.00 | 90.00 |
| 1940 | 16.00 | 15.50 | 15.50 | 20.00 | 20.00 | 23.75 | 26.00 | 40.75 | 50.00 | 50.00 |
| 1941 | 13.75 | 14.00 | 15.00 | 18.00 | 20.25 | 21.75 | 22.00 | 25.00 | 28.00 | 35.00 |
| 1942 | 16.50 | 14.00 | 17.50 | 18.25 | 18.00 | 19.50 | 21.00 | 25.00 | 30.00 | 38.00 |
| 1943 | 13.00 | 14.00 | 17.50 | 17.00 | 18.50 | 22.00 | 25.00 | 25.00 | 28.00 | 40.00 |
| 1944 | 13.00 | 13.65 | 14.00 | 14.75 | 15.25 | 25.00 | 20.75 | 25.00 | 28.50 | 55.00 |
| 1945 | 14.00 | 13.00 | 13.50 | 14.50 | 20.00 | 19.50 | 24.50 | 35.50 | 50.00 | 80.00 |
| 1946 | 16.00 | 17.00 | 19.00 | 24.00 | 21.00 | 22.00 | 29.00 | 55.00 | 110.00 | 110.00 |
| 1947 | 21.00 | 22.75 | 25.00 | 23.00 | 25.00 | 33.00 | 70.00 | 125.00 | 122.50 | 135.00 |
| 1948 | 45.00 | 50.00 | 40.00 | 48.00 | 125.00 | 180.00 | 185.00 | 158.00 | 145.00 | 207.50 |
| 1949 | 300.00 | 225.00 | 215.00 | 450.00 | 725.00 | 485.00 | 387.50 | 340.00 | 480.00 | 435.00 |
| 1950 | 73.00 | 91.00 | 195.00 | 340.00 | 260.00 | 197.50 | 215.00 | 335.00 | 285.00 | 169.50 |
| 1951 | 34.00 | 62.50 | 80.00 | 70.00 | 57.50 | 50.00 | 80.00 | 85.00 | 54.50 | 85.00 |
| 1952 | 35.00 | 42.50 | 70.00 | 47.50 | 39.00 | 52.00 | 50.00 | 38.00 | 37.50 | 42.00 |
| 1953 | 210.00 | 225.00 | 215.00 | 195.00 | 210.00 | 200.00 | 142.00 | 110.00 | 179.50 | 260.00 |
| 1954 | 33.50 | 25.00 | 21.50 | 46.00 | 42.50 | 22.00 | 22.50 | 27.00 | 38.00 | 53.75 |
| 1955 | 158.00 | 140.00 | 167.00 | 155.00 | 117.50 | 110.00 | 110.00 | 130.00 | 149.00 | 140.00 |
| 1956 | 45.00 | 70.00 | 62.00 | 50.00 | 45.00 | 53.00 | 62.00 | 65.00 | 60.00 | |
| 1957 | 52.00 | 45.00 | 36.50 | 33.00 | 33.50 | 40.00 | 60.00 | 60.00 | | |
| 1958 | 50.00 | 32.50 | 35.00 | 35.00 | 45.00 | 64.00 | 57.00 | | | |
| 1959 | 31.50 | 30.00 | 25.00 | 35.00 | 54.00 | 48.00 | | | | |
| 1960 | 26.00 | 23.00 | 30.00 | 48.50 | 44.00 | | | | | |
| 1961 | 21.00 | 30.00 | 45.00 | 44.00 | | | | | | |
| 1962 | 29.00 | 45.00 | 43.00 | | | | | | | |
| 1963 | 37.75 | 43.00 | | | | | | | | |
| 1964 | 39.00 | | | | | | | | | |

## Retail Prices — Uncirculated Rolls of P Half-Dollars

*Face Value of One Roll: $10.00*

| Year Minted | Number of Years After Year Minted | | | | | | | | | |
|---|---|---|---|---|---|---|---|---|---|---|
| | 21 | 22 | 23 | 24 | 25 | 26 | 27 | 28 | 29 | 30 |
| 1935 | $ 26.50 | $ 43.00 | $ 55.00 | $ 70.00 | $ 63.00 | $ 70.00 | $ 80.00 | $110.00 | $120.00 | $125.00 |
| 1936 | 34.00 | 42.50 | 45.00 | 55.00 | 60.00 | 64.00 | 85.00 | 90.00 | 120.00 | 120.00 |
| 1937 | 55.00 | 70.00 | 75.00 | 90.00 | 115.00 | 115.00 | 120.00 | 200.00 | 200.00 | 200.00 |
| 1938 | 80.00 | 90.00 | 90.00 | 95.00 | 120.00 | 160.00 | 450.00 | 450.00 | 460.00 | 500.00 |
| 1939 | 100.00 | 105.00 | 110.00 | 125.00 | 150.00 | 165.00 | 165.00 | 120.00 | 140.00 | 145.00 |
| 1940 | 65.00 | 70.00 | 75.00 | 80.00 | 90.00 | 90.00 | 90.00 | 102.00 | 120.00 | 100.00 |
| 1941 | 42.00 | 50.00 | 65.00 | 95.00 | 95.00 | 80.00 | 90.00 | 100.00 | 83.00 | 85.75 |
| 1942 | 45.00 | 60.00 | 80.00 | 80.00 | 75.00 | 90.00 | 97.50 | 82.00 | 74.50 | 105.00 |
| 1943 | 50.00 | 75.00 | 75.00 | 75.00 | 92.50 | 97.50 | 82.00 | 92.50 | 105.00 | 220.00 |
| 1944 | 80.00 | 80.00 | 77.50 | 90.00 | 97.50 | 82.00 | 74.50 | 111.75 | 220.00 | 300.00 |
| 1945 | · 77.50 | 75.00 | 92.00 | 99.00 | 82.00 | 74.50 | 105.00 | 220.00 | 300.00 | 265.00 |
| 1946 | 85.00 | 105.00 | 110.00 | 90.00 | 85.75 | 126.75 | 268.00 | 360.00 | 317.00 | |
| 1947 | 170.00 | 185.00 | 170.00 | 156.50 | 193.75 | 328.00 | 400.00 | 363.00 | | |
| 1948 | 180.00 | 117.00 | 110.00 | 126.75 | 175.00 | 185.00 | 162.50 | | | |
| 1949 | 299.50 | 270.00 | 325.00 | 575.00 | 612.50 | 490.00 | | | | |
| 1950 | 150.00 | 290.00 | 298.00 | 365.00 | 345.00 | | | | | |
| 1951 | 50.00 | 185.00 | 236.75 | 194.00 | | | | | | |
| 1952 | 78.00 | 175.00 | 129.75 | | | | | | | |
| 1953 | 250.00 | 207.00 | | | | | | | | |
| 1954 | 56.00 | | | | | | | | | |

## Retail Prices — Uncirculated Rolls of P Half-Dollars

*Face Value of One Roll: $10.0(*

| Year Minted | Number of Years After Year Minted | | | | | | | | | |
|---|---|---|---|---|---|---|---|---|---|---|
| | 31 | 32 | 33 | 34 | 35 | 36 | 37 | 38 | 39 | 40 |
| 1935 | $125.00 | $125.00 | $135.00 | $145.00 | $140.00 | $119.00 | $156.50 | $342.50 | $425.00 | $423.00 |
| 1936 | 100.00 | 130.00 | 140.00 | 140.00 | 119.00 | 145.25 | 425.00 | 395.00 | 495.00 | |
| 1937 | 150.00 | 175.00 | 150.00 | 134.00 | 160.25 | 342.50 | 440.00 | 406.00 | | |
| 1938 | 500.00 | 439.50 | 409.75 | 588.50 | 693.00 | 851.00 | 946.00 | | | |
| 1939 | 140.00 | 126.75 | 171.25 | 469.00 | 525.00 | 558.00 | | | | |
| 1940 | 104.25 | 134.00 | 257.00 | 360.00 | 460.00 | | | | | |
| 1941 | 105.00 | 295.00 | 320.00 | 299.00 | | | | | | |
| 1942 | 227.50 | 300.00 | 275.00 | | | | | | | |
| 1943 | 300.00 | 265.00 | | | | | | | | |
| 1944 | 265.00 | | | | | | | | | |

## Retail Prices — Uncirculated Rolls of D Half-Dollars

*Face Value of One Roll: $10.00*

| Year Minted | \ Number of Years After Year Minted | | | | | | | | | |
|---|---|---|---|---|---|---|---|---|---|---|
| | 1 | 2 | 3 | 4 | 5 | 6 | 7 | 8 | 9 | 10 |
| 1935 | $ 10.90 | $ 11.25 | $ 11.35 | $ 13.00 | $ 13.25 | $ 14.85 | $ 16.00 | $ 18.00 | $ 18.00 | $ 22.00 |
| 1936 | 11.00 | 11.25 | 12.75 | 13.50 | 15.00 | 16.00 | 19.00 | 18.50 | 20.50 | 22.25 |
| 1937 | 11.25 | 11.55 | 12.50 | 15.00 | 15.00 | 17.00 | 16.50 | 17.50 | 18.65 | 19.25 |
| 1938 | 12.95 | 14.00 | 20.00 | 30.00 | 40.00 | 55.00 | 70.00 | 85.00 | 100.00 | 120.00 |
| 1939 | 12.00 | 13.50 | 14.00 | 16.50 | 15.00 | 16.00 | 18.50 | 20.75 | 20.75 | 17.50 |
| 1941 | 12.00 | 15.00 | 13.00 | 14.00 | 14.00 | 14.50 | 15.00 | 14.25 | 13.90 | 13.75 |
| 1942 | 13.00 | 13.00 | 13.25 | 13.75 | 14.00 | 15.00 | 14.00 | 14.50 | 14.75 | 16.00 |
| 1943 | 11.50 | 12.50 | 12.00 | 13.00 | 14.50 | 13.25 | 13.25 | 13.25 | 13.25 | 16.50 |
| 1944 | 11.25 | 12.00 | 12.00 | 13.50 | 11.10 | 12.00 | 12.60 | 13.00 | 13.00 | 13.00 |
| 1945 | 11.00 | 11.50 | 12.00 | 11.10 | 12.25 | 13.50 | 13.00 | 13.00 | 13.00 | 13.50 |
| 1946 | 11.00 | 12.00 | 11.10 | 11.85 | 13.00 | 12.25 | 13.00 | 14.00 | 14.60 | 14.00 |
| 1947 | 11.00 | 11.25 | 11.45 | 12.50 | 12.25 | 13.00 | 15.00 | 15.00 | 15.70 | 15.00 |
| 1948 | 11.10 | 11.45 | 12.50 | 12.85 | 13.25 | 16.50 | 19.00 | 23.50 | 21.40 | 18.00 |
| 1949 | 11.25 | 12.50 | 12.45 | 13.00 | 17.50 | 22.00 | 23.00 | 22.25 | 21.00 | 22.00 |
| 1950 | 12.00 | 11.75 | 12.00 | 14.00 | 28.00 | 23.00 | 22.50 | 20.00 | 22.00 | 52.50 |
| 1951 | 11.75 | 12.00 | 12.00 | 12.00 | 18.00 | 17.25 | 16.00 | 18.00 | 22.50 | 30.00 |
| 1952 | 11.75 | 12.00 | 12.75 | 13.50 | 13.50 | 13.00 | 13.75 | 20.00 | 19.50 | 19.50 |
| 1953 | 11.25 | 12.00 | 12.75 | 12.50 | 12.50 | 13.50 | 16.00 | 18.00 | 18.00 | 20.00 |
| 1954 | 11.25 | 11.75 | 12.00 | 12.00 | 12.75 | 17.50 | 15.50 | 15.50 | 18.00 | 22.00 |
| 1957 | 11.00 | 11.75 | 12.50 | 13.00 | 13.00 | 15.00 | 20.00 | 16.00 | 18.50 | 18.50 |
| 1958 | 11.75 | 12.50 | 13.50 | 13.50 | 14.00 | 17.50 | 16.00 | 19.00 | 18.50 | 26.00 |
| 1959 | 12.50 | 13.00 | 15.00 | 23.00 | 24.00 | 23.00 | 23.00 | 23.00 | 25.00 | 29.00 |
| 1960 | 12.00 | 12.00 | 15.00 | 18.00 | 20.00 | 21.00 | 18.00 | 24.00 | 21.00 | 19.00 |
| 1961 | 11.00 | 13.00 | 19.00 | 17.50 | 19.50 | 17.75 | 24.00 | 26.00 | *19.00 | 21.00 |
| 1962 | 13.00 | 16.00 | 12.50 | 15.00 | 15.50 | 21.00 | 20.00 | 17.50 | 17.00 | 20.00 |
| 1963 | 12.50 | 12.50 | 15.00 | 13.75 | 19.00 | 16.00 | 15.00 | 15.00 | 15.50 | 28.00 |
| 1964 | 15.00 | 15.00 | 15.00 | 17.00 | 14.50 | 15.00 | 15.50 | 16.00 | 26.00 | 38.50 |
| 1968 | 12.00 | 11.75 | 12.50 | 12.25 | 15.00 | 20.00 | 18.00 | | | |
| 1969 | 11.50 | 12.50 | 12.00 | 15.00 | 20.00 | 18.00 | | | | |
| 1970 | 165.00 | 200.00 | 350.00 | 350.00 | 310.00 | | | | | |
| 1971 | 11.00 | 14.00 | 17.00 | 14.00 | | | | | | |
| 1972 | 14.00 | 15.00 | 14.00 | | | | | | | |
| 1973 | 14.00 | 14.50 | | | | | | | | |
| 1974 | 14.00 | | | | | | | | | |

## Retail Prices — Uncirculated Rolls of D Half-Dollars

*Face Value of One Roll: $10.00*

| Year Minted | 11 | 12 | 13 | 14 | 15 | 16 | 17 | 18 | 19 | 20 |
|---|---|---|---|---|---|---|---|---|---|---|
| | | | | *Number of Years After Year Minted* | | | | | | |
| 1935 | $ 25.00 | $ 27.50 | $ 29.00 | $ 30.00 | $ 30.00 | $ 35.00 | $ 40.00 | $ 45.00 | $ 55.00 | $ 75.00 |
| 1936 | 23.00 | 22.50 | 22.50 | 24.00 | 22.50 | 22.50 | 23.00 | 24.00 | 24.00 | 30.00 |
| 1937 | 22.95 | 27.00 | 27.50 | 32.00 | 33.75 | 70.00 | 140.00 | 120.00 | 130.00 | 190.00 |
| 1938 | 120.00 | 125.00 | 125.00 | 125.00 | 165.00 | 210.00 | 235.00 | 250.00 | 265.00 | 365.00 |
| 1939 | 18.00 | 18.65 | 18.00 | 22.50 | 21.50 | 33.00 | 36.50 | 35.00 | 36.50 | 40.00 |
| 1941 | 13.50 | 13.50 | 15.00 | 17.00 | 18.00 | 20.00 | 30.50 | 37.00 | 35.00 | 42.50 |
| 1942 | 16.50 | 16.50 | 17.25 | 20.25 | 25.00 | 27.85 | 40.00 | 34.00 | 44.25 | 46.00 |
| 1943 | 16.50 | 16.00 | 16.25 | 20.00 | 22.50 | 40.00 | 50.00 | 54.00 | 54.00 | 54.00 |
| 1944 | 13.00 | 13.95 | 13.00 | 14.00 | 15.50 | 22.50 | 22.50 | 24.00 | 28.00 | 55.00 |
| 1945 | 14.00 | 13.50 | 14.00 | 14.75 | 21.00 | 22.00 | 23.75 | 33.60 | 60.00 | 80.00 |
| 1946 | 16.75 | 20.00 | 22.00 | 22.50 | 30.00 | 30.00 | 57.00 | 120.00 | 205.00 | 200.00 |
| 1947 | 14.50 | 15.75 | 25.00 | 21.00 | 21.00 | 28.00 | 75.00 | 120.00 | 115.00 | 115.00 |
| 1948 | 20.00 | 26.00 | 27.50 | 27.50 | 55.00 | 95.00 | 120.00 | 117.50 | 82.50 | 108.00 |
| 1949 | 70.00 | 80.00 | 80.00 | 100.00 | 225.00 | 195.00 | 185.00 | 210.00 | 385.00 | 375.00 |
| 1950 | 50.00 | 63.00 | 110.25 | 220.00 | 175.00 | 120.00 | 110.00 | 220.00 | 180.00 | 140.00 |
| 1951 | 33.50 | 50.00 | 190.00 | 160.00 | 134.00 | 130.00 | 375.00 | 350.00 | 226.50 | 152.50 |
| 1952 | 25.00 | 30.00 | 32.50 | 30.00 | 30.00 | 47.50 | 47.50 | 28.00 | 30.00 | 38.00 |
| 1953 | 25.00 | 26.00 | 24.00 | 24.00 | 40.00 | 37.50 | 22.00 | 28.50 | 30.00 | 46.00 |
| 1954 | 20.00 | 22.00 | 18.50 | 30.00 | 27.00 | 19.00 | 17.50 | 25.00 | 36.00 | 43.75 |
| 1957 | 23.50 | 22.00 | 20.00 | 21.00 | 21.50 | 34.00 | 52.50 | 44.50 | | |
| 1958 | 23.00 | 17.50 | 19.50 | 27.00 | 34.00 | 46.00 | 44.25 | | | |
| 1959 | 27.50 | 26.00 | 27.00 | 38.00 | 58.00 | 48.00 | | | | |
| 1960 | 22.00 | 22.00 | 30.00 | 50.00 | 44.00 | | | | | |
| 1961 | 21.00 | 30.00 | 48.00 | 45.25 | | | | | | |
| 1962 | 29.00 | 46.50 | 43.00 | | | | | | | |
| 1963 | 37.75 | 43.00 | | | | | | | | |
| 1964 | 39.00 | | | | | | | | | |

## Retail Prices — Uncirculated Rolls of D Half-Dollars

*Face Value of One Roll: $10.00*

| Year Minted | Number of Years After Year Minted | | | | | | | | | |
|---|---|---|---|---|---|---|---|---|---|---|
| | 21 | 22 | 23 | 24 | 25 | 26 | 27 | 28 | 29 | 30 |
| 1935 | $100.00 | $125.00 | $225.00 | $360.00 | $360.00 | $370.00 | $325.00 | $360.00 | $460.00 | $675.00 |
| 1936 | 41.00 | 50.00 | 80.00 | 93.00 | 90.00 | 95.00 | 130.00 | 140.00 | 250.00 | 250.00 |
| 1937 | 240.00 | 300.00 | 300.00 | 320.00 | 320.00 | 390.00 | 470.00 | 850.00 | 850.00 | 850.00 |
| 1938 | 500.00 | 540.00 | 900.00 | 1,500.00 | 1,620.00 | 1,500.00 | 2,150.00 | 2,150.00 | 2,150.00 | 3,200.00 |
| 1939 | 52.50 | 65.00 | 80.00 | 95.00 | 110.00 | 160.00 | 160.00 | 160.00 | 195.00 | 190.00 |
| 1941 | 45.00 | 65.00 | 120.00 | 220.00 | 220.00 | 190.00 | 225.00 | 205.00 | 169.50 | 164.00 |
| 1942 | 56.00 | 70.00 | 225.00 | 215.00 | 195.00 | 235.00 | 275.00 | 220.00 | 208.50 | 238.50 |
| 1943 | 85.00 | 75.00 | 175.00 | 135.00 | 190.00 | 210.00 | 209.50 | 171.25 | 216.00 | 850.00 |
| 1944 | 90.00 | 90.00 | 87.50 | 100.00 | 105.00 | 109.50 | 96.75 | 141.50 | 313.00 | 370.00 |
| 1945 | 80.00 | 80.00 | 100.00 | 103.00 | 90.00 | 82.00 | 125.00 | 380.00 | 370.00 | 337.00 |
| 1946 | 180.00 | 220.00 | 200.00 | 152.50 | 149.00 | 175.00 | 460.00 | 465.00 | 346.00 | |
| 1947 | 130.00 | 137.00 | 117.50 | 111.75 | 149.00 | 450.00 | 400.00 | 346.00 | | |
| 1948 | 92.50 | 63.75 | 67.00 | 82.00 | 88.65 | 175.00 | 134.00 | | | |
| 1949 | 260.00 | 270.00 | 285.00 | 360.00 | 490.00 | 389.50 | | | | |
| 1950 | 152.50 | 295.00 | 450.00 | 255.00 | 245.00 | | | | | |
| 1951 | 195.00 | 405.00 | 360.00 | 362.00 | | | | | | |
| 1952 | 69.00 | 76.50 | 60.25 | | | | | | | |
| 1953 | 66.00 | 67.50 | | | | | | | | |
| 1954 | 47.00 | | | | | | | | | |

## Retail Prices — Uncirculated Rolls of D Half-Dollars

Face Value of One Roll: $10.00

| Year Minted | Number of Years After Year Minted | | | | | | | | | |
|---|---|---|---|---|---|---|---|---|---|---|
| | 31 | 32 | 33 | 34 | 35 | 36 | 37 | 38 | 39 | 40 |
| 1935 | $675.00 | $675.00 | $700.00 | $700.00 | $595.00 | $633.25 | $737.50 | $1,099.00 | $1,482.00 | $2,818.00 |
| 1936 | 250.00 | 275.00 | 275.00 | 269.50 | 260.75 | 327.75 | 536.00 | 659.00 | 1,932.00 | |
| 1937 | 900.00 | 900.00 | 1,045.00 | 1,005.75 | 1,080.25 | 1,639.00 | 2,013.00 | 3,140.00 | | |
| 1938 | 3,200.00 | 2,970.00 | 2,756.50 | 2,756.50 | 3,948.50 | 5,398.00 | 5,555.00 | | | |
| 1939 | 169.50 | 164.00 | 201.25 | 454.50 | 525.00 | 547.00 | | | | |
| 1941 | 193.75 | 440.00 | 580.00 | 499.00 | | | | | | |
| 1942 | 335.25 | 425.00 | 378.00 | | | | | | | |
| 1943 | 560.00 | 523.00 | | | | | | | | |
| 1944 | 305.00 | | | | | | | | | |

# APPENDIX II

## Average Annual Profit Percentage (AAPP) Tables of Standard & Poor's Composite Stock Index

The following pages show the Average Annual Profit Percentage (AAPP), from one to thirty-eight years after year purchased, of Standard & Poor's Composite Stock Index for the years 1935 through 1973 (with monthly reinvestment of dividends).[1]

To determine the AAPP of an average share of stock at any number of years after the date purchased, find the year when the stock was purchased under the *Year Purchased* column and locate the AAPP under the *Number of Years After Date Purchased* column.

For example, if you want to know what the AAPP of an average share of stock purchased on December 31, 1952 was, fourteen years after the date purchased, go to the table on page 148 and find *1952* under the *Year Purchased* column. Across the page under column 14 you will find 12% — the AAPP, fourteen years after the date purchased, of an average share of stock that was purchased on December 31, 1952.

---

[1] Ibbotson and Sinquefield, *op. cit.*, pp. 123-125.

### Average Annual Profit Percentage (AAPP)
### Standard & Poor's Composite Stock Index (with monthly reinvestment of dividends)

| Year Purchased (at December 31) | Number of Years After Date Purchased | | | | | | | | | |
|---|---|---|---|---|---|---|---|---|---|---|
| | 1 | 2 | 3 | 4 | 5 | 6 | 7 | 8 | 9 | 10 |
| 1935 | 33% | -7% | 5% | 3% | 0% | -2% | 1% | 4% | 6% | 8% |
| 1936 | -35 | -7 | -5 | -6 | -8 | -3 | 1 | 3 | 6 | 5 |
| 1937 | 33 | 15 | 6 | 1 | 5 | 8 | 10 | 13 | 10 | 10 |
| 1938 | -1 | -6 | -8 | -1 | 4 | 6 | 10 | 8 | 7 | 7 |
| 1939 | -10 | -11 | -1 | 5 | 8 | 12 | 9 | 8 | 8 | 9 |
| 1940 | -12 | 3 | 10 | 13 | 17 | 12 | 11 | 11 | 11 | 13 |
| 1941 | 21 | 23 | 22 | 26 | 18 | 16 | 14 | 15 | 16 | 17 |
| 1942 | 26 | 23 | 27 | 17 | 15 | 13 | 14 | 16 | 17 | 17 |
| 1943 | 20 | 28 | 14 | 12 | 11 | 12 | 14 | 16 | 16 | 14 |
| 1944 | 36 | 12 | 10 | 9 | 10 | 14 | 15 | 15 | 14 | 17 |
| 1945 | -8 | -2 | 1 | 5 | 9 | 12 | 13 | 11 | 15 | 16 |
| 1946 | 5 | 5 | 9 | 14 | 16 | 17 | 14 | 18 | 20 | 18 |
| 1947 | 5 | 11 | 17 | 19 | 19 | 15 | 20 | 21 | 20 | 16 |
| 1948 | 18 | 24 | 24 | 23 | 18 | 23 | 24 | 22 | 18 | 20 |
| 1949 | 31 | 28 | 24 | 18 | 24 | 25 | 22 | 18 | 20 | 19 |
| 1950 | 25 | 22 | 13 | 22 | 24 | 21 | 16 | 19 | 18 | 16 |
| 1951 | 19 | 8 | 21 | 24 | 20 | 14 | 18 | 17 | 15 | 16 |
| 1952 | -1 | 23 | 26 | 21 | 14 | 18 | 17 | 15 | 16 | 13 |
| 1953 | 52 | 42 | 29 | 18 | 22 | 20 | 17 | 19 | 15 | 16 |
| 1954 | 31 | 18 | 8 | 16 | 15 | 12 | 14 | 11 | 12 | 13 |
| 1955 | 7 | -3 | 11 | 11 | 9 | 12 | 9 | 10 | 11 | 11 |
| 1956 | -11 | 13 | 13 | 10 | 13 | 9 | 11 | 11 | 12 | 9 |
| 1957 | 43 | 27 | 17 | 20 | 13 | 15 | 15 | 15 | 12 | 13 |
| 1958 | 12 | 6 | 13 | 7 | 10 | 11 | 11 | 8 | 10 | 10 |
| 1959 | 1 | 13 | 5 | 9 | 11 | 11 | 8 | 10 | 10 | 8 |
| 1960 | 27 | 8 | 12 | 13 | 13 | 9 | 11 | 11 | 9 | 8 |
| 1961 | -9 | 6 | 9 | 10 | 6 | 9 | 9 | 7 | 6 | 7 |
| 1962 | 23 | 20 | 17 | 10 | 12 | 12 | 9 | 8 | 9 | 10 |
| 1963 | 16 | 14 | 6 | 10 | 10 | 7 | 6 | 7 | 9 | 6 |
| 1964 | 12 | 1 | 8 | 9 | 5 | 5 | 6 | 8 | 5 | |
| 1965 | -10 | 6 | 7 | 3 | 3 | 5 | 7 | 4 | | |
| 1966 | 24 | 17 | 8 | 7 | 8 | 10 | 6 | | | |
| 1967 | 11 | 1 | 2 | 5 | 8 | 4 | | | | |
| 1968 | -9 | -3 | 3 | 7 | 2 | | | | | |
| 1969 | 4 | 9 | 12 | 5 | | | | | | |
| 1970 | 14 | 17 | 5 | | | | | | | |
| 1971 | 19 | 1 | | | | | | | | |
| 1972 | -15 | | | | | | | | | |

### Average Annual Profit Percentage (AAPP)
### Standard & Poor's Composite Stock Index (with monthly reinvestment of dividends)

| Year Purchased (at December 31) | 11 | 12 | 13 | 14 | 15 | 16 | 17 | 18 | 19 | 20 |
|---|---|---|---|---|---|---|---|---|---|---|
| | | | | | Number of Years After Date Purchased | | | | | |
| 1935 | 7% | 7% | 7% | 7% | 9% | 10% | 10% | 10% | 11% | 12% |
| 1936 | 5 | 5 | 6 | 7 | 8 | 9 | 8 | 10 | 11 | 11 |
| 1937 | 9 | 10 | 11 | 12 | 13 | 12 | 14 | 15 | 14 | 13 |
| 1938 | 8 | 10 | 11 | 11 | 11 | 13 | 14 | 13 | 12 | 13 |
| 1939 | 11 | 12 | 12 | 11 | 14 | 15 | 14 | 13 | 14 | 14 |
| 1940 | 14 | 15 | 13 | 16 | 17 | 16 | 14 | 16 | 15 | 15 |
| 1941 | 17 | 16 | 18 | 19 | 18 | 16 | 18 | 17 | 16 | 17 |
| 1942 | 15 | 18 | 19 | 18 | 16 | 17 | 17 | 16 | 17 | 15 |
| 1943 | 17 | 18 | 17 | 15 | 17 | 16 | 15 | 16 | 15 | 15 |
| 1944 | 18 | 17 | 15 | 17 | 16 | 15 | 16 | 14 | 15 | 15 |
| 1945 | 16 | 13 | 15 | 15 | 14 | 15 | 13 | 14 | 14 | 14 |
| 1946 | 15 | 17 | 17 | 16 | 16 | 15 | 15 | 15 | 15 | 14 |
| 1947 | 19 | 18 | 17 | 17 | 15 | 16 | 16 | 16 | 14 | 15 |
| 1948 | 19 | 18 | 18 | 16 | 16 | 16 | 16 | 15 | 15 | 15 |
| 1949 | 17 | 18 | 16 | 16 | 16 | 16 | 14 | 15 | 15 | 13 |
| 1950 | 17 | 15 | 15 | 15 | 15 | 13 | 14 | 14 | 13 | 12 |
| 1951 | 14 | 15 | 15 | 15 | 13 | 13 | 13 | 12 | 12 | 12 |
| 1952 | 14 | 14 | 14 | 12 | 13 | 13 | 12 | 11 | 11 | 12 |
| 1953 | 16 | 16 | 13 | 14 | 14 | 12 | 12 | 12 | 12 | 11 |
| 1954 | 13 | 11 | 12 | 12 | 10 | 10 | 10 | 11 | 9 | |
| 1955 | 9 | 10 | 10 | 9 | 8 | 9 | 9 | 8 | | |
| 1956 | 10 | 11 | 9 | 9 | 9 | 10 | 8 | | | |
| 1957 | 13 | 11 | 10 | 11 | 11 | 9 | | | | |
| 1958 | 8 | 8 | 8 | 9 | 7 | | | | | |
| 1959 | 7 | 8 | 9 | 7 | | | | | | |
| 1960 | 9 | 10 | 7 | | | | | | | |
| 1961 | 8 | 6 | | | | | | | | |
| 1962 | 7 | | | | | | | | | |

## Average Annual Profit Percentage (AAPP)
## Standard & Poor's Composite Stock Index (with monthly reinvestment of dividends)

| Year Purchased (at December 31) | 21 | 22 | 23 | 24 | 25 | 26 | 27 | 28 | 29 | 30 |
|---|---|---|---|---|---|---|---|---|---|---|
| 1935 | 12% | 11% | 12% | 12% | 12% | 12% | 11% | 12% | 12% | 12% |
| 1936 | 10 | 11 | 11 | 11 | 11 | 11 | 11 | 11 | 11 | 11 |
| 1937 | 14 | 14 | 14 | 14 | 13 | 13 | 13 | 13 | 13 | 13 |
| 1938 | 13 | 13 | 13 | 12 | 13 | 13 | 13 | 12 | 12 | 12 |
| 1939 | 13 | 14 | 13 | 13 | 13 | 13 | 12 | 13 | 13 | 12 |
| 1940 | 15 | 14 | 14 | 14 | 14 | 13 | 14 | 14 | 13 | 12 |
| 1941 | 15 | 16 | 16 | 16 | 14 | 15 | 15 | 14 | 13 | 13 |
| 1942 | 15 | 16 | 15 | 14 | 15 | 14 | 14 | 13 | 13 | 13 |
| 1943 | 15 | 15 | 14 | 14 | 14 | 13 | 13 | 13 | 13 | 12 |
| 1944 | 15 | 13 | 14 | 14 | 13 | 12 | 13 | 13 | 12 | |
| 1945 | 12 | 13 | 13 | 12 | 12 | 12 | 12 | 11 | | |
| 1946 | 14 | 14 | 13 | 12 | 13 | 13 | 12 | | | |
| 1947 | 14 | 13 | 13 | 13 | 13 | 12 | | | | |
| 1948 | 14 | 13 | 13 | 13 | 12 | | | | | |
| 1949 | 13 | 13 | 13 | 12 | | | | | | |
| 1950 | 12 | 13 | 11 | | | | | | | |
| 1951 | 12 | 11 | | | | | | | | |
| 1952 | 10 | | | | | | | | | |

150/High Profits Without Risk

### Average Annual Profit Percentage (AAPP)
### Standard & Poor's Composite Stock Index (with monthly reinvestment o dividends)

| Year Purchased (at December 31) | Number of Years After Date Purchased | | | | | | | |
|---|---|---|---|---|---|---|---|---|
| | 31 | 32 | 33 | 34 | 35 | 36 | 37 | 38 |
| 1935 | 11% | 12% | 12% | 11% | 11% | 11% | 11% | 10% |
| 1936 | 11 | 11 | 10 | 10 | 10 | 10 | 10 | |
| 1937 | 13 | 12 | 12 | 12 | 12 | 11 | | |
| 1938 | 11 | 11 | 11 | 12 | 11 | | | |
| 1939 | 12 | 12 | 12 | 11 | | | | |
| 1940 | 13 | 13 | 12 | | | | | |
| 1941 | 14 | 13 | | | | | | |
| 1942 | 12 | | | | | | | |

# APPENDIX III

## Average Annual Profit Percentage (AAPP) Tables of High Grade, Long Term Corporate Bonds

The following pages show the Average Annual Profit Percentage (AAPP), from one to thirty-eight years after year purchased, of high grade, long term corporate bonds for the years 1935 through 1973 (with monthly reinvestment of dividends).[1]

To determine the AAPP of an average corporate bond at any number of years after the date purchased, find the year when the bond was purchased under the *Year Purchased* column and locate the AAPP under the *Number of Years After Date Purchased* column.

For example, if you want to know what the AAPP of an average corporate bond purchased at December 31, 1957 was, ten years after the date purchased, go to the table on page 153 and find *1957* under the *Year Purchased* column. Across the page under column 10 you will find 2% — the AAPP, ten years after the date purchased, of an average corporate bond that was purchased on December 31, 1957.

---

[1]Ibbotson and Sinquefield, *op. cit.*, pp. 128-130.

## Average Annual Profit Percentage (AAPP)
## High Grade, Long Term Corporate Bonds (with monthly reinvestment of dividends)

| Year Purchased (at December 31) | Number of Years After Date Purchased | | | | | | | | | |
|---|---|---|---|---|---|---|---|---|---|---|
| | 1 | 2 | 3 | 4 | 5 | 6 | 7 | 8 | 9 | 10 |
| 1935 | 8% | 5% | 5% | 5% | 5% | 5% | 4% | 4% | 4% | 4% |
| 1936 | 2 | 4 | 4 | 4 | 4 | 4 | 4 | 4 | 4 | 4 |
| 1937 | 6 | 5 | 5 | 5 | 4 | 4 | 4 | 4 | 4 | 3 |
| 1938 | 5 | 5 | 4 | 4 | 4 | 4 | 4 | 4 | 3 | 3 |
| 1939 | 5 | 4 | 3 | 3 | 4 | 4 | 4 | 3 | 3 | 3 |
| 1940 | 3 | 3 | 3 | 3 | 4 | 3 | 3 | 3 | 3 | 3 |
| 1941 | 3 | 3 | 4 | 4 | 3 | 3 | 3 | 3 | 3 | 2 |
| 1942 | 3 | 4 | 4 | 4 | 2 | 3 | 3 | 3 | 2 | 2 |
| 1943 | 4 | 5 | 4 | 2 | 3 | 3 | 3 | 2 | 2 | 2 |
| 1944 | 5 | 3 | 2 | 2 | 2 | 2 | 2 | 2 | 2 | 2 |
| 1945 | 2 | 0 | 1 | 2 | 2 | 1 | 1 | 2 | 2 | 2 |
| 1946 | -2 | 1 | 2 | 2 | 1 | 1 | 2 | 2 | 2 | 1 |
| 1947 | 4 | 4 | 3 | 2 | 2 | 2 | 3 | 2 | 1 | 2 |
| 1948 | 3 | 3 | 1 | 2 | 2 | 3 | 2 | 1 | 2 | 1 |
| 1949 | 2 | 0 | 1 | 2 | 2 | 2 | 1 | 2 | 1 | 1 |
| 1950 | -3 | 0 | 1 | 2 | 2 | 0 | 2 | 1 | 1 | 2 |
| 1951 | 4 | 3 | 4 | 3 | 1 | 2 | 2 | 1 | 2 | 2 |
| 1952 | 3 | 4 | 3 | 0 | 2 | 1 | 1 | 2 | 2 | 3 |
| 1953 | 6 | 3 | 0 | 2 | 1 | 1 | 2 | 2 | 3 | 3 |
| 1954 | 0 | -3 | 0 | 0 | -1 | 1 | 2 | 2 | 2 | 3 |
| 1955 | -7 | 0 | -1 | -1 | 1 | 2 | 3 | 3 | 3 | 2 |
| 1956 | 8 | 3 | 1 | 3 | 3 | 4 | 4 | 4 | 4 | 3 |
| 1957 | -2 | -2 | 2 | 2 | 3 | 3 | 3 | 3 | 3 | 2 |
| 1958 | -2 | 4 | 4 | 5 | 4 | 4 | 4 | 3 | 2 | 2 |
| 1959 | 9 | 7 | 7 | 6 | 6 | 5 | 4 | 3 | 2 | 1 |
| 1960 | 5 | 6 | 5 | 5 | 4 | 3 | 2 | 2 | 1 | 2 |
| 1961 | 8 | 5 | 5 | 4 | 3 | 1 | 1 | 0 | 2 | 3 |
| 1962 | 3 | 4 | 2 | 2 | 0 | 0 | -1 | 1 | 2 | 3 |
| 1963 | 5 | 2 | 1 | -1 | 0 | -2 | 1 | 2 | 3 | 3 |
| 1964 | -1 | -1 | -2 | -1 | -3 | 0 | 2 | 3 | 2 | |
| 1965 | -1 | -3 | -2 | -4 | 1 | 2 | 3 | 3 | | |
| 1966 | -6 | -2 | -5 | 1 | 3 | 4 | 3 | | | |
| 1967 | 1 | -4 | 3 | 5 | 6 | 5 | | | | |
| 1968 | -9 | 4 | 6 | 7 | 6 | | | | | |
| 1969 | 19 | 15 | 12 | 9 | | | | | | |
| 1970 | 11 | 9 | 6 | | | | | | | |
| 1971 | 7 | 4 | | | | | | | | |
| 1972 | 1 | | | | | | | | | |

## Average Annual Profit Percentage (AAPP)
## High Grade, Long Term Corporate Bonds (with monthly reinvestment of dividends)

| Year Purchased (at December 31) | Number of Years After Date Purchased | | | | | | | | | |
|---|---|---|---|---|---|---|---|---|---|---|
| | 11 | 12 | 13 | 14 | 15 | 16 | 17 | 18 | 19 | 20 |
| 1935 | 4% | 4% | 4% | 4% | 4% | 3% | 3% | 3% | 3% | 3 |
| 1936 | 3 | 3 | 3 | 3 | 3 | 3 | 3 | 3 | 3 | 2 |
| 1937 | 3 | 3 | 3 | 3 | 3 | 3 | 3 | 3 | 2 | 3 |
| 1938 | 3 | 3 | 3 | 3 | 3 | 3 | 3 | 2 | 3 | 2 |
| 1939 | 3 | 2 | 3 | 3 | 3 | 3 | 2 | 2 | 2 | 2 |
| 1940 | 2 | 2 | 2 | 3 | 2 | 2 | 2 | 2 | 2 | 2 |
| 1941 | 2 | 2 | 3 | 2 | 2 | 2 | 2 | 2 | 2 | 2 |
| 1942 | 2 | 3 | 2 | 2 | 2 | 2 | 2 | 2 | 2 | 2 |
| 1943 | 3 | 2 | 2 | 2 | 2 | 2 | 2 | 2 | 2 | 2 |
| 1944 | 2 | 1 | 2 | 2 | 1 | 2 | 2 | 2 | 2 | 2 |
| 1945 | 1 | 2 | 1 | 1 | 2 | 2 | 2 | 2 | 2 | 2 |
| 1946 | 2 | 1 | 1 | 2 | 2 | 2 | 2 | 2 | 2 | 2 |
| 1947 | 2 | 1 | 2 | 2 | 2 | 3 | 3 | 2 | 2 | 2 |
| 1948 | 1 | 2 | 2 | 2 | 2 | 3 | 2 | 2 | 2 | 2 |
| 1949 | 2 | 2 | 2 | 2 | 2 | 2 | 2 | 2 | 2 | 1 |
| 1950 | 2 | 2 | 2 | 2 | 2 | 2 | 2 | 2 | 1 | 2 |
| 1951 | 3 | 3 | 3 | 3 | 2 | 2 | 2 | 1 | 2 | 3 |
| 1952 | 3 | 3 | 3 | 2 | 2 | 2 | 1 | 2 | 2 | 3 |
| 1953 | 3 | 3 | 2 | 2 | 2 | 1 | 2 | 2 | 3 | 3 |
| 1954 | 2 | 2 | 1 | 1 | 1 | 2 | 2 | 3 | 2 | |
| 1955 | 2 | 1 | 1 | 1 | 2 | 2 | 3 | 3 | | |
| 1956 | 2 | 2 | 1 | 2 | 3 | 3 | 3 | | | |
| 1957 | 2 | 1 | 2 | 3 | 3 | 3 | | | | |
| 1958 | 1 | 2 | 3 | 3 | 3 | | | | | |
| 1959 | 3 | 3 | 4 | 4 | | | | | | |
| 1960 | 3 | 3 | 3 | | | | | | | |
| 1961 | 3 | 3 | | | | | | | | |
| 1962 | 3 | | | | | | | | | |

## Average Annual Profit Percentage (AAPP)
### igh Grade, Long Term Corporate Bonds (with monthly reinvestment of dividends)

| Year Purchased (December 31) | 21 | 22 | 23 | 24 | 25 | 26 | 27 | 28 | 29 | 30 |
|---|---|---|---|---|---|---|---|---|---|---|
| 1935 | 3% | 3% | 3% | 2% | 3% | 3% | 3% | 3% | 3% | 3% |
| 1936 | 3 | 2 | 2 | 3 | 3 | 3 | 3 | 3 | 3 | 3 |
| 1937 | 2 | 2 | 3 | 3 | 3 | 3 | 3 | 3 | 3 | 2 |
| 1938 | 2 | 2 | 2 | 3 | 3 | 3 | 3 | 3 | 2 | 2 |
| 1939 | 2 | 2 | 3 | 3 | 3 | 3 | 2 | 2 | 2 | 2 |
| 1940 | 2 | 2 | 3 | 3 | 2 | 2 | 2 | 2 | 2 | 2 |
| 1941 | 2 | 3 | 3 | 2 | 2 | 2 | 2 | 2 | 2 | 2 |
| 1942 | 2 | 3 | 2 | 2 | 2 | 2 | 2 | 2 | 2 | 3 |
| 1943 | 3 | 2 | 2 | 2 | 2 | 1 | 2 | 2 | 3 | 2 |
| 1944 | 2 | 2 | 2 | 2 | 1 | 2 | 2 | 2 | 2 | |
| 1945 | 2 | 2 | 2 | 1 | 2 | 2 | 2 | 2 | | |
| 1946 | 2 | 2 | 1 | 2 | 2 | 2 | 2 | | | |
| 1947 | 2 | 1 | 2 | 2 | 3 | 3 | | | | |
| 1948 | 1 | 2 | 2 | 3 | 2 | | | | | |
| 1949 | 2 | 2 | 2 | 2 | | | | | | |
| 1950 | 2 | 3 | 2 | | | | | | | |
| 1951 | 3 | 3 | | | | | | | | |
| 1952 | 3 | | | | | | | | | |

## Average Annual Profit Percentage (AAPP)
### High Grade, Long Term Corporate Bonds (with monthly reinvestment of dividends)

| Year Purchased (at December 31) | 31 | 32 | 33 | 34 | 35 | 36 | 37 | 38 |
|---|---|---|---|---|---|---|---|---|
| 1935 | 3% | 3% | 2% | 2% | 3% | 3% | 3% | 3% |
| 1936 | 2 | 2 | 2 | 2 | 3 | 3 | 3 | |
| 1937 | 2 | 2 | 2 | 3 | 3 | 3 | | |
| 1938 | 2 | 2 | 3 | 3 | 3 | | | |
| 1939 | 2 | 3 | 3 | 3 | | | | |
| 1940 | 2 | 3 | 3 | | | | | |
| 1941 | 3 | 3 | | | | | | |
| 1942 | 3 | | | | | | | |

# APPENDIX IV

## Average Annual Profit Percentage (AAPP) Tables of Uncirculated Coin Rolls

The following pages show the Average Annual Profit Percentage (AAPP), from one to forty years after the year minted, of uncirculated rolls of all coins that were minted between 1935 and 1974 (except S nickels, S dimes, S quarters, and S half-dollars which, on the date this book was written, were no longer minted for general circulation).

To determine the AAPP of one roll of uncirculated coins of any denomination and mintage at any number of years after the year minted, go to the table for that mintage coin, find the date of the coin under the *Year Minted* column and locate the AAPP under the *Number of Years After Year Minted* column.

For example, if you want to know the AAPP of a roll of uncirculated 1951 *D* half-dollars, thirteen years after the year minted, go to the *Average Annual Profit Percentage (AAPP) — Uncirculated Rolls of D Half-Dollars* table on page 200 and find *1951* under the *Year Minted* column.

Across the page under column 13 you will find 103% — the AAPP of one roll of uncirculated 1951 *D* half-dollars, thirteen years after the year the coins were minted.

## Average Annual Profit Percentage (AAPP)
## Uncirculated Rolls of P Cents

| Year Minted | Number of Years After Year Minted | | | | | | | | | |
|---|---|---|---|---|---|---|---|---|---|---|
| | 1 | 2 | 3 | 4 | 5 | 6 | 7 | 8 | 9 | 10 |
| 35 | 56% | 98% | 63% | 47% | 38% | 22% | 36% | 46% | 41% | 25% |
| 36 | 174 | 87 | 58 | 44 | 27 | 18 | 30 | 27 | 25 | 27 |
| 37 | 24 | 28 | 32 | 24 | 24 | 35 | 23 | 22 | 19 | 21 |
| 38 | 40 | 28 | 32 | 24 | 38 | 35 | 41 | 41 | 41 | 38 |
| 39 | 18 | 40 | 27 | 34 | 19 | 25 | 24 | 21 | 20 | 18 |
| 40 | 56 | 28 | 32 | 24 | 19 | 16 | 17 | 17 | 19 | 12 |
| 41 | 32 | 36 | 24 | 18 | 16 | 16 | 16 | 14 | 12 | 13 |
| 42 | 40 | 20 | 19 | 14 | 11 | 12 | 8 | 5 | 4 | 6 |
| 43 | 18 | 12 | 19 | 14 | 14 | 9 | 20 | 25 | 15 | 6 |
| 44 | 18 | 12 | 8 | 10 | 8 | 5 | 6 | 5 | 4 | 4 |
| 45 | 18 | 9 | 11 | 6 | 6 | 7 | 6 | 5 | 4 | 5 |
| 46 | 10 | 16 | 8 | 5 | 4 | 4 | 3 | 5 | 4 | 4 |
| 47 | 18 | 9 | 6 | 8 | 6 | 9 | 50 | 46 | 41 | 43 |
| 48 | 10 | 9 | 11 | 10 | 11 | 42 | 41 | 40 | 44 | 68 |
| 49 | 18 | 16 | 11 | 14 | 20 | 76 | 68 | 66 | 110 | 341 |
| | 32 | 16 | 11 | 73 | 58 | 50 | 45 | 66 | 206 | 279 |
| | 18 | 12 | 16 | 14 | 27 | 35 | 97 | 339 | 336 | 263 |
| | 18 | 20 | 19 | 28 | 42 | 113 | 264 | 300 | 232 | 224 |
| | 24 | 20 | 11 | 20 | 27 | 81 | 197 | 114 | 110 | 146 |
| | 10 | 59 | 58 | 102 | 323 | 347 | 264 | 446 | 544 | 614 |
| | 24 | 36 | 53 | 112 | 183 | 126 | 108 | 153 | 128 | 95 |
| | 18 | 20 | 45 | 151 | 74 | 61 | 119 | 105 | 67 | 60 |
| | 32 | 48 | 149 | 83 | 74 | 139 | 108 | 56 | 41 | 45 |
| | 32 | 204 | 89 | 77 | 183 | 139 | 86 | 56 | 41 | 29 |
| | 134 | 67 | 32 | 102 | 74 | 29 | 8 | 12 | 6 | 6 |
| | 56 | 28 | 55 | 63 | 19 | 16 | 8 | 7 | 4 | 6 |
| | 32 | 48 | 58 | 34 | 11 | 9 | 8 | 7 | 6 | 6 |
| | 64 | 106 | 45 | 34 | 18 | 9 | 8 | 7 | 6 | 6 |
| | 24 | 12 | 19 | 14 | 11 | 9 | 8 | 7 | 6 | 10 |
| | 18 | 20 | 19 | 14 | 11 | 9 | 8 | 7 | 11 | 10 |
| | 32 | 20 | 19 | 14 | 11 | 9 | 10 | 22 | 41 | 29 |
| | 32 | 24 | 19 | 14 | 11 | 15 | 25 | 56 | 34 | |
| | 48 | 28 | 19 | 14 | 19 | 29 | 64 | 45 | | |
| | 56 | 28 | 19 | 14 | 58 | 74 | 51 | | | |
| | 40 | 28 | 19 | 44 | 183 | 117 | | | | |
| | 32 | 20 | 45 | 112 | 64 | | | | | |
| | 32 | 87 | 84 | 40 | | | | | | |
| | 80 | 67 | 24 | | | | | | | |
| | 56 | 24 | | | | | | | | |
| | 48 | | | | | | | | | |

## Average Annual Profit Percentage (AAPP)
## Uncirculated Rolls of P Cents

| Year Minted | Number of Years After Year Minted | | | | | | | | | |
|---|---|---|---|---|---|---|---|---|---|---|
| | 11 | 12 | 13 | 14 | 15 | 16 | 17 | 18 | 19 | 20 |
| 1935 | 24% | 24% | 24% | 24% | 22% | 22% | 22% | 23% | 28% | 47 |
| 1936 | 30 | 28 | 19 | 18 | 18 | 18 | 18 | 20 | 52 | 58 |
| 1937 | 23 | 15 | 13 | 12 | 12 | 11 | 12 | 38 | 32 | 65 |
| 1938 | 26 | 26 | 24 | 22 | 22 | 26 | 49 | 81 | 159 | 291 |
| 1939 | 16 | 15 | 13 | 12 | 14 | 38 | 40 | 38 | 85 | 108 |
| 1940 | 12 | 13 | 13 | 15 | 31 | 34 | 72 | 98 | 118 | 128 |
| 1941 | 12 | 13 | 14 | 33 | 34 | 62 | 68 | 103 | 106 | 124 |
| 1942 | 5 | 5 | 7 | 10 | 24 | 52 | 81 | 94 | 89 | 93 |
| 1943 | 5 | 8 | 22 | 37 | 61 | 86 | 90 | 68 | 67 | 89 |
| 1944 | 4 | 4 | 10 | 18 | 71 | 91 | 58 | 64 | 69 | 69 |
| 1945 | 4 | 10 | 16 | 76 | 170 | 101 | 95 | 98 | 126 | 73 |
| 1946 | 14 | 18 | 64 | 76 | 51 | 47 | 72 | 81 | 60 | 56 |
| 1947 | 69 | 245 | 322 | 249 | 243 | 277 | 315 | 202 | 155 | 137 |
| 1948 | 168 | 265 | 196 | 171 | 181 | 150 | 132 | 81 | 60 | 8 |
| 1949 | 353 | 239 | 280 | 327 | 326 | 189 | 132 | 111 | 122 | 10 |
| 1950 | 175 | 180 | 208 | 171 | 123 | 91 | 77 | 107 | 97 | 8 |
| 1951 | 303 | 330 | 376 | 238 | 186 | 150 | 157 | 148 | 108 | 11 |
| 1952 | 246 | 382 | 292 | 216 | 181 | 147 | 132 | 90 | 77 | 9 |
| 1953 | 147 | 109 | 76 | 60 | 64 | 55 | 31 | 25 | 34 | 3 |
| 1954 | 445 | 349 | 232 | 188 | 149 | 104 | 68 | 90 | 110 | 9 |
| 1955 | 62 | 50 | 46 | 43 | 30 | 13 | 22 | 36 | 36 | |
| 1956 | 41 | 37 | 22 | 15 | 4 | 7 | 10 | 42 | 26 | |
| 1957 | 26 | 18 | 14 | 4 | 9 | 13 | 21 | 16 | | |
| 1958 | 19 | 15 | 4 | 12 | 17 | 23 | 12 | | | |
| 1959 | 5 | 5 | 4 | 10 | 6 | 3 | | | | |
| 1960 | 5 | 5 | 7 | 7 | 3 | | | | | |
| 1961 | 5 | 8 | 7 | 3 | | | | | | |
| 1962 | 9 | 8 | 4 | | | | | | | |
| 1963 | 9 | 4 | | | | | | | | |
| 1964 | 4 | | | | | | | | | |

## Average Annual Profit Percentage (AAPP)
## Uncirculated Rolls of P Cents

| Year Minted | Number of Years After Year Minted | | | | | | | | | |
|---|---|---|---|---|---|---|---|---|---|---|
| | 21 | 22 | 23 | 24 | 25 | 26 | 27 | 28 | 29 | 30 |
| 935 | 55% | 65% | 118% | 142% | 152% | 200% | 227% | 331% | 279% | 184% |
| 936 | 61 | 109 | 125 | 207 | 171 | 176 | 227 | 191 | 126 | 106 |
| 937 | 81 | 102 | 138 | 113 | 127 | 215 | 199 | 108 | 104 | 101 |
| 938 | 285 | 322 | 253 | 308 | 570 | 356 | 227 | 205 | 185 | 184 |
| 939 | 129 | 109 | 125 | 201 | 199 | 131 | 97 | 91 | 131 | 116 |
| 940 | 122 | 166 | 226 | 175 | 136 | 95 | 83 | 86 | 77 | 54 |
| 941 | 185 | 235 | 233 | 165 | 99 | 92 | 95 | 94 | 68 | 53 |
| 942 | 118 | 144 | 63 | 54 | 46 | 50 | 48 | 34 | 28 | 40 |
| 943 | 103 | 84 | 57 | 61 | 55 | 47 | 35 | 29 | 34 | 69 |
| 944 | 51 | 45 | 36 | 40 | 33 | 18 | 17 | 34 | 23 | 38 |
| 945 | 77 | 66 | 60 | 51 | 38 | 34 | 32 | 48 | 56 | 35 |
| 946 | 40 | 43 | 36 | 20 | 13 | 36 | 30 | 35 | 36 | |
| 947 | 125 | 116 | 77 | 67 | 69 | 101 | 118 | 81 | | |
| 948 | 81 | 65 | 50 | 71 | 83 | 98 | 56 | | | |
| 949 | 77 | 66 | 87 | 113 | 189 | 95 | | | | |
| 50 | 55 | 81 | 94 | 85 | 66 | | | | | |
| 51 | 203 | 279 | 406 | 269 | | | | | | |
| 52 | 103 | 144 | 125 | | | | | | | |
| 53 | 44 | 22 | | | | | | | | |
| 54 | 79 | | | | | | | | | |

## Average Annual Profit Percentage (AAPP)
## Uncirculated Rolls of P Cents

| Year Minted | 31 | 32 | 33 | 34 | 35 | 36 | 37 | 38 | 39 | 40 |
|---|---|---|---|---|---|---|---|---|---|---|
| | | | | Number of Years After Year Minted | | | | | | |
| 1935 | 158% | 143% | 174% | 176% | 141% | 106% | 98% | 88% | 141% | 111% |
| 1936 | 102 | 153 | 144 | 99 | 77 | 69 | 61 | 145 | 107 | |
| 1937 | 135 | 143 | 102 | 77 | 71 | 60 | 187 | 67 | | |
| 1938 | 185 | 118 | 82 | 88 | 117 | 171 | 141 | | | |
| 1939 | 85 | 60 | 86 | 77 | 126 | 84 | | | | |
| 1940 | 42 | 46 | 63 | 130 | 80 | | | | | |
| 1941 | 72 | 68 | 106 | 69 | | | | | | |
| 1942 | 45 | 51 | 46 | | | | | | | |
| 1943 | 97 | 71 | | | | | | | | |
| 1944 | 29 | | | | | | | | | |

## Average Annual Profit Percentage (AAPP)
## Uncirculated Rolls of D Cents

| Year Minted | Number of Years After Year Minted | | | | | | | | | |
|---|---|---|---|---|---|---|---|---|---|---|
| | 1 | 2 | 3 | 4 | 5 | 6 | 7 | 8 | 9 | 10 |
| 1935 | 48% | 75% | 45% | 40% | 42% | 42% | 36% | 46% | 41% | 29% |
| 1936 | 72 | 36 | 32 | 44 | 35 | 26 | 36 | 27 | 28 | 27 |
| 1937 | 24 | 28 | 32 | 32 | 24 | 29 | 25 | 22 | 19 | 20 |
| 1938 | 24 | 28 | 11 | 18 | 38 | 35 | 39 | 39 | 38 | 37 |
| 1939 | 18 | 36 | 24 | 44 | 58 | 61 | 66 | 56 | 58 | 49 |
| 1940 | 56 | 24 | 32 | 24 | 19 | 18 | 18 | 17 | 15 | 12 |
| 1941 | 32 | 36 | 24 | 18 | 22 | 18 | 16 | 14 | 11 | 10 |
| 1942 | 40 | 20 | 13 | 14 | 11 | 12 | 8 | 5 | 4 | 6 |
| 1943 | 18 | 12 | 19 | 14 | 14 | 9 | 8 | 9 | 8 | 6 |
| 1944 | 18 | 12 | 8 | 10 | 5 | 3 | 3 | 5 | 4 | 4 |
| 1945 | 18 | 9 | 11 | 6 | 4 | 3 | 5 | 4 | 4 | 4 |
| 1946 | 10 | 16 | 8 | 5 | 4 | 4 | 3 | 5 | 4 | 5 |
| 1947 | 18 | 9 | 6 | 5 | 5 | 9 | 8 | 22 | 17 | 25 |
| 1948 | 10 | 9 | 6 | 6 | 11 | 16 | 41 | 40 | 45 | 52 |
| 1949 | 18 | 9 | 11 | 14 | 97 | 81 | 64 | 58 | 76 | 138 |
| 1950 | 18 | 9 | 11 | 12 | 52 | 50 | 46 | 51 | 102 | 154 |
| 1951 | 24 | 12 | 16 | 14 | 19 | 24 | 41 | 85 | 154 | 84 |
| 1952 | 18 | 20 | 19 | 14 | 18 | 42 | 81 | 144 | 76 | 68 |
| 1953 | 24 | 20 | 11 | 10 | 27 | 74 | 142 | 85 | 76 | 107 |
| 1954 | 18 | 12 | 13 | 34 | 82 | 139 | 86 | 75 | 145 | 115 |
| 1955 | 18 | 12 | 32 | 73 | 183 | 107 | 86 | 153 | 119 | 84 |
| 1956 | 48 | 20 | 45 | 131 | 66 | 48 | 64 | 46 | 19 | 10 |
| 1957 | 32 | 48 | 123 | 44 | 35 | 68 | 41 | 17 | 11 | 10 |
| 1958 | 32 | 126 | 45 | 34 | 38 | 48 | 19 | 12 | 11 | 7 |
| 1959 | 56 | 28 | 27 | 53 | 50 | 16 | 8 | 7 | 6 | 6 |
| 1960 | 32 | 28 | 32 | 44 | 19 | 9 | 8 | 7 | 4 | 6 |
| 1961 | 32 | 40 | 27 | 14 | 11 | 9 | 8 | 7 | 6 | 6 |
| 1962 | 64 | 36 | 19 | 14 | 11 | 9 | 8 | 7 | 6 | 6 |
| 1963 | 18 | 9 | 19 | 14 | 11 | 9 | 8 | 7 | 6 | 10 |
| 1964 | 18 | 20 | 19 | 14 | 11 | 9 | 8 | 9 | 11 | 10 |
| 1968 | 56 | 28 | 19 | 14 | 50 | 42 | 11 | | | |
| 1969 | 56 | 28 | 19 | 44 | 30 | 12 | | | | |
| 1970 | 32 | 20 | 45 | 73 | 39 | | | | | |
| 1971 | 32 | 59 | 84 | 36 | | | | | | |
| 1972 | 56 | 67 | 34 | | | | | | | |
| 1973 | 56 | 24 | | | | | | | | |
| 1974 | 48 | | | | | | | | | |

## Average Annual Profit Percentage (AAPP)
## Uncirculated Rolls of D Cents

| Year Minted | Number of Years After Year Minted | | | | | | | | | |
|---|---|---|---|---|---|---|---|---|---|---|
| | 11 | 12 | 13 | 14 | 15 | 16 | 17 | 18 | 19 | 20 |
| 1935 | 26% | 31% | 40% | 37% | 25% | 33% | 37% | 40% | 52% | 84 |
| 1936 | 30 | 28 | 19 | 19 | 18 | 18 | 18 | 20 | 57 | 57 |
| 1937 | 21 | 15 | 13 | 12 | 12 | 11 | 19 | 34 | 33 | 95 |
| 1938 | 26 | 28 | 25 | 24 | 22 | 30 | 49 | 64 | 159 | 190 |
| 1939 | 47 | 43 | 40 | 43 | 64 | 82 | 191 | 384 | 528 | 736 |
| 1940 | 11 | 11 | 13 | 15 | 51 | 52 | 54 | 103 | 138 | 135 |
| 1941 | 10 | 13 | 13 | 33 | 38 | 67 | 72 | 124 | 122 | 124 |
| 1942 | 5 | 5 | 7 | 10 | 14 | 43 | 63 | 77 | 60 | 93 |
| 1943 | 5 | 8 | 28 | 35 | 66 | 116 | 118 | 85 | 85 | 190 |
| 1944 | 4 | 4 | 8 | 20 | 71 | 91 | 58 | 64 | 85 | 112 |
| 1945 | 4 | 9 | 16 | 65 | 118 | 72 | 68 | 168 | 159 | 112 |
| 1946 | 12 | 18 | 64 | 82 | 45 | 50 | 86 | 159 | 122 | 61 |
| 1947 | 33 | 128 | 118 | 71 | 92 | 111 | 141 | 81 | 56 | 50 |
| 1948 | 154 | 141 | 88 | 115 | 173 | 150 | 123 | 81 | 65 | 54 |
| 1949 | 154 | 109 | 148 | 372 | 279 | 179 | 123 | 111 | 101 | 89 |
| 1950 | 104 | 115 | 112 | 115 | 77 | 72 | 68 | 42 | 44 | 26 |
| 1951 | 76 | 96 | 82 | 60 | 45 | 33 | 38 | 38 | 19 | 11 |
| 1952 | 97 | 76 | 52 | 37 | 35 | 28 | 24 | 20 | 11 | 24 |
| 1953 | 76 | 50 | 37 | 29 | 22 | 21 | 17 | 12 | 23 | 30 |
| 1954 | 76 | 57 | 37 | 32 | 25 | 18 | 17 | 27 | 32 | 44 |
| 1955 | 62 | 44 | 22 | 21 | 6 | 4 | 15 | 23 | 28 | 15 |
| 1956 | 9 | 8 | 7 | 7 | 4 | 7 | 10 | 20 | 16 | |
| 1957 | 7 | 5 | 4 | 4 | 6 | 8 | 20 | 11 | | |
| 1958 | 5 | 5 | 4 | 7 | 9 | 13 | 9 | | | |
| 1959 | 5 | 5 | 4 | 10 | 6 | 3 | | | | |
| 1960 | 5 | 5 | 7 | 7 | 3 | | | | | |
| 1961 | 5 | 8 | 7 | 3 | | | | | | |
| 1962 | 9 | 8 | 4 | | | | | | | |
| 1963 | 9 | 4 | | | | | | | | |
| 1964 | 4 | | | | | | | | | |

## Average Annual Profit Percentage (AAPP)
## Uncirculated Rolls of D Cents

| Year Minted | Number of Years After Year Minted | | | | | | | | | |
|---|---|---|---|---|---|---|---|---|---|---|
| | 21 | 22 | 23 | 24 | 25 | 26 | 27 | 28 | 29 | 30 |
| 935 | 136% | 155% | 233% | 246% | 230% | 266% | 516% | 832% | 615% | 517% |
| 936 | 61 | 151 | 165 | 191 | 171 | 236 | 719 | 470 | 400 | 309 |
| 937 | 122 | 109 | 104 | 106 | 140 | 476 | 285 | 233 | 174 | 168 |
| 938 | 214 | 222 | 233 | 334 | 963 | 806 | 603 | 498 | 454 | 301 |
| 939 | 775 | 882 | 1,115 | 1,702 | 1,494 | 1,091 | 898 | 721 | 723 | 621 |
| 940 | 144 | 173 | 331 | 337 | 230 | 164 | 126 | 133 | 118 | 84 |
| 941 | 244 | 456 | 403 | 288 | 214 | 167 | 213 | 205 | 161 | 167 |
| 942 | 140 | 155 | 97 | 67 | 58 | 50 | 48 | 33 | 29 | 62 |
| 943 | 200 | 137 | 131 | 126 | 111 | 104 | 66 | 58 | 69 | 90 |
| 944 | 70 | 45 | 36 | 40 | 30 | 17 | 15 | 23 | 32 | 38 |
| 945 | 77 | 66 | 60 | 54 | 38 | 34 | 27 | 48 | 136 | 64 |
| 946 | 47 | 50 | 36 | 20 | 15 | 28 | 34 | 35 | 30 | |
| 947 | 51 | 42 | 28 | 28 | 30 | 41 | 48 | 46 | | |
| 948 | 51 | 34 | 26 | 24 | 40 | 62 | 43 | | | |
| 949 | 55 | 45 | 60 | 93 | 118 | 92 | | | | |
| 950 | 21 | 36 | 40 | 41 | 33 | | | | | |
| 951 | 23 | 27 | 40 | 27 | | | | | | |
| 952 | 27 | 29 | 19 | | | | | | | |
| 953 | 29 | 20 | | | | | | | | |
| 954 | 27 | | | | | | | | | |

## *Average Annual Profit Percentage (AAPP)*
## *Uncirculated Rolls of D Cents*

| Year Minted | Number of Years After Year Minted 31 | 32 | 33 | 34 | 35 | 36 | 37 | 38 | 39 | 40 |
|---|---|---|---|---|---|---|---|---|---|---|
| 1935 | 349% | 326% | 233% | 215% | 150% | 106% | 103% | 137% | 221% | 157% |
| 1936 | 299 | 216 | 210 | 135 | 89 | 84 | 128 | 166 | 129 | |
| 1937 | 173 | 148 | 102 | 76 | 81 | 114 | 229 | 141 | | |
| 1938 | 261 | 189 | 154 | 120 | 271 | 327 | 178 | | | |
| 1939 | 412 | 314 | 434 | 309 | 577 | 387 | | | | |
| 1940 | 71 | 55 | 96 | 167 | 144 | | | | | |
| 1941 | 211 | 197 | 399 | 268 | | | | | | |
| 1942 | 50 | 70 | 40 | | | | | | | |
| 1943 | 123 | 124 | | | | | | | | |
| 1944 | 35 | | | | | | | | | |

## Average Annual Profit Percentage (AAPP)
### Uncirculated Rolls of S Cents

| Year Minted | Number of Years After Year Minted | | | | | | | | | |
|---|---|---|---|---|---|---|---|---|---|---|
| | 1 | 2 | 3 | 4 | 5 | 6 | 7 | 8 | 9 | 10 |
| 1935 | 56% | 59% | 39% | 34% | 35% | 42% | 36% | 44% | 50% | 52% |
| 1936 | 110 | 55 | 37 | 44 | 42 | 29 | 36 | 27 | 28 | 27 |
| 1937 | 24 | 36 | 32 | 24 | 24 | 35 | 30 | 27 | 24 | 21 |
| 1938 | 48 | 28 | 13 | 18 | 38 | 35 | 36 | 41 | 38 | 37 |
| 1939 | 18 | 9 | 19 | 34 | 27 | 31 | 30 | 27 | 25 | 18 |
| 1940 | 56 | 24 | 32 | 24 | 19 | 18 | 18 | 17 | 15 | 12 |
| 1941 | 32 | 36 | 24 | 24 | 27 | 20 | 19 | 17 | 11 | 19 |
| 1942 | 80 | 67 | 136 | 190 | 160 | 139 | 119 | 100 | 63 | 52 |
| 1943 | 24 | 75 | 97 | 63 | 53 | 44 | 36 | 46 | 37 | 29 |
| 1944 | 18 | 12 | 8 | 10 | 8 | 5 | 3 | 5 | 4 | 4 |
| 1945 | 18 | 9 | 11 | 6 | 4 | 3 | 5 | 4 | 4 | 3 |
| 1946 | 10 | 12 | 8 | 5 | 4 | 4 | 3 | 5 | 4 | 5 |
| 1947 | 18 | 9 | 6 | 8 | 6 | 9 | 8 | 22 | 18 | 37 |
| 1948 | 10 | 9 | 11 | 8 | 6 | 16 | 11 | 40 | 63 | 84 |
| 1949 | 18 | 16 | 11 | 14 | 74 | 61 | 81 | 105 | 188 | 388 |
| 1950 | 32 | 16 | 11 | 12 | 52 | 50 | 37 | 134 | 187 | 380 |
| 1951 | 24 | 28 | 16 | 115 | 74 | 100 | 185 | 426 | 509 | 458 |
| 1952 | 56 | 67 | 97 | 83 | 89 | 126 | 320 | 358 | 318 | 419 |
| 1953 | 24 | 20 | 63 | 73 | 105 | 230 | 264 | 212 | 323 | 411 |
| 1954 | 40 | 44 | 32 | 63 | 113 | 165 | 142 | 358 | 440 | 341 |
| 1955 | 150 | 79 | 65 | 258 | 292 | 328 | 766 | 816 | 648 | 427 |
| 1968 | 96 | 28 | 19 | 14 | 27 | 29 | 11 | | | |
| 1969 | 56 | 28 | 19 | 44 | 35 | 17 | | | | |
| 1970 | 32 | 20 | 45 | 61 | 32 | | | | | |
| 1971 | 134 | 126 | 89 | 51 | | | | | | |
| 1972 | 56 | 67 | 24 | | | | | | | |
| 1973 | 134 | 28 | | | | | | | | |
| 1974 | 258 | | | | | | | | | |

## Average Annual Profit Percentage (AAPP)
## Uncirculated Rolls of S Cents

| Year Minted | 11 | 12 | 13 | 14 | 15 | 16 | 17 | 18 | 19 | 20 |
|---|---|---|---|---|---|---|---|---|---|---|
| 1935 | 60% | 57% | 52% | 49% | 45% | 43% | 41% | 40% | 52% | 10⁵ |
| 1936 | 41 | 37 | 28 | 21 | 21 | 20 | 20 | 29 | 60 | 5ᶜ |
| 1937 | 23 | 15 | 13 | 12 | 12 | 11 | 19 | 38 | 44 | 13 |
| 1938 | 30 | 25 | 25 | 24 | 22 | 38 | 46 | 98 | 192 | 29 |
| 1939 | 16 | 21 | 23 | 26 | 32 | 67 | 77 | 81 | 159 | 17 |
| 1940 | 16 | 15 | 13 | 15 | 51 | 45 | 58 | 98 | 118 | 12 |
| 1941 | 19 | 22 | 22 | 44 | 53 | 82 | 102 | 124 | 134 | 15 |
| 1942 | 57 | 57 | 52 | 82 | 149 | 277 | 357 | 358 | 512 | 97 |
| 1943 | 41 | 91 | 88 | 138 | 305 | 335 | 315 | 298 | 315 | 40 |
| 1944 | 4 | 4 | 13 | 26 | 82 | 94 | 68 | 98 | 163 | 17 |
| 1945 | 4 | 19 | 28 | 96 | 97 | 82 | 109 | 168 | 184 | 14 |
| 1946 | 19 | 31 | 76 | 82 | 56 | 108 | 159 | 168 | 97 | 5 |
| 1947 | 73 | 154 | 148 | 93 | 243 | 250 | 435 | 254 | 159 | 9 |
| 1948 | 168 | 304 | 232 | 294 | 545 | 749 | 499 | 332 | 241 | 24 |
| 1949 | 544 | 414 | 532 | 840 | 903 | 676 | 453 | 384 | 323 | 30 |
| 1950 | 246 | 317 | 364 | 411 | 357 | 257 | 201 | 129 | 110 | 8 |
| 1951 | 587 | 707 | 712 | 528 | 279 | 213 | 246 | 224 | 134 | 1 |
| 1952 | 416 | 479 | 316 | 216 | 160 | 140 | 132 | 98 | 85 | |
| 1953 | 381 | 265 | 172 | 127 | 77 | 72 | 45 | 46 | 52 | |
| 1954 | 218 | 154 | 112 | 76 | 71 | 35 | 31 | 40 | 44 | |
| 1955 | 317 | 226 | 196 | 168 | 108 | 91 | 102 | 98 | 130 | |

## Average Annual Profit Percentage (AAPP)
## Uncirculated Rolls of S Cents

| Year Minted | Number of Years After Year Minted | | | | | | | | | |
|---|---|---|---|---|---|---|---|---|---|---|
| | 21 | 22 | 23 | 24 | 25 | 26 | 27 | 28 | 29 | 30 |
| 1935 | 136% | 144% | 233% | 321% | 402% | 458% | 863% | 1,417% | 1,072% | 881% |
| 1936 | 61 | 173 | 196 | 256 | 246 | 320 | 921 | 665 | 508 | 428 |
| 1937 | 144 | 155 | 162 | 155 | 221 | 686 | 487 | 386 | 282 | 257 |
| 1938 | 292 | 329 | 389 | 776 | 1,316 | 1,076 | 661 | 554 | 481 | 376 |
| 1939 | 174 | 155 | 233 | 483 | 417 | 311 | 175 | 164 | 147 | 134 |
| 1940 | 136 | 159 | 284 | 256 | 146 | 116 | 92 | 86 | 77 | 54 |
| 1941 | 322 | 456 | 403 | 256 | 214 | 176 | 213 | 205 | 196 | 181 |
| 1942 | 1,630 | 1,555 | 1,250 | 906 | 745 | 764 | 690 | 470 | 416 | 722 |
| 1943 | 441 | 315 | 233 | 223 | 202 | 176 | 141 | 129 | 179 | 199 |
| 1944 | 125 | 73 | 57 | 58 | 49 | 37 | 30 | 41 | 40 | 64 |
| 1945 | 96 | 66 | 60 | 58 | 38 | 32 | 63 | 48 | 93 | 55 |
| 1946 | 49 | 50 | 43 | 20 | 18 | 56 | 109 | 97 | 80 | |
| 1947 | 118 | 109 | 106 | 110 | 121 | 134 | 147 | 86 | | |
| 1948 | 207 | 134 | 111 | 119 | 133 | 185 | 96 | | | |
| 1949 | 188 | 166 | 199 | 197 | 333 | 212 | | | | |
| 1950 | 66 | 95 | 118 | 92 | 77 | | | | | |
| 1951 | 181 | 162 | 213 | 152 | | | | | | |
| 1952 | 84 | 166 | 152 | | | | | | | |
| 1953 | 99 | 77 | | | | | | | | |
| 1954 | 35 | | | | | | | | | |

## Average Annual Profit Percentage (AAPP)
## Uncirculated Rolls of S Cents

| Year Minted | Number of Years After Year Minted | | | | | | | | | |
|---|---|---|---|---|---|---|---|---|---|---|
| | 31 | 32 | 33 | 34 | 35 | 36 | 37 | 38 | 39 | 40 |
| 1935 | 802% | 765% | 482% | 479% | 309% | 246% | 385% | 396% | 777% | 649% |
| 1936 | 399 | 324 | 269 | 147 | 112 | 197 | 162 | 211 | 147 | |
| 1937 | 185 | 180 | 118 | 76 | 106 | 121 | 229 | 145 | | |
| 1938 | 349 | 241 | 194 | 362 | 363 | 431 | 292 | | | |
| 1939 | 99 | 77 | 115 | 153 | 282 | 173 | | | | |
| 1940 | 50 | 87 | 80 | 112 | 95 | | | | | |
| 1941 | 347 | 353 | 564 | 360 | | | | | | |
| 1942 | 638 | 1,021 | 588 | | | | | | | |
| 1943 | 309 | 274 | | | | | | | | |
| 1944 | 50 | | | | | | | | | |

## Average Annual Profit Percentage (AAPP)
## Uncirculated Rolls of P Nickels

| Year Minted | Number of Years After Year Minted | | | | | | | | | |
|---|---|---|---|---|---|---|---|---|---|---|
| | 1 | 2 | 3 | 4 | 5 | 6 | 7 | 8 | 9 | 10 |
| 1935 | 8% | 7% | 5% | 6% | 9% | 13% | 18% | 19% | 17% | 22% |
| 1936 | 10 | 12 | 8 | 17 | 13 | 11 | 9 | 16 | 14 | 13 |
| 1937 | 0 | 2 | 8 | 6 | 9 | 8 | 15 | 14 | 12 | 11 |
| 1938 | 4 | 11 | 8 | 7 | 17 | 18 | 20 | 19 | 17 | 15 |
| 1939 | 46 | 23 | 53 | 41 | 46 | 42 | 39 | 42 | 35 | 32 |
| 1940 | 14 | 13 | 11 | 17 | 14 | 14 | 12 | 12 | 10 | 9 |
| 1941 | 14 | 23 | 19 | 16 | 13 | 11 | 9 | 7 | 8 | 9 |
| *1942 | 201 | 96 | 91 | 69 | 42 | 35 | 24 | 24 | 21 | 15 |
| *1942 | 14 | 2 | 5 | 6 | 5 | 4 | 4 | 3 | 2 | 2 |
| 1943 | 0 | 2 | 5 | 6 | 5 | 2 | 3 | 3 | 2 | 2 |
| 1944 | 0 | 2 | 5 | 4 | 5 | 2 | 2 | 2 | 1 | 3 |
| 1945 | 2 | 7 | 5 | 2 | 3 | 2 | 2 | 2 | 2 | 2 |
| 1946 | 14 | 7 | 3 | 2 | 4 | 3 | 2 | 2 | 2 | 3 |
| 1947 | 14 | 4 | 1 | 4 | 3 | 2 | 2 | 2 | 2 | 5 |
| 1948 | 4 | 2 | 3 | 3 | 3 | 8 | 7 | 6 | 6 | 9 |
| 1949 | 2 | 1 | 1 | 4 | 13 | 13 | 9 | 13 | 14 | 13 |
| 1950 | 35 | 18 | 62 | 95 | 76 | 63 | 69 | 76 | 104 | 301 |
| 1951 | 8 | 7 | 3 | 2 | 30 | 28 | 24 | 34 | 104 | 56 |
| 1952 | 4 | 2 | 3 | 5 | 5 | 25 | 21 | 71 | 53 | 48 |
| 1953 | 4 | 4 | 3 | 6 | 11 | 11 | 57 | 39 | 30 | 65 |
| 1954 | 4 | 5 | 5 | 11 | 22 | 60 | 39 | 29 | 53 | 52 |
| 1955 | 274 | 148 | 98 | 79 | 374 | 232 | 282 | 750 | 611 | 364 |
| 1956 | 25 | 13 | 12 | 58 | 34 | 25 | 81 | 55 | 28 | 19 |
| 1957 | 19 | 23 | 64 | 45 | 28 | 80 | 72 | 50 | 26 | 10 |
| 1958 | 87 | 231 | 84 | 100 | 254 | 239 | 164 | 91 | 38 | 42 |
| 1959 | 232 | 49 | 36 | 141 | 96 | 66 | 33 | 16 | 17 | 13 |
| 1960 | 46 | 13 | 50 | 43 | 13 | 6 | 5 | 4 | 3 | 3 |
| 1961 | 14 | 23 | 29 | 17 | 5 | 4 | 5 | 6 | 3 | 3 |
| 1962 | 31 | 28 | 12 | 6 | 3 | 4 | 4 | 3 | 3 | 3 |
| 1963 | 4 | 7 | 5 | 4 | 5 | 4 | 4 | 3 | 3 | 3 |
| 1964 | 8 | 13 | 5 | 4 | 5 | 4 | 4 | 3 | 6 | 7 |
| 1965 | 35 | 5 | 5 | 6 | 4 | 3 | 4 | 8 | 7 | 7 |
| 1966 | 10 | 7 | 8 | 5 | 3 | 4 | 9 | 8 | 8 | |
| 1967 | 14 | 13 | 6 | 4 | 5 | 10 | 9 | 12 | | |
| 1971 | 16 | 23 | 22 | 30 | | | | | | |
| 1972 | 46 | 33 | 32 | | | | | | | |
| 1973 | 66 | 33 | | | | | | | | |
| 1974 | 35 | | | | | | | | | |

* Pre-War (made of nickel)
Wartime alloy

## Average Annual Profit Percentage (AAPP)
## Uncirculated Rolls of P Nickels

| Year Minted | Number of Years After Year Minted | | | | | | | | | |
|---|---|---|---|---|---|---|---|---|---|---|
| | 11 | 12 | 13 | 14 | 15 | 16 | 17 | 18 | 19 | 20 |
| 1935 | 30% | 35% | 29% | 26% | 21% | 20% | 19% | 19% | 21% | 22% |
| 1936 | 12 | 11 | 10 | 9 | 9 | 9 | 9 | 8 | 19 | 26 |
| 1937 | 10 | 9 | 8 | 8 | 7 | 7 | 9 | 11 | 15 | 26 |
| 1938 | 14 | 12 | 11 | 9 | 9 | 8 | 11 | 13 | 24 | 26 |
| 1939 | 29 | 30 | 25 | 22 | 20 | 37 | 65 | 64 | 82 | 161 |
| 1940 | 8 | 7 | 7 | 8 | 13 | 15 | 16 | 22 | 38 | 41 |
| 1941 | 6 | 6 | 8 | 14 | 10 | 12 | 14 | 22 | 33 | 39 |
| *1942 | 14 | 11 | 10 | 17 | 18 | 20 | 31 | 59 | 60 | 57 |
| **1942 | 2 | 2 | 4 | 5 | 4 | 34 | 153 | 248 | 187 | 224 |
| 1943 | 2 | 3 | 2 | 3 | 7 | 79 | 80 | 48 | 49 | 151 |
| 1944 | 2 | 2 | 5 | 8 | 85 | 85 | 62 | 54 | 180 | 244 |
| 1945 | 2 | 4 | 7 | 73 | 75 | 48 | 55 | 173 | 333 | 203 |
| 1946 | 4 | 6 | 7 | 24 | 21 | 20 | 33 | 46 | 28 | 13 |
| 1947 | 8 | 7 | 23 | 21 | 20 | 38 | 55 | 38 | 12 | 11 |
| 1948 | 17 | 26 | 27 | 23 | 43 | 56 | 38 | 18 | 10 | 23 |
| 1949 | 123 | 75 | 69 | 82 | 140 | 123 | 67 | 35 | 37 | 31 |
| 1950 | 189 | 217 | 695 | 556 | 381 | 214 | 141 | 190 | 148 | 102 |
| 1951 | 48 | 241 | 216 | 126 | 90 | 50 | 58 | 59 | 42 | 28 |
| 1952 | 48 | 75 | 56 | 23 | 15 | 37 | 32 | 24 | 13 | 14 |
| 1953 | 63 | 35 | 18 | 11 | 13 | 11 | 9 | 4 | 5 | 18 |
| 1954 | 38 | 14 | 7 | 12 | 11 | 7 | 6 | 3 | 6 | 7 |
| 1955 | 246 | 165 | 158 | 141 | 92 | 65 | 73 | 75 | 82 | 39 |
| 1956 | 7 | 12 | 8 | 6 | 4 | 3 | 4 | 4 | 3 | |
| 1957 | 14 | 11 | 7 | 5 | 3 | 4 | 4 | 4 | | |
| 1958 | 36 | 32 | 16 | 9 | 13 | 24 | 9 | | | |
| 1959 | 9 | 6 | 4 | 7 | 4 | 3 | | | | |
| 1960 | 2 | 2 | 4 | 5 | 3 | | | | | |
| 1961 | 2 | 3 | 5 | 3 | | | | | | |
| 1962 | 3 | 6 | 3 | | | | | | | |
| 1963 | 6 | 3 | | | | | | | | |
| 1964 | 4 | | | | | | | | | |

*Pre-War (made of nickel)
**Wartime alloy

## Average Annual Profit Percentage (AAPP)
## Uncirculated Rolls of P Nickels

| Year Minted | Number of Years After Year Minted | | | | | | | | | |
|---|---|---|---|---|---|---|---|---|---|---|
| | 21 | 22 | 23 | 24 | 25 | 26 | 27 | 28 | 29 | 30 |
| 935 | 25% | 33% | 44% | 65% | 54% | 65% | 119% | 174% | 190% | 170% |
| 936 | 35 | 46 | 59 | 56 | 59 | 96 | 127 | 182 | 175 | 170 |
| 937 | 30 | 33 | 54 | 70 | 91 | 156 | 219 | 211 | 204 | 128 |
| 938 | 64 | 109 | 77 | 74 | 162 | 196 | 150 | 93 | 65 | 66 |
| 939 | 143 | 137 | 131 | 117 | 104 | 52 | 49 | 41 | 57 | 58 |
| 940 | 45 | 52 | 52 | 61 | 46 | 41 | 29 | 37 | 32 | 22 |
| 941 | 37 | 43 | 59 | 43 | 39 | 30 | 33 | 32 | 23 | 16 |
| 942 | 203 | 152 | 95 | 56 | 50 | 64 | 65 | 52 | 38 | 35 |
| 942 | 717 | 750 | 492 | 402 | 262 | 427 | 391 | 228 | 204 | 250 |
| 943 | 153 | 123 | 95 | 62 | 75 | 64 | 50 | 41 | 57 | 75 |
| 944 | 213 | 170 | 104 | 117 | 108 | 71 | 54 | 67 | 99 | 94 |
| 945 | 189 | 118 | 176 | 165 | 112 | 80 | 89 | 115 | 100 | 80 |
| 946 | 8 | 14 | 10 | 8 | 4 | 6 | 13 | 14 | 10 | |
| 947 | 25 | 16 | 8 | 5 | 6 | 11 | 10 | 8 | | |
| 948 | 17 | 12 | 5 | 8 | 16 | 23 | 12 | | | |
| 949 | 25 | 17 | 16 | 21 | 24 | 25 | | | | |
| 950 | 87 | 88 | 99 | 118 | 61 | | | | | |
| 951 | 55 | 39 | 53 | 31 | | | | | | |
| 952 | 17 | 29 | 14 | | | | | | | |
| 953 | 13 | 6 | | | | | | | | |
| 954 | 4 | | | | | | | | | |

re-War (made of nickel)
artime Alloy

## Average Annual Profit Percentage (AAPP)
## Uncirculated Rolls of P Nickels

| Year Minted | \multicolumn{10}{c}{Number of Years After Year Minted} | | | | | | | | | |
|---|---|---|---|---|---|---|---|---|---|---|
| | 31 | 32 | 33 | 34 | 35 | 36 | 37 | 38 | 39 | 40 |
| 1935 | 164% | 159% | 154% | 162% | 104% | 130% | 140% | 265% | 418% | 315% |
| 1936 | 164 | 146 | 135 | 100 | 99 | 111 | 222 | 391 | 267 | |
| 1937 | 144 | 140 | 105 | 126 | 139 | 246 | 379 | 284 | | |
| 1938 | 60 | 40 | 28 | 37 | 40 | 47 | 35 | | | |
| 1939 | 33 | 29 | 26 | 26 | 47 | 35 | | | | |
| 1940 | 15 | 14 | 21 | 28 | 26 | | | | | |
| 1941 | 15 | 20 | 26 | 21 | | | | | | |
| *1942 | 45 | 71 | 64 | | | | | | | |
| **1942 | 398 | 516 | 392 | | | | | | | |
| 1943 | 86 | 62 | | | | | | | | |
| 1944 | 70 | | | | | | | | | |

*Pre-War (made of nickel)
**Wartime Alloy

## Average Annual Profit Percentage (AAPP)
## Uncirculated Rolls of D Nickels

| Year Minted | Number of Years After Year Minted | | | | | | | | | |
|---|---|---|---|---|---|---|---|---|---|---|
| | 1 | 2 | 3 | 4 | 5 | 6 | 7 | 8 | 9 | 10 |
| 1935 | 4% | 7% | 5% | 6% | 26% | 20% | 18% | 19% | 17% | 23% |
| 1936 | 10 | 7 | 10 | 17 | 13 | 11 | 15 | 16 | 14 | 27 |
| 1937 | 0 | 3 | 8 | 6 | 5 | 17 | 15 | 16 | 26 | 26 |
| 1938 | 14 | 10 | 8 | 6 | 19 | 9 | 9 | 7 | 7 | 7 |
| 1938 | 6 | 5 | 6 | 12 | 19 | 18 | 24 | 29 | 42 | 36 |
| 1939 | 66 | 262 | 198 | 183 | 146 | 232 | 282 | 377 | 219 | 245 |
| 1940 | 10 | 12 | 10 | 19 | 19 | 18 | 18 | 17 | 14 | 13 |
| 1941 | 14 | 18 | 19 | 16 | 13 | 11 | 9 | 8 | 10 | 9 |
| 1942 | 344 | 168 | 250 | 255 | 291 | 260 | 178 | 143 | 116 | 115 |
| 1943 | 0 | 7 | 8 | 6 | 5 | 4 | 3 | 6 | 3 | 2 |
| 1944 | 14 | 7 | 5 | 4 | 2 | 2 | 2 | 2 | 2 | 3 |
| 1945 | 2 | 7 | 5 | 2 | 3 | 2 | 2 | 2 | 2 | 3 |
| 1946 | 14 | 7 | 1 | 1 | 2 | 2 | 2 | 2 | 2 | 3 |
| 1947 | 10 | 5 | 1 | 3 | 3 | 1 | 2 | 2 | 3 | 5 |
| 1948 | 4 | 0 | 5 | 4 | 3 | 9 | 7 | 3 | 6 | 7 |
| 1949 | 2 | 1 | 2 | 4 | 13 | 13 | 9 | 8 | 11 | 12 |
| 1950 | 129 | 65 | 46 | 30 | 57 | 73 | 131 | 159 | 335 | 779 |
| 1951 | 10 | 7 | 4 | 54 | 38 | 32 | 30 | 50 | 289 | 135 |
| 1952 | 10 | 4 | 36 | 27 | 34 | 32 | 282 | 610 | 335 | 447 |
| 1953 | 4 | 3 | 3 | 4 | 11 | 18 | 81 | 39 | 35 | 86 |
| 1954 | 0 | 2 | 3 | 12 | 15 | 60 | 39 | 27 | 53 | 32 |
| 1955 | 8 | 7 | 5 | 6 | 88 | 44 | 33 | 133 | 81 | 48 |
| 1956 | 4 | 7 | 12 | 58 | 34 | 25 | 63 | 34 | 10 | 7 |
| 1957 | 19 | 18 | 57 | 43 | 22 | 39 | 15 | 6 | 3 | 5 |
| 1958 | 25 | 33 | 22 | 17 | 38 | 15 | 9 | 4 | 3 | 4 |
| 1959 | 14 | 18 | 12 | 22 | 13 | 4 | 4 | 3 | 3 | 3 |
| 1960 | 14 | 13 | 15 | 12 | 5 | 4 | 4 | 3 | 3 | 3 |
| 1961 | 14 | 20 | 15 | 6 | 5 | 2 | 4 | 3 | 3 | 3 |
| 1962 | 31 | 18 | 8 | 6 | 3 | 4 | 4 | 3 | 3 | 3 |
| 1963 | 0 | 2 | 1 | 4 | 5 | 4 | 4 | 3 | 3 | 3 |
| 1964 | 4 | 13 | 5 | 4 | 5 | 4 | 4 | 4 | 6 | 7 |
| 1968 | 19 | 6 | 5 | 6 | 11 | 11 | 9 | | | |
| 1969 | 12 | 7 | 5 | 13 | 13 | 11 | | | | |
| 1970 | 14 | 8 | 15 | 17 | 13 | | | | | |
| 1971 | 16 | 23 | 22 | 17 | | | | | | |
| 1972 | 46 | 33 | 22 | | | | | | | |
| 1973 | 66 | 33 | | | | | | | | |
| 1974 | 46 | | | | | | | | | |

Buffalo nickel
Jefferson nickel

## Average Annual Profit Percentage (AAPP)
### Uncirculated Rolls of D Nickels

| Year Minted | Number of Years After Year Minted | | | | | | | | | |
|---|---|---|---|---|---|---|---|---|---|---|
| | 11 | 12 | 13 | 14 | 15 | 16 | 17 | 18 | 19 | 20 |
| 1935 | 29% | 33% | 27% | 26% | 27% | 33% | 31% | 29% | 38% | 41% |
| 1936 | 36 | 23 | 21 | 19 | 17 | 16 | 15 | 33 | 33 | 32 |
| 1937 | 24 | 22 | 20 | 19 | 18 | 16 | 15 | 15 | 15 | 31 |
| *1938 | 6 | 5 | 5 | 4 | 4 | 4 | 4 | 7 | 28 | 31 |
| **1938 | 31 | 23 | 31 | 20 | 17 | 16 | 36 | 38 | 30 | 29 |
| 1939 | 228 | 208 | 216 | 200 | 229 | 227 | 348 | 513 | 694 | 1,448 |
| 1940 | 11 | 11 | 15 | 23 | 35 | 31 | 30 | 28 | 59 | 73 |
| 1941 | 6 | 6 | 11 | 14 | 10 | 12 | 14 | 29 | 49 | 64 |
| 1942 | 115 | 113 | 129 | 150 | 242 | 383 | 726 | 1,147 | 759 | 804 |
| 1943 | 2 | 3 | 11 | 14 | 27 | 85 | 104 | 82 | 93 | 327 |
| 1944 | 2 | 2 | 2 | 11 | 63 | 85 | 62 | 66 | 169 | 166 |
| 1945 | 2 | 4 | 7 | 23 | 68 | 46 | 48 | 137 | 148 | 120 |
| 1946 | 2 | 7 | 18 | 27 | 21 | 20 | 53 | 82 | 82 | 62 |
| 1947 | 8 | 7 | 24 | 23 | 21 | 92 | 102 | 75 | 45 | 34 |
| 1948 | 8 | 54 | 56 | 49 | 159 | 208 | 122 | 71 | 75 | 94 |
| 1949 | 63 | 64 | 63 | 123 | 180 | 130 | 80 | 68 | 80 | 62 |
| 1950 | 821 | 1,444 | 2,626 | 2,809 | 1,916 | 1,498 | 1,038 | 1,147 | 1,054 | 701 |
| 1951 | 161 | 286 | 280 | 208 | 118 | 59 | 86 | 68 | 71 | 57 |
| 1952 | 547 | 632 | 519 | 326 | 201 | 201 | 165 | 107 | 85 | 83 |
| 1953 | 63 | 44 | 21 | 10 | 10 | 15 | 16 | 9 | 9 | 20 |
| 1954 | 17 | 16 | 7 | 9 | 9 | 5 | 1 | 2 | 6 | 11 |
| 1955 | 29 | 12 | 14 | 15 | 6 | 4 | 6 | 4 | 7 | 8 |
| 1956 | 4 | 6 | 4 | 3 | 4 | 3 | 4 | 4 | 3 | |
| 1957 | 6 | 4 | 4 | 5 | 3 | 4 | 4 | 4 | | |
| 1958 | 2 | 1 | 2 | 3 | 3 | 4 | 5 | | | |
| 1959 | 2 | 4 | 2 | 3 | 4 | 3 | | | | |
| 1960 | 2 | 2 | 4 | 5 | 3 | | | | | |
| 1961 | 2 | 3 | 5 | 3 | | | | | | |
| 1962 | 3 | 6 | 3 | | | | | | | |
| 1963 | 6 | 3 | | | | | | | | |
| 1964 | 4 | | | | | | | | | |

*Buffalo nickel
**Jefferson nickel

## Average Annual Profit Percentage (AAPP)
## Uncirculated Rolls of D Nickels

| Year Minted | Number of Years After Year Minted | | | | | | | | | |
|---|---|---|---|---|---|---|---|---|---|---|
| | 21 | 22 | 23 | 24 | 25 | 26 | 27 | 28 | 29 | 30 |
| 1935 | 76% | 90% | 86% | 100% | 150% | 188% | 319% | 404% | 426% | 384% |
| 1936 | 45 | 52 | 77 | 82 | 89 | 112 | 150 | 197 | 175 | 170 |
| 1937 | 35 | 62 | 68 | 88 | 109 | 132 | 211 | 182 | 175 | 170 |
| 1938 | 45 | 43 | 46 | 112 | 162 | 196 | 173 | 159 | 154 | 142 |
| 1938 | 64 | 165 | 149 | 212 | 585 | 539 | 358 | 271 | 190 | 204 |
| 1939 | 3,157 | 2,259 | 2,522 | 3,886 | 4,146 | 3,268 | 2,417 | 1,479 | 2,000 | 1,795 |
| 1940 | 69 | 66 | 86 | 91 | 75 | 68 | 46 | 52 | 47 | 38 |
| 1941 | 60 | 62 | 77 | 78 | 52 | 38 | 39 | 41 | 34 | 23 |
| 1942 | 1,339 | 1,033 | 826 | 636 | 436 | 451 | 411 | 337 | 275 | 246 |
| 1943 | 361 | 269 | 203 | 130 | 262 | 244 | 131 | 86 | 139 | 163 |
| 1944 | 173 | 145 | 104 | 151 | 135 | 104 | 85 | 89 | 123 | 118 |
| 1945 | 89 | 61 | 89 | 81 | 64 | 53 | 55 | 77 | 77 | 59 |
| 1946 | 32 | 35 | 29 | 27 | 37 | 25 | 22 | 32 | 17 | |
| 1947 | 45 | 38 | 32 | 23 | 29 | 37 | 33 | 22 | | |
| 1948 | 74 | 50 | 54 | 60 | 49 | 51 | 29 | | | |
| 1949 | 64 | 40 | 36 | 25 | 47 | 41 | | | | |
| 1950 | 628 | 597 | 717 | 644 | 511 | | | | | |
| 1951 | 58 | 86 | 101 | 53 | | | | | | |
| 1952 | 130 | 107 | 71 | | | | | | | |
| 1953 | 17 | 9 | | | | | | | | |
| 1954 | 6 | | | | | | | | | |

Buffalo nickel
Jefferson nickel

## Average Annual Profit Percentage (AAPP)
## Uncirculated Rolls of D Nickels

| Year Minted | Number of Years After Year Minted | | | | | | | | | |
|---|---|---|---|---|---|---|---|---|---|---|
| | 31 | 32 | 33 | 34 | 35 | 36 | 37 | 38 | 39 | 40 |
| 1935 | 372% | 360% | 368% | 357% | 300% | 320% | 301% | 467% | 689% | 666% |
| 1936 | 164 | 159 | 135 | 102 | 101 | 114 | 216 | 434 | 300 | |
| 1937 | 144 | 140 | 106 | 119 | 110 | 251 | 440 | 279 | | |
| *1938 | 137 | 100 | 110 | 113 | 258 | 222 | 154 | | | |
| **1938 | 244 | 188 | 136 | 121 | 228 | 222 | 127 | | | |
| 1939 | 1,289 | 1,047 | 934 | 2,188 | 2,072 | 1,306 | | | | |
| | | | | | | | | | | |
| 1940 | 22 | 19 | 27 | 58 | 42 | | | | | |
| 1941 | 24 | 29 | 40 | 33 | | | | | | |
| 1942 | 378 | 516 | 340 | | | | | | | |
| 1943 | 137 | 97 | | | | | | | | |
| 1944 | 66 | | | | | | | | | |

*Buffalo nickel
**Jefferson nickel

### Average Annual Profit Percentage (AAPP)
### Uncirculated Rolls of P Dimes

| Year Minted | Number of Years After Year Minted | | | | | | | | | |
|---|---|---|---|---|---|---|---|---|---|---|
| | 1 | 2 | 3 | 4 | 5 | 6 | 7 | 8 | 9 | 10 |
| 1935 | 0% | 0% | 0% | 0% | 0% | 2% | 6% | 5% | 5% | 6% |
| 1936 | 0 | 0 | 0 | 0 | 4 | 7 | 9 | 6 | 8 | 8 |
| 1937 | 0 | 0 | 0 | 2 | 5 | 7 | 4 | 4 | 7 | 4 |
| 1938 | 0 | 4 | 3 | 7 | 9 | 4 | 6 | 7 | 7 | 4 |
| 1939 | 0 | 0 | 6 | 7 | 4 | 4 | 5 | 5 | 5 | 3 |
| 1940 | 0 | 6 | 6 | 3 | 3 | 2 | 2 | 3 | 3 | 3 |
| 1941 | 3 | 6 | 2 | 3 | 3 | 3 | 3 | 2 | 2 | 2 |
| 1942 | 3 | 2 | 2 | 5 | 3 | 3 | 2 | 2 | 2 | 2 |
| 1943 | 0 | 2 | 4 | 0 | 1 | 1 | 1 | 1 | 1 | 1 |
| 1944 | 0 | 0 | 0 | 0 | 0 | 0 | 1 | 1 | 0 | 1 |
| 1945 | 0 | 0 | 0 | 0 | 0 | 0 | 0 | 0 | 0 | 2 |
| 1946 | 0 | 0 | 0 | 0 | 1 | 0 | 0 | 1 | 9 | 9 |
| 1947 | 0 | 0 | 0 | 0 | 0 | 0 | 8 | 31 | 31 | 28 |
| 1948 | 0 | 0 | 0 | 0 | 1 | 10 | 36 | 45 | 40 | 36 |
| 1949 | 0 | 0 | 0 | 3 | 12 | 57 | 51 | 45 | 40 | 37 |
| 1950 | 0 | 0 | 0 | 19 | 64 | 57 | 51 | 45 | 42 | 140 |
| 1951 | 0 | 0 | 1 | 13 | 8 | 8 | 7 | 7 | 26 | 18 |
| 1952 | 0 | 0 | 0 | 5 | 5 | 4 | 6 | 22 | 13 | 14 |
| 1953 | 0 | 0 | 0 | 1 | 1 | 2 | 20 | 11 | 13 | 85 |
| 1954 | 0 | 0 | 0 | 1 | 2 | 11 | 6 | 5 | 17 | 14 |
| 1955 | 0 | 2 | 14 | 18 | 100 | 52 | 65 | 136 | 226 | 140 |
| 1956 | 0 | 0 | 0 | 5 | 5 | 4 | 11 | 17 | 7 | 3 |
| 1957 | 0 | 0 | 5 | 4 | 4 | 10 | 8 | 3 | 3 | 2 |
| 1958 | 0 | 92 | 30 | 23 | 78 | 102 | 70 | 47 | 21 | 45 |
| 1959 | 0 | 0 | 0 | 5 | 12 | 4 | 4 | 2 | 8 | 6 |
| 1960 | 0 | 0 | 19 | 19 | 8 | 5 | 3 | 7 | 6 | 3 |
| 1961 | 0 | 92 | 40 | 23 | 12 | 3 | 8 | 10 | 3 | 2 |
| 1962 | 0 | 29 | 9 | 7 | 2 | 7 | 8 | 3 | 1 | 3 |
| 1963 | 3 | 6 | 4 | 1 | 8 | 7 | 3 | 2 | 2 | 11 |
| 1964 | 0 | 0 | 1 | 7 | 1 | 3 | 3 | 3 | 12 | 25 |
| 1965 | 0 | 0 | 4 | 0 | 0 | 2 | 2 | 3 | 5 | 5 |
| 1966 | 0 | 0 | 0 | 0 | 2 | 2 | 3 | 5 | 6 | |
| 1967 | 0 | 0 | 0 | 3 | 2 | 3 | 6 | 7 | | |
| 1968 | 0 | 0 | 4 | 4 | 4 | 7 | 9 | | | |
| 1969 | 0 | 4 | 4 | 5 | 8 | 14 | | | | |
| 1970 | 0 | 4 | 4 | 11 | 11 | | | | | |
| 1971 | 3 | 10 | 14 | 17 | | | | | | |
| 1972 | 11 | 21 | 19 | | | | | | | |
| 1973 | 42 | 19 | | | | | | | | |
| 1974 | 25 | | | | | | | | | |

## Average Annual Profit Percentage (AAPP)
### Uncirculated Rolls of P Dimes

| Year Minted | Number of Years After Year Minted | | | | | | | | | |
|---|---|---|---|---|---|---|---|---|---|---|
| | 11 | 12 | 13 | 14 | 15 | 16 | 17 | 18 | 19 | 20 |
| 1935 | 7% | 7% | 6% | 6% | 6% | 6% | 6% | 8% | 12% | 15% |
| 1936 | 7 | 6 | 5 | 5 | 5 | 4 | 5 | 6 | 9 | 9 |
| 1937 | 4 | 4 | 3 | 2 | 3 | 2 | 6 | 6 | 7 | 9 |
| 1938 | 4 | 4 | 4 | 4 | 4 | 6 | 6 | 9 | 9 | 15 |
| 1939 | 3 | 3 | 3 | 5 | 4 | 5 | 6 | 9 | 12 | 17 |
| 1940 | 3 | 3 | 3 | 4 | 9 | 9 | 12 | 13 | 22 | 21 |
| 1941 | 2 | 2 | 1 | 5 | 10 | 13 | 14 | 14 | 13 | 20 |
| 1942 | 1 | 2 | 3 | 2 | 6 | 6 | 6 | 10 | 9 | 9 |
| 1943 | 2 | 3 | 2 | 2 | 4 | 5 | 8 | 9 | 10 | 12 |
| 1944 | 2 | 2 | 1 | 1 | 2 | 9 | 9 | 11 | 13 | 23 |
| 1945 | 2 | 2 | 2 | 2 | 9 | 10 | 10 | 12 | 24 | 40 |
| 1946 | 7 | 6 | 7 | 14 | 7 | 8 | 13 | 13 | 8 | 7 |
| 1947 | 25 | 25 | 96 | 39 | 40 | 78 | 59 | 34 | 18 | 17 |
| 1948 | 34 | 156 | 65 | 72 | 199 | 142 | 87 | 65 | 36 | 54 |
| 1949 | 508 | 301 | 266 | 529 | 452 | 389 | 289 | 196 | 232 | 248 |
| 1950 | 99 | 97 | 144 | 94 | 62 | 31 | 27 | 43 | 45 | 50 |
| 1951 | 17 | 137 | 90 | 55 | 41 | 21 | 29 | 21 | 18 | 18 |
| 1952 | 23 | 29 | 20 | 14 | 9 | 28 | 17 | 11 | 9 | 7 |
| 1953 | 70 | 50 | 26 | 15 | 23 | 23 | 11 | 11 | 16 | 33 |
| 1954 | 8 | 5 | 3 | 11 | 8 | 4 | 2 | 2 | 8 | 14 |
| 1955 | 96 | 67 | 76 | 63 | 38 | 25 | 24 | 31 | 30 | 19 |
| 1956 | 2 | 6 | 7 | 3 | 2 | 7 | 11 | 15 | 12 | |
| 1957 | 5 | 5 | 3 | 2 | 2 | 9 | 15 | 14 | | |
| 1958 | 28 | 15 | 7 | 12 | 13 | 20 | 15 | | | |
| 1959 | 3 | 2 | 2 | 8 | 17 | 14 | | | | |
| 1960 | 2 | 2 | 9 | 18 | 15 | | | | | |
| 1961 | 4 | 9 | 19 | 15 | | | | | | |
| 1962 | 10 | 21 | 17 | | | | | | | |
| 1963 | 23 | 18 | | | | | | | | |
| 1964 | 20 | | | | | | | | | |

## Average Annual Profit Percentage (AAPP)
### Uncirculated Rolls of P Dimes

| Year Minted | 21 | 22 | 23 | 24 | 25 | 26 | 27 | 28 | 29 | 30 |
|---|---|---|---|---|---|---|---|---|---|---|
| 1935 | 17% | 19% | 30% | 29% | 24% | 39% | 46% | 53% | 59% | 57% |
| 1936 | 8 | 17 | 23 | 21 | 23 | 22 | 26 | 26 | 42 | 40 |
| 1937 | 9 | 19 | 18 | 16 | 18 | 27 | 28 | 50 | 48 | 48 |
| 1938 | 20 | 17 | 24 | 29 | 43 | 51 | 46 | 44 | 43 | 70 |
| 1939 | 14 | 24 | 23 | 25 | 37 | 51 | 52 | 47 | 46 | 41 |
| 1940 | 22 | 25 | 24 | 29 | 53 | 49 | 40 | 42 | 39 | 33 |
| 1941 | 20 | 20 | 27 | 34 | 28 | 20 | 24 | 23 | 17 | 14 |
| 1942 | 11 | 24 | 32 | 32 | 21 | 24 | 23 | 18 | 14 | 15 |
| 1943 | 22 | 33 | 32 | 18 | 23 | 24 | 19 | 14 | 16 | 36 |
| 1944 | 29 | 28 | 18 | 24 | 24 | 19 | 14 | 16 | 38 | 63 |
| 1945 | 39 | 19 | 25 | 25 | 20 | 16 | 17 | 39 | 65 | 59 |
| 1946 | 3 | 7 | 7 | 4 | 4 | 4 | 9 | 10 | 12 | |
| 1947 | 25 | 20 | 14 | 9 | 8 | 26 | 16 | 15 | | |
| 1948 | 67 | 41 | 23 | 25 | 55 | 49 | 43 | | | |
| 1949 | 172 | 152 | 202 | 318 | 317 | 245 | | | | |
| 1950 | 40 | 46 | 61 | 51 | 36 | | | | | |
| 1951 | 27 | 54 | 41 | 27 | | | | | | |
| 1952 | 25 | 15 | 16 | | | | | | | |
| 1953 | 19 | 18 | | | | | | | | |
| 1954 | 13 | | | | | | | | | |

*Average Annual Profit Percentage (AAPP)*
*Uncirculated Rolls of P Dimes*

| Year Minted | \multicolumn{10}{c}{Number of Years After Year Minted} |
|---|

| Year Minted | 31 | 32 | 33 | 34 | 35 | 36 | 37 | 38 | 39 | 40 |
|---|---|---|---|---|---|---|---|---|---|---|
| 1935 | 55% | 54% | 54% | 54% | 47% | 43% | 46% | 59% | 109% | 156 |
| 1936 | 39 | 46 | 40 | 26 | 29 | 32 | 53 | 91 | 80 | |
| 1937 | 38 | 34 | 27 | 21 | 25 | 43 | 81 | 83 | | |
| 1938 | 71 | 50 | 47 | 46 | 64 | 116 | 131 | | | |
| 1939 | 32 | 27 | 26 | 38 | 69 | 72 | | | | |
| 1940 | 28 | 27 | 47 | 62 | 58 | | | | | |
| 1941 | 13 | 36 | 64 | 60 | | | | | | |
| 1942 | 35 | 59 | 53 | | | | | | | |
| 1943 | 60 | 56 | | | | | | | | |
| 1944 | 56 | | | | | | | | | |

## Average Annual Profit Percentage (AAPP)
## Uncirculated Rolls of D Dimes

| Year minted | Number of Years After Year Minted | | | | | | | | | |
|---|---|---|---|---|---|---|---|---|---|---|
| | 1 | 2 | 3 | 4 | 5 | 6 | 7 | 8 | 9 | 10 |
| 935 | 0% | 0% | 1% | 2% | 1% | 3% | 6% | 7% | 9% | 10% |
| 936 | 0 | 0 | 0 | 1 | 4 | 7 | 8 | 7 | 6 | 7 |
| 937 | 0 | 0 | 2 | 5 | 5 | 4 | 4 | 6 | 6 | 7 |
| 938 | 0 | 4 | 6 | 7 | 5 | 4 | 5 | 4 | 5 | 4 |
| 939 | 0 | 0 | 6 | 11 | 5 | 4 | 6 | 4 | 5 | 3 |
| 940 | 0 | 6 | 6 | 3 | 2 | 2 | 2 | 3 | 3 | 3 |
| 941 | 0 | 6 | 2 | 3 | 4 | 1 | 3 | 2 | 2 | 2 |
| 942 | 11 | 2 | 2 | 3 | 0 | 3 | 0 | 1 | 2 | 2 |
| 943 | 0 | 4 | 4 | 0 | 1 | 0 | 0 | 0 | 0 | 0 |
| 944 | 0 | 0 | 0 | 0 | 0 | 0 | 0 | 0 | 0 | 1 |
| 945 | 0 | 0 | 0 | 0 | 0 | 0 | 0 | 0 | 0 | 2 |
| 946 | 0 | 0 | 1 | 2 | 1 | 0 | 0 | 1 | 11 | 10 |
| 947 | 0 | 0 | 0 | 0 | 0 | 0 | 2 | 32 | 31 | 28 |
| 948 | 0 | 0 | 0 | 0 | 1 | 2 | 40 | 35 | 31 | 31 |
| 949 | 0 | 0 | 0 | 1 | 4 | 23 | 17 | 15 | 13 | 14 |
| 950 | 0 | 0 | 0 | 1 | 21 | 15 | 13 | 15 | 15 | 30 |
| 951 | 0 | 0 | 1 | 13 | 8 | 7 | 6 | 7 | 26 | 23 |
| 952 | 0 | 0 | 6 | 6 | 5 | 6 | 6 | 24 | 17 | 15 |
| 953 | 0 | 0 | 0 | 1 | 1 | 2 | 11 | 9 | 8 | 22 |
| 954 | 0 | 0 | 0 | 0 | 2 | 11 | 6 | 5 | 15 | 14 |
| 955 | 0 | 0 | 0 | 4 | 97 | 36 | 42 | 106 | 121 | 93 |
| 956 | 0 | 0 | 0 | 5 | 4 | 3 | 6 | 7 | 2 | 2 |
| 957 | 0 | 0 | 5 | 4 | 4 | 7 | 7 | 7 | 6 | 5 |
| 958 | 0 | 2 | 1 | 1 | 2 | 8 | 4 | 3 | 2 | 7 |
| 959 | 0 | 0 | 0 | 1 | 2 | 1 | 3 | 2 | 6 | 4 |
| 960 | 0 | 0 | 11 | 3 | 1 | 1 | 2 | 5 | 5 | 3 |
| 961 | 0 | 10 | 1 | 0 | 2 | 2 | 7 | 5 | 3 | 2 |
| 962 | 0 | 0 | 0 | 6 | 1 | 7 | 6 | 3 | 2 | 3 |
| 963 | 0 | 0 | 0 | 1 | 8 | 7 | 3 | 2 | 2 | 11 |
| 964 | 0 | 0 | 1 | 3 | 1 | 3 | 3 | 3 | 12 | 25 |
| 68 | 0 | 0 | 4 | 4 | 4 | 7 | 8 | | | |
| 69 | 0 | 4 | 4 | 5 | 8 | 10 | | | | |
| 70 | 0 | 4 | 4 | 11 | 10 | | | | | |
| 71 | 3 | 6 | 14 | 14 | | | | | | |
| 72 | 11 | 21 | 17 | | | | | | | |
| 73 | 42 | 17 | | | | | | | | |
| 74 | 25 | | | | | | | | | |

## Average Annual Profit Percentage (AAPP)
### Uncirculated Rolls of D Dimes

| Year Minted | Number of Years After Year Minted | | | | | | | | | |
|---|---|---|---|---|---|---|---|---|---|---|
| | 11 | 12 | 13 | 14 | 15 | 16 | 17 | 18 | 19 | 20 |
| 1935 | 14% | 13% | 20% | 18% | 19% | 18% | 22% | 26% | 41% | 79% |
| 1936 | 11 | 14 | 17 | 19 | 19 | 18 | 27 | 38 | 40 | 42 |
| 1937 | 8 | 10 | 12 | 12 | 11 | 13 | 15 | 22 | 30 | 35 |
| 1938 | 4 | 4 | 3 | 4 | 4 | 6 | 12 | 25 | 32 | 31 |
| 1939 | 3 | 2 | 2 | 3 | 3 | 7 | 9 | 14 | 20 | 19 |
| 1940 | 3 | 3 | 3 | 4 | 14 | 14 | 15 | 16 | 22 | 19 |
| 1941 | 2 | 2 | 9 | 7 | 10 | 13 | 16 | 18 | 16 | 24 |
| 1942 | 1 | 2 | 3 | 2 | 3 | 7 | 7 | 10 | 17 | 16 |
| 1943 | 2 | 3 | 2 | 2 | 4 | 5 | 10 | 16 | 16 | 19 |
| 1944 | 2 | 2 | 2 | 1 | 2 | 10 | 12 | 11 | 14 | 27 |
| 1945 | 2 | 2 | 2 | 3 | 10 | 10 | 10 | 13 | 24 | 31 |
| 1946 | 8 | 6 | 7 | 15 | 7 | 12 | 17 | 43 | 26 | 14 |
| 1947 | 25 | 25 | 41 | 22 | 22 | 43 | 48 | 36 | 17 | 17 |
| 1948 | 28 | 48 | 29 | 28 | 40 | 58 | 50 | 25 | 18 | 34 |
| 1949 | 63 | 77 | 59 | 128 | 151 | 107 | 96 | 73 | 86 | 78 |
| 1950 | 21 | 22 | 43 | 66 | 67 | 31 | 22 | 30 | 40 | 74 |
| 1951 | 20 | 51 | 65 | 38 | 23 | 12 | 18 | 25 | 16 | 14 |
| 1952 | 24 | 25 | 29 | 35 | 17 | 21 | 15 | 14 | 14 | 13 |
| 1953 | 21 | 10 | 8 | 3 | 11 | 5 | 3 | 5 | 6 | 16 |
| 1954 | 8 | 4 | 3 | 13 | 9 | 4 | 2 | 2 | 8 | 13 |
| 1955 | 61 | 50 | 56 | 44 | 18 | 12 | 13 | 17 | 18 | 18 |
| 1956 | 1 | 6 | 9 | 8 | 3 | 3 | 9 | 15 | 12 | |
| 1957 | 34 | 13 | 13 | 14 | 14 | 15 | 17 | 15 | | |
| 1958 | 10 | 4 | 2 | 5 | 8 | 16 | 13 | | | |
| 1959 | 3 | 2 | 2 | 8 | 17 | 14 | | | | |
| 1960 | 2 | 2 | 9 | 18 | 14 | | | | | |
| 1961 | 4 | 9 | 19 | 15 | | | | | | |
| 1962 | 10 | 21 | 17 | | | | | | | |
| 1963 | 23 | 17 | | | | | | | | |
| 1964 | 19 | | | | | | | | | |

### Average Annual Profit Percentage (AAPP)
### Uncirculated Rolls of D Dimes

| Year Minted | Number of Years After Year Minted | | | | | | | | | |
|---|---|---|---|---|---|---|---|---|---|---|
| | 21 | 22 | 23 | 24 | 25 | 26 | 27 | 28 | 29 | 30 |
| 1935 | 82% | 96% | 128% | 147% | 148% | 148% | 192% | 264% | 405% | 563% |
| 1936 | 52 | 90 | 133 | 141 | 141 | 148 | 186 | 279 | 310 | 300 |
| 1937 | 45 | 53 | 58 | 85 | 81 | 96 | 116 | 123 | 119 | 115 |
| 1938 | 29 | 35 | 40 | 52 | 100 | 188 | 260 | 236 | 214 | 213 |
| 1939 | 22 | 17 | 24 | 41 | 37 | 45 | 49 | 47 | 40 | 39 |
| 1940 | 25 | 28 | 32 | 39 | 47 | 43 | 40 | 43 | 42 | 33 |
| 1941 | 25 | 33 | 47 | 75 | 72 | 45 | 44 | 39 | 34 | 15 |
| 1942 | 16 | 31 | 39 | 30 | 21 | 24 | 28 | 19 | 16 | 15 |
| 1943 | 25 | 35 | 33 | 20 | 24 | 24 | 20 | 16 | 16 | 43 |
| 1944 | 27 | 26 | 18 | 25 | 24 | 20 | 17 | 16 | 44 | 65 |
| 1945 | 31 | 21 | 27 | 29 | 21 | 17 | 17 | 46 | 81 | 65 |
| 1946 | 10 | 13 | 11 | 8 | 6 | 11 | 28 | 14 | 14 | |
| 1947 | 35 | 31 | 23 | 19 | 20 | 40 | 29 | 24 | | |
| 1948 | 32 | 20 | 18 | 19 | 37 | 31 | 24 | | | |
| 1949 | 67 | 57 | 82 | 177 | 148 | 136 | | | | |
| 1950 | 62 | 49 | 55 | 46 | 27 | | | | | |
| 1951 | 13 | 33 | 30 | 18 | | | | | | |
| 1952 | 33 | 22 | 20 | | | | | | | |
| 1953 | 16 | 12 | | | | | | | | |
| 1954 | 13 | | | | | | | | | |

## Average Annual Profit Percentage (AAPP)
### Uncirculated Rolls of D Dimes

| Year Minted | Number of Years After Year Minted | | | | | | | | | |
|---|---|---|---|---|---|---|---|---|---|---|
| | 31 | 32 | 33 | 34 | 35 | 36 | 37 | 38 | 39 | 40 |
| 1935 | 545% | 528% | 512% | 497% | 358% | 281% | 334% | 461% | 722% | 1,376 |
| 1936 | 290 | 343 | 356 | 274 | 226 | 266 | 416 | 525 | 678 | |
| 1937 | 124 | 120 | 97 | 78 | 84 | 143 | 279 | 342 | | |
| 1938 | 206 | 140 | 123 | 119 | 159 | 250 | 243 | | | |
| 1939 | 31 | 29 | 28 | 70 | 101 | 118 | | | | |
| 1940 | 28 | 27 | 123 | 164 | 135 | | | | | |
| 1941 | 28 | 56 | 100 | 96 | | | | | | |
| 1942 | 41 | 70 | 76 | | | | | | | |
| 1943 | 71 | 60 | | | | | | | | |
| 1944 | 62 | | | | | | | | | |

## Average Annual Profit Percentage (AAPP)
## Uncirculated Rolls of P Quarters

| Year minted | Number of Years After Year Minted | | | | | | | | | |
|---|---|---|---|---|---|---|---|---|---|---|
| | 1 | 2 | 3 | 4 | 5 | 6 | 7 | 8 | 9 | 10 |
| 35 | 0% | 0% | 0% | 0% | 1% | 4% | 9% | 8% | 10% | 11% |
| 36 | 0 | 0 | 0 | 0 | 2 | 7 | 7 | 7 | 6 | 9 |
| 37 | 0 | 0 | 0 | 3 | 5 | 5 | 5 | 7 | 8 | 7 |
| 38 | 0 | 1 | 2 | 5 | 6 | 5 | 11 | 13 | 18 | 20 |
| 39 | 0 | 0 | 3 | 6 | 4 | 5 | 6 | 7 | 10 | 10 |
| 40 | 0 | 0 | 6 | 5 | 4 | 14 | 26 | 35 | 27 | 22 |
| 41 | 0 | 7 | 0 | 3 | 3 | 2 | 3 | 2 | 2 | 1 |
| 42 | 0 | 0 | 1 | 3 | 2 | 2 | 1 | 1 | 1 | 1 |
| 43 | 0 | 0 | 0 | 2 | 2 | 1 | 1 | 1 | 1 | 1 |
| 44 | 0 | 0 | 0 | 0 | 0 | 0 | 0 | 0 | 0 | 0 |
| 45 | 0 | 0 | 0 | 0 | 0 | 0 | 0 | 0 | 0 | 0 |
| 46 | 0 | 0 | 0 | 0 | 0 | 0 | 0 | 0 | 1 | 1 |
| 47 | 0 | 0 | 0 | 0 | 0 | 0 | 0 | 0 | 1 | 1 |
| 48 | 0 | 0 | 0 | 0 | 0 | 0 | 0 | 1 | 0 | 0 |
| 49 | 0 | 0 | 0 | 0 | 2 | 2 | 2 | 4 | 8 | 11 |
| 50 | 0 | 0 | 0 | 2 | 4 | 5 | 5 | 5 | 6 | 6 |
| 51 | 0 | 0 | 0 | 0 | 0 | 4 | 4 | 4 | 4 | 5 |
| 52 | 0 | 0 | 0 | 0 | 0 | 9 | 12 | 7 | 5 | 5 |
| 53 | 0 | 0 | 0 | 0 | 0 | 0 | 5 | 5 | 7 | 62 |
| 54 | 0 | 0 | 0 | 0 | 0 | 3 | 3 | 2 | 2 | 5 |
| 55 | 0 | 0 | 0 | 0 | 13 | 15 | 13 | 35 | 35 | 26 |
| 56 | 0 | 0 | 0 | 2 | 1 | 3 | 4 | 7 | 2 | 3 |
| 57 | 0 | 0 | 0 | 0 | 1 | 2 | 2 | 1 | 2 | 1 |
| 58 | 3 | 19 | 5 | 7 | 41 | 78 | 54 | 49 | 25 | 36 |
| 59 | 0 | 0 | 1 | 2 | 10 | 4 | 3 | 1 | 5 | 7 |
| 60 | 0 | 0 | 0 | 2 | 3 | 2 | 1 | 6 | 5 | 3 |
| 61 | 0 | 0 | 1 | 1 | 3 | 1 | 7 | 7 | 4 | 1 |
| 62 | 0 | 0 | 2 | 6 | 2 | 4 | 4 | 4 | 1 | 2 |
| 63 | 0 | 0 | 2 | 0 | 7 | 5 | 2 | 1 | 2 | 11 |
| 64 | 0 | 0 | 2 | 3 | 2 | 2 | 3 | 2 | 12 | 23 |
| 65 | 0 | 0 | 0 | 1 | 0 | 1 | 0 | 2 | 4 | 3 |
| 66 | 0 | 0 | 0 | 0 | 1 | 1 | 5 | 5 | 4 | |
| 67 | 0 | 0 | 0 | 1 | 1 | 2 | 5 | 4 | | |
| 68 | 0 | 0 | 1 | 3 | 3 | 6 | 4 | | | |
| 69 | 0 | 0 | 0 | 4 | 7 | 5 | | | | |
| 70 | 0 | 0 | 2 | 6 | 4 | | | | | |
| 71 | 0 | 7 | 7 | 6 | | | | | | |
| 72 | 0 | 11 | 7 | | | | | | | |
| 73 | 22 | 7 | | | | | | | | |
| 74 | 6 | | | | | | | | | |

## Average Annual Profit Percentage (AAPP)
## Uncirculated Rolls of P Quarters

| Year Minted | Number of Years After Year Minted | | | | | | | | | |
|---|---|---|---|---|---|---|---|---|---|---|

| Year Minted | 11 | 12 | 13 | 14 | 15 | 16 | 17 | 18 | 19 | 20 |
|---|---|---|---|---|---|---|---|---|---|---|
| 1935 | 12% | 13% | 13% | 19% | 17% | 14% | 13% | 13% | 13% | 14 |
| 1936 | 8 | 8 | 11 | 10 | 10 | 13 | 12 | 11 | 13 | 18 |
| 1937 | 17 | 19 | 14 | 13 | 12 | 12 | 11 | 11 | 19 | 25 |
| 1938 | 20 | 17 | 17 | 15 | 17 | 18 | 32 | 51 | 72 | 124 |
| 1939 | 9 | 8 | 9 | 9 | 11 | 20 | 28 | 30 | 31 | 48 |
| 1940 | 19 | 17 | 19 | 23 | 31 | 41 | 43 | 45 | 55 | 46 |
| 1941 | 1 | 2 | 1 | 2 | 3 | 3 | 3 | 3 | 11 | 12 |
| 1942 | 1 | 1 | 0 | 1 | 9 | 15 | 14 | 13 | 18 | 14 |
| 1943 | 1 | 1 | 1 | 2 | 2 | 3 | 8 | 7 | 9 | 10 |
| 1944 | 0 | 0 | 0 | 0 | 0 | 6 | 3 | 9 | 9 | 12 |
| 1945 | 0 | 0 | 0 | 0 | 6 | 3 | 4 | 5 | 11 | 6 |
| 1946 | 0 | 0 | 0 | 2 | 2 | 4 | 4 | 13 | 10 | 6 |
| 1947 | 0 | 0 | 3 | 3 | 3 | 8 | 25 | 22 | 18 | 11 |
| 1948 | 0 | 2 | 3 | 3 | 6 | 13 | 9 | 5 | 5 | 7 |
| 1949 | 53 | 93 | 95 | 96 | 259 | 229 | 182 | 138 | 115 | 101 |
| 1950 | 10 | 12 | 45 | 28 | 19 | 10 | 9 | 13 | 11 | 6 |
| 1951 | 5 | 8 | 16 | 11 | 7 | 5 | 8 | 7 | 4 | 6 |
| 1952 | 4 | 14 | 10 | 5 | 5 | 7 | 8 | 3 | 7 | 7 |
| 1953 | 50 | 36 | 22 | 14 | 20 | 20 | 11 | 15 | 14 | 29 |
| 1954 | 1 | 2 | 1 | 8 | 5 | 2 | 1 | 2 | 8 | 12 |
| 1955 | 15 | 6 | 22 | 18 | 7 | 6 | 8 | 16 | 15 | 12 |
| 1956 | 2 | 9 | 4 | 3 | 1 | 2 | 8 | 13 | 11 | |
| 1957 | 5 | 5 | 5 | 1 | 2 | 8 | 14 | 11 | | |
| 1958 | 25 | 19 | 13 | 17 | 16 | 20 | 16 | | | |
| 1959 | 3 | 2 | 2 | 9 | 16 | 13 | | | | |
| 1960 | 2 | 2 | 9 | 17 | 13 | | | | | |
| 1961 | 2 | 9 | 18 | 14 | | | | | | |
| 1962 | 10 | 20 | 15 | | | | | | | |
| 1963 | 21 | 17 | | | | | | | | |
| 1964 | 18 | | | | | | | | | |

## *Average Annual Profit Percentage (AAPP)*
## *Uncirculated Rolls of P Quarters*

| Year Minted | Number of Years After Year Minted | | | | | | | | | |
|---|---|---|---|---|---|---|---|---|---|---|
| | 21 | 22 | 23 | 24 | 25 | 26 | 27 | 28 | 29 | 30 |
| 1935 | 19% | 21% | 37% | 35% | 36% | 50% | 55% | 58% | 62% | 60% |
| 1936 | 19 | 27 | 24 | 23 | 37 | 49 | 50 | 64 | 69 | 66 |
| 1937 | 31 | 47 | 67 | 51 | 61 | 66 | 60 | 58 | 56 | 54 |
| 1938 | 183 | 182 | 326 | 376 | 482 | 435 | 461 | 444 | 324 | 351 |
| 1939 | 46 | 56 | 65 | 70 | 66 | 59 | 57 | 51 | 40 | 32 |
| 1940 | 64 | 82 | 95 | 123 | 78 | 74 | 64 | 60 | 48 | 28 |
| 1941 | 11 | 13 | 22 | 20 | 19 | 11 | 12 | 11 | 8 | 7 |
| 1942 | 19 | 28 | 22 | 21 | 11 | 11 | 10 | 7 | 6 | 7 |
| 1943 | 12 | 11 | 11 | 9 | 20 | 17 | 11 | 13 | 13 | 26 |
| 1944 | 12 | 9 | 5 | 8 | 8 | 5 | 7 | 8 | 13 | 13 |
| 1945 | 6 | 5 | 7 | 7 | 5 | 4 | 4 | 13 | 20 | 13 |
| 1946 | 4 | 7 | 7 | 5 | 4 | 7 | 13 | 13 | 12 | |
| 1947 | 13 | 15 | 10 | 9 | 9 | 18 | 22 | 17 | | |
| 1948 | 7 | 5 | 5 | 5 | 14 | 13 | 14 | | | |
| 1949 | 84 | 78 | 78 | 134 | 157 | 134 | | | | |
| 1950 | 6 | 7 | 15 | 15 | 22 | | | | | |
| 1951 | 8 | 14 | 16 | 16 | | | | | | |
| 1952 | 13 | 18 | 19 | | | | | | | |
| 1953 | 21 | 19 | | | | | | | | |
| 1954 | 11 | | | | | | | | | |

## Average Annual Profit Percentage (AAPP)
## Uncirculated Rolls of P Quarters

| Year Minted | Number of Years After Year Minted | | | | | | | | | |
|---|---|---|---|---|---|---|---|---|---|---|
| | 31 | 32 | 33 | 34 | 35 | 36 | 37 | 38 | 39 | 40 |
| 1935 | 58% | 68% | 55% | 53% | 36% | 32% | 34% | 46% | 92% | 112% |
| 1936 | 68 | 56 | 50 | 38 | 33 | 38 | 53 | 92 | 94 | |
| 1937 | 51 | 49 | 36 | 37 | 42 | 66 | 136 | 114 | | |
| 1938 | 340 | 233 | 221 | 180 | 237 | 308 | 285 | | | |
| 1939 | 24 | 30 | 31 | 42 | 68 | 76 | | | | |
| 1940 | 31 | 33 | 32 | 75 | 81 | | | | | |
| 1941 | 8 | 29 | 42 | 37 | | | | | | |
| 1942 | 21 | 28 | 30 | | | | | | | |
| 1943 | 27 | 25 | | | | | | | | |
| 1944 | 11 | | | | | | | | | |

## Average Annual Profit Percentage (AAPP)
## Uncirculated Rolls of D Quarters

| Year Minted | Number of Years After Year Minted | | | | | | | | | |
|---|---|---|---|---|---|---|---|---|---|---|
| | 1 | 2 | 3 | 4 | 5 | 6 | 7 | 8 | 9 | 10 |
| 1935 | 0% | 0% | 0% | 0% | 1% | 2% | 9% | 9% | 10% | 10% |
| 1936 | 0 | 0 | 0 | 0 | 1 | 7 | 7 | 11 | 14 | 28 |
| 1937 | 0 | 0 | 0 | 2 | 5 | 6 | 4 | 8 | 8 | 11 |
| 1939 | 0 | 0 | 3 | 4 | 4 | 6 | 5 | 5 | 6 | 7 |
| 1940 | 0 | 0 | 6 | 5 | 4 | 5 | 18 | 35 | 35 | 32 |
| 1941 | 0 | 7 | 2 | 3 | 3 | 4 | 2 | 2 | 2 | 2 |
| 1942 | 0 | 0 | 0 | 4 | 3 | 2 | 2 | 1 | 1 | 1 |
| 1943 | 0 | 0 | 0 | 2 | 2 | 1 | 1 | 1 | 1 | 1 |
| 1944 | 0 | 0 | 0 | 0 | 0 | 0 | 0 | 0 | 0 | 0 |
| 1945 | 0 | 0 | 0 | 0 | 0 | 0 | 0 | 0 | 0 | 0 |
| 1946 | 0 | 0 | 0 | 0 | 0 | 0 | 0 | 0 | 0 | 1 |
| 1947 | 0 | 0 | 0 | 0 | 0 | 0 | 0 | 0 | 1 | 1 |
| 1948 | 0 | 0 | 0 | 0 | 0 | 0 | 0 | 0 | 0 | 1 |
| 1949 | 0 | 0 | 0 | 0 | 0 | 0 | 1 | 0 | 0 | 0 |
| 1950 | 0 | 0 | 0 | 2 | 1 | 1 | 0 | 0 | 1 | 3 |
| 1951 | 0 | 0 | 0 | 0 | 0 | 0 | 0 | 0 | 4 | 3 |
| 1952 | 0 | 0 | 0 | 0 | 0 | 0 | 0 | 3 | 3 | 4 |
| 1953 | 0 | 0 | 0 | 0 | 0 | 0 | 4 | 3 | 3 | 4 |
| 1954 | 0 | 0 | 0 | 0 | 0 | 4 | 3 | 2 | 31 | 17 |
| 1955 | 14 | 3 | 1 | 4 | 41 | 23 | 35 | 125 | 124 | 100 |
| 1956 | 0 | 0 | 0 | 2 | 4 | 7 | 4 | 7 | 5 | 3 |
| 1957 | 0 | 0 | 0 | 0 | 1 | 2 | 1 | 0 | 2 | 1 |
| 1958 | 0 | 7 | 1 | 2 | 1 | 2 | 0 | 1 | 0 | 4 |
| 1959 | 0 | 0 | 0 | 4 | 3 | 0 | 0 | 0 | 5 | 4 |
| 1960 | 0 | 0 | 0 | 0 | 0 | 2 | 1 | 6 | 2 | 3 |
| 1961 | 0 | 0 | 0 | 0 | 2 | 1 | 5 | 4 | 4 | 1 |
| 1962 | 0 | 0 | 0 | 2 | 1 | 7 | 4 | 4 | 1 | 2 |
| 1963 | 0 | 0 | 2 | 0 | 7 | 4 | 2 | 1 | 2 | 11 |
| 1964 | 0 | 0 | 2 | 1 | 1 | 2 | 3 | 3 | 12 | 23 |
| 1968 | 0 | 0 | 5 | 13 | 13 | 14 | 9 | | | |
| 1969 | 0 | 0 | 17 | 28 | 18 | 14 | | | | |
| 1970 | 0 | 0 | 2 | 6 | 4 | | | | | |
| 1971 | 0 | 0 | 7 | 5 | | | | | | |
| 1972 | 0 | 11 | 6 | | | | | | | |
| 1973 | 22 | 5 | | | | | | | | |
| 1974 | 6 | | | | | | | | | |

## Average Annual Profit Percentage (AAPP)
## Uncirculated Rolls of D Quarters

| Year Minted | Number of Years After Year Minted | | | | | | | | | |
|---|---|---|---|---|---|---|---|---|---|---|
| | 11 | 12 | 13 | 14 | 15 | 16 | 17 | 18 | 19 | 20 |
| 1935 | 10% | 11% | 16% | 15% | 16% | 15% | 14% | 16% | 34% | 33% |
| 1936 | 50 | 55 | 62 | 74 | 95 | 108 | 151 | 222 | 315 | 375 |
| 1937 | 12 | 9 | 8 | 8 | 9 | 10 | 9 | 18 | 25 | 25 |
| 1939 | 8 | 8 | 7 | 8 | 6 | 13 | 21 | 26 | 31 | 33 |
| 1940 | 31 | 34 | 32 | 30 | 39 | 51 | 51 | 66 | 95 | 120 |
| 1941 | 2 | 2 | 2 | 2 | 14 | 12 | 14 | 18 | 19 | 27 |
| 1942 | 1 | 1 | 0 | 1 | 1 | 2 | 10 | 13 | 11 | 13 |
| 1943 | 1 | 2 | 2 | 2 | 1 | 3 | 11 | 10 | 9 | 12 |
| 1944 | 0 | 1 | 0 | 0 | 0 | 8 | 5 | 9 | 10 | 48 |
| 1945 | 1 | 0 | 0 | 0 | 5 | 4 | 4 | 7 | 27 | 29 |
| 1946 | 0 | 0 | 0 | 3 | 3 | 5 | 8 | 49 | 33 | 33 |
| 1947 | 0 | 1 | 2 | 3 | 3 | 6 | 28 | 22 | 13 | 10 |
| 1948 | 1 | 3 | 3 | 4 | 5 | 27 | 21 | 13 | 10 | 16 |
| 1949 | 4 | 23 | 31 | 36 | 54 | 60 | 49 | 28 | 54 | 56 |
| 1950 | 3 | 6 | 10 | 23 | 19 | 9 | 8 | 16 | 14 | 9 |
| 1951 | 4 | 5 | 19 | 9 | 4 | 4 | 6 | 8 | 6 | 8 |
| 1952 | 5 | 14 | 5 | 4 | 3 | 8 | 7 | 4 | 4 | 4 |
| 1953 | 9 | 4 | 2 | 2 | 7 | 6 | 2 | 3 | 3 | 9 |
| 1954 | 8 | 3 | 2 | 9 | 6 | 2 | 1 | 2 | 8 | 12 |
| 1955 | 78 | 65 | 80 | 74 | 41 | 39 | 31 | 37 | 45 | 40 |
| 1956 | 2 | 8 | 5 | 3 | 1 | 2 | 9 | 13 | 11 | |
| 1957 | 5 | 2 | 3 | 1 | 2 | 8 | 14 | 11 | | |
| 1958 | 3 | 1 | 2 | 1 | 8 | 15 | 12 | | | |
| 1959 | 1 | 2 | 2 | 9 | 16 | 13 | | | | |
| 1960 | 2 | 2 | 9 | 17 | 13 | | | | | |
| 1961 | 2 | 9 | 18 | 14 | | | | | | |
| 1962 | 10 | 20 | 15 | | | | | | | |
| 1963 | 21 | 17 | | | | | | | | |
| 1964 | 18 | | | | | | | | | |

## Average Annual Profit Percentage (AAPP)
## Uncirculated Rolls of D Quarters

| Year Minted | Number of Years After Year Minted | | | | | | | | | |
|---|---|---|---|---|---|---|---|---|---|---|
| | *21* | *22* | *23* | *24* | *25* | *26* | *27* | *28* | *29* | *30* |
| 35 | 39% | 51% | 78% | 116% | 116% | 201% | 207% | 254% | 259% | 155% |
| 36 | 404 | 565 | 723 | 724 | 1,060 | 1,282 | 1,516 | 2,114 | 2,041 | 1,922 |
| 37 | 24 | 27 | 22 | 59 | 64 | 84 | 91 | 87 | 84 | 82 |
| 39 | 35 | 51 | 55 | 75 | 81 | 88 | 85 | 74 | 78 | 70 |
| 40 | 209 | 251 | 326 | 376 | 452 | 435 | 348 | 349 | 331 | 249 |
| 41 | 30 | 28 | 60 | 50 | 48 | 27 | 27 | 41 | 49 | 35 |
| 42 | 12 | 27 | 41 | 39 | 11 | 25 | 23 | 20 | 17 | 21 |
| 43 | 40 | 35 | 34 | 20 | 26 | 23 | 20 | 19 | 24 | 64 |
| 44 | 40 | 33 | 12 | 26 | 24 | 19 | 16 | 23 | 26 | 41 |
| 45 | 28 | 21 | 25 | 24 | 17 | 16 | 22 | 34 | 35 | 23 |
| 46 | 24 | 35 | 27 | 19 | 14 | 16 | 23 | 70 | 33 | |
| 47 | 13 | 14 | 9 | 7 | 11 | 20 | 21 | 19 | | |
| 48 | 24 | 16 | 25 | 22 | 25 | 21 | 19 | | | |
| 49 | 31 | 27 | 27 | 73 | 77 | 55 | | | | |
| 50 | 7 | 8 | 24 | 38 | 30 | | | | | |
| 51 | 11 | 14 | 23 | 18 | | | | | | |
| 52 | 10 | 14 | 11 | | | | | | | |
| 53 | 12 | 11 | | | | | | | | |
| 54 | 10 | | | | | | | | | |

## Average Annual Profit Percentage (AAPP)
### Uncirculated Rolls of D Quarters

| Year Minted | Number of Years After Year Minted | | | | | | | | | |
|---|---|---|---|---|---|---|---|---|---|---|
| | 31 | 32 | 33 | 34 | 35 | 36 | 37 | 38 | 39 | 40 |
| 1935 | 182% | 145% | 365% | 355% | 399% | 379% | 451% | 381% | 497% | 515 |
| 1936 | 1,909 | 1,659 | 1,609 | 1,562 | 1,416 | 1,376 | 1,482 | 1,707 | 1,614 | |
| 1937 | 89 | 92 | 66 | 56 | 56 | 137 | 158 | 163 | | |
| 1939 | 46 | 40 | 41 | 46 | 145 | 125 | | | | |
| 1940 | 218 | 244 | 298 | 342 | 317 | | | | | |
| 1941 | 48 | 84 | 135 | 112 | | | | | | |
| 1942 | 100 | 151 | 89 | | | | | | | |
| 1943 | 80 | 67 | | | | | | | | |
| 1944 | 35 | | | | | | | | | |

## Average Annual Profit Percentage (AAPP)
### Uncirculated Rolls of P Half-Dollars

| Year Minted | Number of Years After Year Minted | | | | | | | | | |
|---|---|---|---|---|---|---|---|---|---|---|
| | 1 | 2 | 3 | 4 | 5 | 6 | 7 | 8 | 9 | 10 |
| 35 | 0% | 0% | 0% | 0% | 0% | 3% | 3% | 3% | 2% | 5% |
| 36 | 0 | 0 | 0 | 0 | 3 | 4 | 5 | 5 | 6 | 7 |
| 37 | 0 | 0 | 0 | 2 | 3 | 5 | 3 | 5 | 5 | 7 |
| 38 | 0 | 0 | 2 | 2 | 5 | 4 | 4 | 3 | 4 | 5 |
| 39 | 0 | 2 | 2 | 6 | 5 | 6 | 7 | 7 | 10 | 13 |
| 40 | 0 | 0 | 5 | 2 | 3 | 4 | 4 | 3 | 3 | 2 |
| 41 | 0 | 7 | 0 | 0 | 1 | 2 | 2 | 1 | 1 | 1 |
| 42 | 0 | 0 | 1 | 1 | 1 | 2 | 1 | 2 | 2 | 1 |
| 43 | 0 | 0 | 0 | 0 | 1 | 0 | 0 | 0 | 0 | 0 |
| 44 | 0 | 0 | 0 | 0 | 0 | 0 | 0 | 0 | 0 | 1 |
| 45 | 0 | 0 | 0 | 0 | 0 | 0 | 0 | 0 | 0 | 0 |
| 46 | 0 | 0 | 0 | 0 | 0 | 0 | 0 | 1 | 0 | 0 |
| 47 | 0 | 0 | 0 | 0 | 4 | 9 | 13 | 9 | 8 | 7 |
| 48 | 0 | 0 | 0 | 4 | 6 | 21 | 35 | 26 | 27 | 22 |
| 49 | 0 | 6 | 40 | 42 | 51 | 78 | 67 | 64 | 90 | 112 |
| 50 | 0 | 0 | 0 | 18 | 14 | 13 | 10 | 30 | 56 | 77 |
| 51 | 0 | 0 | 0 | 0 | 7 | 6 | 4 | 5 | 10 | 14 |
| 52 | 0 | 0 | 0 | 1 | 1 | 0 | 1 | 8 | 6 | 6 |
| 53 | 0 | 7 | 5 | 11 | 16 | 34 | 32 | 26 | 31 | 47 |
| 54 | 0 | 0 | 0 | 0 | 0 | 4 | 3 | 3 | 2 | 11 |
| 55 | 0 | 0 | 0 | 0 | 21 | 10 | 13 | 30 | 107 | 115 |
| 56 | 0 | 0 | 0 | 6 | 2 | 5 | 9 | 40 | 52 | 36 |
| 57 | 0 | 0 | 1 | 0 | 1 | 6 | 26 | 28 | 21 | 15 |
| 58 | 0 | 7 | 5 | 4 | 16 | 47 | 51 | 33 | 21 | 34 |
| 59 | 0 | 0 | 1 | 6 | 16 | 34 | 24 | 12 | 25 | 17 |
| 60 | 0 | 0 | 5 | 21 | 37 | 28 | 12 | 21 | 16 | 7 |
| 61 | 0 | 1 | 17 | 23 | 18 | 9 | 22 | 11 | 7 | 7 |
| 62 | 0 | 32 | 22 | 25 | 9 | 24 | 14 | 8 | 6 | 5 |
| 63 | 6 | 2 | 7 | 3 | 9 | 5 | 2 | 2 | 2 | 11 |
| 64 | 0 | 0 | 1 | 6 | 1 | 2 | 3 | 2 | 11 | 19 |
| 65 | 0 | 0 | 17 | 18 | 3 | 1 | 1 | 2 | 6 | 5 |
| 66 | 0 | 7 | 0 | 0 | 0 | 0 | 3 | 7 | 5 | |
| 67 | 6 | 0 | 0 | 0 | 0 | 2 | 7 | 5 | | |
| 68 | 0 | 7 | 11 | 7 | | | | | | |
| 69 | 6 | 7 | 7 | | | | | | | |
| 70 | 6 | 3 | | | | | | | | |
| 71 | 6 | | | | | | | | | |

## Average Annual Profit Percentage (AAPP)
## Uncirculated Rolls of P Half-Dollars

| Year Minted | Number of Years After Year Minted | | | | | | | | |
|---|---|---|---|---|---|---|---|---|---|
| | 11 | 12 | 13 | 14 | 15 | 16 | 17 | 18 | 19 |
| 1935 | 7% | 9% | 7% | 6% | 5% | 5% | 4% | 4% | 5% |
| 1936 | 7 | 8 | 5 | 5 | 5 | 4 | 4 | 4 | 3 |
| 1937 | 6 | 5 | 5 | 5 | 5 | 6 | 5 | 11 | 11 |
| 1938 | 6 | 6 | 7 | 8 | 8 | 13 | 12 | 11 | 12 |
| 1939 | 8 | 7 | 7 | 7 | 7 | 9 | 12 | 19 | 25 |
| 1940 | 2 | 2 | 1 | 4 | 3 | 5 | 6 | 12 | 15 |
| 1941 | 0 | 1 | 1 | 3 | 4 | 4 | 4 | 5 | 6 |
| 1942 | 2 | 1 | 3 | 3 | 2 | 3 | 4 | 5 | 7 |
| 1943 | 0 | 1 | 3 | 2 | 3 | 4 | 5 | 5 | 6 |
| 1944 | 0 | 0 | 0 | 1 | 1 | 6 | 3 | 5 | 6 |
| 1945 | 1 | 0 | 0 | 1 | 3 | 3 | 5 | 9 | 15 |
| 1946 | 2 | 2 | 3 | 6 | 4 | 4 | 7 | 18 | 39 |
| 1947 | 5 | 6 | 7 | 5 | 6 | 9 | 25 | 47 | 44 |
| 1948 | 22 | 23 | 16 | 19 | 57 | 79 | 77 | 61 | 53 |
| 1949 | 198 | 134 | 118 | 237 | 361 | 224 | 167 | 138 | 187 |
| 1950 | 41 | 49 | 106 | 177 | 125 | 88 | 90 | 136 | 109 |
| 1951 | 14 | 31 | 39 | 31 | 22 | 18 | 30 | 30 | 17 |
| 1952 | 15 | 19 | 33 | 19 | 13 | 18 | 16 | 11 | 10 |
| 1953 | 136 | 134 | 118 | 99 | 100 | 89 | 58 | 41 | 67 |
| 1954 | 14 | 8 | 5 | 18 | 15 | 4 | 4 | 6 | 10 |
| 1955 | 100 | 80 | 90 | 77 | 53 | 46 | 43 | 49 | 54 |
| 1956 | 22 | 36 | 29 | 20 | 16 | 19 | 22 | 22 | 19 |
| 1957 | 27 | 20 | 14 | 11 | 10 | 13 | 21 | 20 | |
| 1958 | 25 | 12 | 13 | 12 | 16 | 24 | 20 | | |
| 1959 | 13 | 11 | 7 | 12 | 21 | 17 | | | |
| 1960 | 9 | 6 | 10 | 19 | 16 | | | | |
| 1961 | 5 | 11 | 19 | 17 | | | | | |
| 1962 | 11 | 20 | 17 | | | | | | |
| 1963 | 17 | 19 | | | | | | | |
| 1964 | 18 | | | | | | | | |

*Average Annual Profit Percentage (AAPP)*
*Uncirculated Rolls of P Half-Dollars*

| Year Minted | Number of Years After Year Minted | | | | | | | | | |
|---|---|---|---|---|---|---|---|---|---|---|
| | 21 | 22 | 23 | 24 | 25 | 26 | 27 | 28 | 29 | 30 |
| 1935 | 5% | 10% | 14% | 18% | 15% | 17% | 19% | 26% | 28% | 28% |
| 1936 | 8 | 10 | 11 | 13 | 14 | 15 | 20 | 21 | 28 | 27 |
| 1937 | 15 | 20 | 20 | 24 | 31 | 30 | 30 | 51 | 49 | 47 |
| 1938 | 24 | 27 | 25 | 26 | 32 | 43 | 123 | 119 | 117 | 123 |
| 1939 | 31 | 32 | 32 | 35 | 42 | 44 | 43 | 29 | 33 | 33 |
| 1940 | 19 | 20 | 20 | 21 | 23 | 22 | 22 | 24 | 28 | 22 |
| 1941 | 10 | 13 | 17 | 26 | 25 | 20 | 22 | 24 | 18 | 18 |
| 1942 | 12 | 16 | 22 | 21 | 19 | 22 | 24 | 19 | 16 | 23 |
| 1943 | 13 | 21 | 20 | 20 | 24 | 25 | 19 | 22 | 24 | 52 |
| 1944 | 24 | 23 | 21 | 24 | 26 | 20 | 17 | 27 | 54 | 73 |
| 1945 | 23 | 21 | 26 | 27 | 21 | 18 | 26 | 56 | 75 | 64 |
| 1946 | 26 | 32 | 32 | 24 | 22 | 33 | 72 | 94 | 80 | |
| 1947 | 57 | 59 | 52 | 45 | 55 | 92 | 109 | 95 | | |
| 1948 | 60 | 36 | 32 | 36 | 49 | 50 | 42 | | | |
| 1949 | 104 | 89 | 103 | 178 | 182 | 139 | | | | |
| 1950 | 50 | 96 | 94 | 111 | 101 | | | | | |
| 1951 | 13 | 59 | 74 | 57 | | | | | | |
| 1952 | 23 | 56 | 39 | | | | | | | |
| 1953 | 86 | 67 | | | | | | | | |
| 1954 | 16 | | | | | | | | | |

### Average Annual Profit Percentage (AAPP)
### Uncirculated Rolls of P Half-Dollars

| Year Minted | Number of Years After Year Minted | | | | | | | | | |
|---|---|---|---|---|---|---|---|---|---|---|
| | 31 | 32 | 33 | 34 | 35 | 36 | 37 | 38 | 39 | 40 |
| 1935 | 27% | 27% | 28% | 29% | 28% | 22% | 29% | 66% | 80% | 78 |
| 1936 | 21 | 28 | 29 | 28 | 23 | 28 | 85 | 76 | 94 | |
| 1937 | 34 | 38 | 32 | 27 | 32 | 70 | 88 | 79 | | |
| 1938 | 119 | 101 | 91 | 129 | 148 | 177 | 192 | | | |
| 1939 | 31 | 27 | 36 | 102 | 111 | 115 | | | | |
| 1940 | 22 | 29 | 56 | 78 | 97 | | | | | |
| 1941 | 23 | 67 | 71 | 64 | | | | | | |
| 1942 | 53 | 68 | 60 | | | | | | | |
| 1943 | 70 | 60 | | | | | | | | |
| 1944 | 62 | | | | | | | | | |

## Average Annual Profit Percentage (AAPP)
## Uncirculated Rolls of D Half-Dollars

| Year Minted | Number of Years After Year Minted | | | | | | | | | |
|---|---|---|---|---|---|---|---|---|---|---|
| | 1 | 2 | 3 | 4 | 5 | 6 | 7 | 8 | 9 | 10 |
| 1935 | 0% | 0% | 0% | 0% | 0% | 2% | 3% | 5% | 4% | 7% |
| 1936 | 0 | 0 | 0 | 1 | 3 | 4 | 6 | 5 | 6 | 7 |
| 1937 | 0 | 0 | 0 | 4 | 3 | 5 | 4 | 4 | 5 | 5 |
| 1938 | 0 | 3 | 17 | 32 | 41 | 53 | 62 | 68 | 73 | 81 |
| 1939 | 0 | 2 | 2 | 6 | 3 | 4 | 6 | 7 | 6 | 3 |
| 1941 | 0 | 7 | 0 | 2 | 1 | 2 | 2 | 1 | 1 | 1 |
| 1942 | 0 | 0 | 0 | 1 | 1 | 2 | 1 | 1 | 1 | 2 |
| 1943 | 0 | 0 | 0 | 0 | 2 | 0 | 0 | 0 | 0 | 3 |
| 1944 | 0 | 0 | 0 | 1 | 0 | 0 | 0 | 0 | 0 | 0 |
| 1945 | 0 | 0 | 0 | 0 | 0 | 1 | 0 | 0 | 0 | 0 |
| 1946 | 0 | 0 | 0 | 0 | 0 | 0 | 0 | 1 | 1 | 1 |
| 1947 | 0 | 0 | 0 | 0 | 0 | 0 | 2 | 2 | 2 | 1 |
| 1948 | 0 | 0 | 0 | 0 | 0 | 4 | 6 | 10 | 7 | 4 |
| 1949 | 0 | 0 | 0 | 0 | 7 | 11 | 11 | 9 | 7 | 7 |
| 1950 | 0 | 0 | 0 | 2 | 23 | 13 | 10 | 7 | 7 | 30 |
| 1951 | 0 | 0 | 0 | 0 | 7 | 5 | 3 | 5 | 8 | 13 |
| 1952 | 0 | 0 | 0 | 1 | 1 | 0 | 1 | 7 | 5 | 5 |
| 1953 | 0 | 0 | 0 | 0 | 0 | 1 | 3 | 5 | 4 | 5 |
| 1954 | 0 | 0 | 0 | 0 | 0 | 6 | 3 | 2 | 4 | 7 |
| 1957 | 0 | 0 | 0 | 0 | 0 | 2 | 7 | 3 | 5 | 4 |
| 1958 | 0 | 0 | 1 | 1 | 1 | 6 | 3 | 6 | 5 | 10 |
| 1959 | 0 | 0 | 5 | 19 | 16 | 13 | 11 | 9 | 10 | 12 |
| 1960 | 0 | 0 | 5 | 9 | 10 | 10 | 5 | 10 | 7 | 4 |
| 1961 | 0 | 1 | 15 | 8 | 10 | 6 | 12 | 12 | 5 | 6 |
| 1962 | 0 | 11 | 0 | 4 | 4 | 10 | 7 | 4 | 3 | 5 |
| 1963 | 0 | 0 | 5 | 1 | 9 | 4 | 2 | 2 | 2 | 11 |
| 1964 | 14 | 7 | 5 | 7 | 2 | 2 | 3 | 3 | 11 | 19 |
| 1968 | 0 | 0 | 0 | 0 | 3 | 9 | 5 | | | |
| 1969 | 0 | 0 | 0 | 4 | 10 | 6 | | | | |
| 1970 | 1,154 | 710 | 853 | 640 | 451 | | | | | |
| 1971 | 0 | 3 | 10 | 2 | | | | | | |
| 1972 | 6 | 7 | 2 | | | | | | | |
| 1973 | 6 | 5 | | | | | | | | |
| 1974 | 6 | | | | | | | | | |

## Average Annual Profit Percentage (AAPP)
## Uncirculated Rolls of D Half-Dollars

| Year Minted | Number of Years After Year Minted | | | | | | | | | |
|---|---|---|---|---|---|---|---|---|---|---|
| | 11 | 12 | 13 | 14 | 15 | 16 | 17 | 18 | 19 | 20 |
| 1935 | 8% | 9% | 9% | 9% | 9% | 10% | 12% | 13% | 17% | 24 |
| 1936 | 7 | 6 | 5 | 6 | 5 | 4 | 4 | 5 | 4 | 6 |
| 1937 | 7 | 9 | 8 | 10 | 10 | 27 | 57 | 45 | 47 | 67 |
| 1938 | 74 | 71 | 65 | 61 | 77 | 94 | 99 | 100 | 101 | 134 |
| 1939 | 3 | 4 | 3 | 5 | 4 | 9 | 10 | 9 | 9 | 10 |
| 1941 | 0 | 0 | 1 | 2 | 2 | 3 | 8 | 10 | 9 | 11 |
| 1942 | 2 | 2 | 2 | 4 | 6 | 7 | 12 | 9 | 12 | 13 |
| 1943 | 2 | 2 | 2 | 4 | 5 | 13 | 16 | 17 | 16 | 16 |
| 1944 | 0 | 1 | 0 | 0 | 1 | 4 | 4 | 5 | 6 | 16 |
| 1945 | 1 | 0 | 0 | 1 | 4 | 4 | 5 | 9 | 19 | 25 |
| 1946 | 2 | 4 | 5 | 5 | 9 | 8 | 20 | 45 | 77 | 7 |
| 1947 | 1 | 2 | 7 | 4 | 4 | 7 | 28 | 45 | 41 | 39 |
| 1948 | 5 | 8 | 8 | 8 | 21 | 39 | 48 | 44 | 28 | 36 |
| 1949 | 39 | 42 | 39 | 47 | 107 | 86 | 77 | 83 | 149 | 138 |
| 1950 | 25 | 32 | 57 | 112 | 82 | 51 | 43 | 87 | 67 | 48 |
| 1951 | 14 | 23 | 103 | 80 | 61 | 56 | 162 | 142 | 85 | 53 |
| 1952 | 8 | 11 | 11 | 9 | 9 | 16 | 15 | 6 | 7 | 9 |
| 1953 | 8 | 8 | 6 | 6 | 14 | 12 | 4 | 7 | 7 | 13 |
| 1954 | 5 | 6 | 3 | 9 | 7 | 3 | 2 | 5 | 9 | 13 |
| 1957 | 7 | 6 | 4 | 4 | 4 | 10 | 18 | 13 | | |
| 1958 | 7 | 3 | 4 | 8 | 11 | 16 | 14 | | | |
| 1959 | 10 | 8 | 8 | 14 | 23 | 17 | | | | |
| 1960 | 6 | 6 | 10 | 20 | 16 | | | | | |
| 1961 | 5 | 11 | 20 | 17 | | | | | | |
| 1962 | 11 | 21 | 17 | | | | | | | |
| 1963 | 17 | 19 | | | | | | | | |
| 1964 | 18 | | | | | | | | | |

## Average Annual Profit Percentage (AAPP)
## Uncirculated Rolls of D Half-Dollars

| Year Minted | Number of Years After Year Minted | | | | | | | | | |
|---|---|---|---|---|---|---|---|---|---|---|
| | 21 | 22 | 23 | 24 | 25 | 26 | 27 | 28 | 29 | 30 |
| 1935 | 31% | 39% | 70% | 110% | 105% | 104% | 88% | 94% | 117% | 168% |
| 1936 | 10 | 13 | 22 | 25 | 23 | 24 | 33 | 34 | 62 | 60 |
| 1937 | 82 | 99 | 95 | 97 | 93 | 110 | 129 | 227 | 219 | 212 |
| 1938 | 176 | 182 | 293 | 471 | 488 | 435 | 601 | 580 | 560 | 807 |
| 1939 | 14 | 18 | 22 | 26 | 29 | 43 | 41 | 40 | 48 | 45 |
| 1941 | 12 | 18 | 35 | 66 | 63 | 52 | 60 | 52 | 41 | 38 |
| 1942 | 16 | 20 | 70 | 64 | 55 | 65 | 74 | 56 | 51 | 57 |
| 1943 | 26 | 21 | 53 | 39 | 54 | 58 | 55 | 43 | 53 | 212 |
| 1944 | 28 | 27 | 25 | 28 | 28 | 28 | 24 | 35 | 79 | 90 |
| 1945 | 24 | 23 | 29 | 28 | 23 | 20 | 31 | 100 | 94 | 82 |
| 1946 | 60 | 71 | 62 | 44 | 41 | 47 | 126 | 123 | 87 | |
| 1947 | 42 | 43 | 34 | 31 | 41 | 128 | 109 | 90 | | |
| 1948 | 29 | 18 | 18 | 22 | 23 | 47 | 34 | | | |
| 1949 | 89 | 89 | 90 | 110 | 145 | 110 | | | | |
| 1950 | 50 | 97 | 144 | 77 | 70 | | | | | |
| 1951 | 66 | 135 | 115 | 110 | | | | | | |
| 1952 | 20 | 22 | 16 | | | | | | | |
| 1953 | 19 | 19 | | | | | | | | |
| 1954 | 12 | | | | | | | | | |

Average Annual Profit Percentage (AAPP)
Uncirculated Rolls of D Half-Dollars

| Year Minted | Number of Years After Year Minted | | | | | | | | | |
|---|---|---|---|---|---|---|---|---|---|---|
| | 31 | 32 | 33 | 34 | 35 | 36 | 37 | 38 | 39 | 40 |
| 1935 | 162% | 157% | 158% | 154% | 126% | 131% | 149% | 217% | 286% | 533% |
| 1936 | 58 | 62 | 60 | 57 | 54 | 66 | 107 | 129 | 374 | |
| 1937 | 217 | 211 | 238 | 222 | 232 | 343 | 411 | 625 | | |
| 1938 | 781 | 702 | 632 | 613 | 855 | 1,137 | 1,138 | | | |
| 1939 | 38 | 36 | 43 | 99 | 111 | 113 | | | | |
| 1941 | 44 | 101 | 131 | 109 | | | | | | |
| 1942 | 79 | 98 | 84 | | | | | | | |
| 1943 | 134 | 121 | | | | | | | | |
| 1944 | 72 | | | | | | | | | |

# APPENDIX V

## Median Wholesale Values of $100
## Face Value of Rolls of Uncirculated Coins
## of Each Denomination and Mintage

The following pages show the median wholesale values, from one to thirty-five years after the year minted, of $100 face value of rolls of all coins that were minted between 1935 and 1974 (except S nickels, S dimes, S quarters, and S half-dollars which, on the date this book was written, were no longer minted for general circulation).

To determine the probable value at any future date of an investment of $100 in current-year uncirculated coin rolls of any denomination and mintage, find the denomination and mintage coin and locate the average value under the *Number of Years After Date Purchased* column.

For example, if you want to know the probable value, seventeen years after the date purchased, of an investment of $100 in current-year uncirculated S cents, go to the table on page 206 and find the S *Cents* line. Across the page under column 17 you will find $1,814 — the probable value of an investment of $100 in current-year uncirculated S cents, seventeen years after the date purchased.

Of course, if you want to know the value of an investment of $500 instead of $100, merely multiply the result ($1,814) by 5.

## Median Wholesale Value* of $100 Face Value
## of Rolls of Uncirculated Coins of Each Denomination and Mintage

| | Number of Years After Date Purchased | | | | | | | | | |
| | 1 | 2 | 3 | 4 | 5 | 6 | 7 | 8 | 9 | 10 |
|---|---|---|---|---|---|---|---|---|---|---|
| Cents | $132 | $156 | $164 | $196 | $200 | $250 | $294 | $312 | $366 | $352 |
| Cents | 132 | 146 | 156 | 166 | 218 | 226 | 234 | 254 | 242 | 208 |
| Cents | 138 | 156 | 172 | 234 | 274 | 312 | 352 | 430 | 444 | 468 |
| verage Cents | 134 | 153 | 164 | 199 | 231 | 263 | 293 | 332 | 351 | 343 |
| Nickels | 114 | 123 | 125 | 125 | 151 | 166 | 166 | 202 | 208 | 203 |
| Nickels | 114 | 114 | 125 | 146 | 166 | 166 | 166 | 166 | 187 | 166 |
| verage Nickels | 114 | 119 | 125 | 136 | 159 | 166 | 166 | 184 | 198 | 185 |
| Dimes | 100 | 100 | 105 | 115 | 118 | 126 | 142 | 142 | 164 | 158 |
| Dimes | 100 | 100 | 103 | 111 | 111 | 122 | 142 | 142 | 154 | 166 |
| verage Dimes | 100 | 100 | 104 | 113 | 115 | 124 | 142 | 142 | 159 | 162 |
| Quarters | 100 | 100 | 100 | 105 | 110 | 118 | 127 | 133 | 137 | 152 |
| Quarters | 100 | 100 | 100 | 103 | 106 | 114 | 112 | 114 | 122 | 129 |
| verage Quarters | 100 | 100 | 100 | 104 | 108 | 116 | 120 | 124 | 130 | 141 |
| Half-Dollars | 100 | 100 | 100 | 106 | 114 | 129 | 129 | 143 | 152 | 171 |
| Half-Dollars | 100 | 100 | 100 | 103 | 112 | 122 | 122 | 137 | 141 | 152 |
| verage Half-Dollars | 100 | 100 | 100 | 105 | 113 | 126 | 126 | 140 | 147 | 162 |

ounded to nearest whole dollar

### Median Wholesale Value* of $100 Face Value
### of Rolls of Uncirculated Coins of Each Denomination and Mintage

| | \multicolumn{10}{c}{Number of Years After Date Purchased} |
|---|---|---|---|---|---|---|---|---|---|---|
| | 11 | 12 | 13 | 14 | 15 | 16 | 17 | 18 | 19 | 20 |
| P Cents | $332 | $312 | $ 372 | $ 430 | $ 590 | $ 936 | $1,248 | $1,560 | $1,638 | $1,872 |
| D Cents | 226 | 274 | 372 | 508 | 546 | 624 | 976 | 1,248 | 1,216 | 1,778 |
| S Cents | 726 | 780 | 1,092 | 1,248 | 1,326 | 1,560 | 1,814 | 1,872 | 2,652 | 2,730 |
| Average Cents | 428 | 455 | 612 | 729 | 821 | 1,040 | 1,346 | 1,560 | 1,835 | 2,127 |
| P Nickels | 208 | 229 | 208 | 260 | 291 | 446 | 644 | 633 | 727 | 695 |
| D Nickels | 187 | 208 | 291 | 363 | 415 | 509 | 706 | 991 | 1,121 | 1,349 |
| Average Nickels | 198 | 219 | 250 | 312 | 353 | 478 | 675 | 812 | 924 | 1,022 |
| P Dimes | 176 | 174 | 186 | 217 | 233 | 237 | 292 | 308 | 338 | 442 |
| D Dimes | 198 | 213 | 213 | 277 | 288 | 300 | 348 | 411 | 446 | 474 |
| Average Dimes | 187 | 194 | 200 | 247 | 261 | 269 | 320 | 360 | 392 | 458 |
| P Quarters | 160 | 190 | 224 | 228 | 219 | 266 | 264 | 342 | 323 | 342 |
| D Quarters | 141 | 156 | 160 | 184 | 190 | 236 | 285 | 361 | 361 | 623 |
| Average Quarters | 151 | 173 | 192 | 206 | 205 | 251 | 275 | 352 | 342 | 483 |
| P Half-Dollars | 209 | 209 | 193 | 251 | 241 | 251 | 302 | 310 | 380 | 555 |
| D Half-Dollars | 175 | 184 | 190 | 207 | 228 | 276 | 361 | 340 | 418 | 570 |
| Average Half-Dollars | 192 | 197 | 192 | 229 | 235 | 264 | 332 | 325 | 399 | 565 |

*Rounded to nearest whole dollar

### Median Wholesale Value* of $100 Face Value
### of Rolls of Uncirculated Coins of Each Denomination and Mintage

| | \multicolumn{10}{c}{Number of Years After Date Purchased} | | | | | | | | |
| | 21 | 22 | 23 | 24 | 25 | 26 | 27 | 28 | 29 | 30 |
|---|---|---|---|---|---|---|---|---|---|---|
| P Cents | $1,794 | $2,340 | $2,536 | $2,808 | $2,380 | $2,574 | $2,126 | $2,496 | $2,204 | $2,184 |
| D Cents | 1,472 | 1,560 | 1,912 | 2,340 | 2,964 | 2,808 | 2,692 | 3,822 | 4,408 | 5,110 |
| S Cents | 2,964 | 3,510 | 4,642 | 4,836 | 5,304 | 4,914 | 4,446 | 4,680 | 5,538 | 6,084 |
| Average Cents | 2,077 | 2,470 | 3,030 | 3,328 | 3,549 | 3,432 | 3,088 | 3,666 | 4,050 | 4,459 |
| P Nickels | 872 | 1,079 | 1,453 | 1,577 | 1,577 | 1,764 | 1,567 | 1,769 | 1,972 | 2,418 |
| D Nickels | 1,453 | 1,505 | 2,075 | 2,241 | 2,822 | 2,905 | 3,632 | 3,580 | 4,565 | 5,084 |
| Average Nickels | 1,163 | 1,292 | 1,764 | 1,909 | 2,200 | 2,335 | 2,600 | 2,675 | 3,269 | 3,751 |
| P Dimes | 541 | 537 | 648 | 711 | 711 | 774 | 770 | 830 | 1,264 | 1,343 |
| D Dimes | 691 | 790 | 853 | 1,027 | 1,027 | 1,217 | 1,035 | 1,296 | 1,343 | 2,054 |
| Average Dimes | 616 | 664 | 751 | 869 | 869 | 996 | 903 | 1,063 | 1,304 | 1,699 |
| P Quarters | 380 | 494 | 570 | 570 | 625 | 570 | 585 | 578 | 969 | 931 |
| D Quarters | 608 | 684 | 722 | 1,030 | 851 | 770 | 722 | 1,653 | 1,512 | 2,109 |
| Average Quarters | 494 | 589 | 646 | 800 | 738 | 670 | 654 | 1,116 | 1,241 | 1,520 |
| P Half-Dollars | 591 | 684 | 692 | 722 | 732 | 741 | 770 | 849 | 988 | 1,102 |
| D Half-Dollars | 684 | 646 | 1,330 | 1,397 | 1,444 | 1,520 | 1,710 | 2,151 | 2,379 | 2,687 |
| Average Half-Dollars | 638 | 665 | 1,011 | 1,060 | 1,088 | 1,131 | 1,240 | 1,500 | 1,684 | 1,895 |

*Rounded to nearest whole dollar

### Median Wholesale Value* of $100 Face Value
### of Rolls of Uncirculated Coins of Each Denomination and Mintage

| | Number of Years After Date Purchased | | | | |
|---|---|---|---|---|---|
| | 31 | 32 | 33 | 34 | 35 |
| P Cents | $ 2,926 | $2,380 | $3,198 | $3,082 | $3,550 |
| D Cents | 6,046 | 6,162 | 6,104 | 5,772 | 5,246 |
| S Cents | 10,258 | 8,854 | 7,742 | 5,304 | 7,002 |
| Average Cents | 6,410 | 5,799 | 5,681 | 4,719 | 5,266 |
| P Nickels | 2,283 | 2,221 | 2,200 | 1,349 | 2,656 |
| D Nickels | 4,565 | 4,877 | 4,565 | 4,044 | 8,093 |
| Average Nickels | 3,424 | 3,549 | 3,383 | 2,697 | 5,375 |
| P Dimes | 1,284 | 1,580 | 1,659 | 1,659 | 1,932 |
| D Dimes | 2,161 | 2,354 | 4,148 | 4,148 | 5,244 |
| Average Dimes | 1,723 | 1,967 | 2,904 | 2,904 | 3,588 |
| P Quarters | 1,003 | 1,163 | 1,385 | 1,531 | 2,027 |
| D Quarters | 2,850 | 3,895 | 4,560 | 7,832 | 11,180 |
| Average Quarters | 1,927 | 2,529 | 2,973 | 4,682 | 6,604 |
| P Half-Dollars | 1,102 | 1,330 | 1,638 | 2,272 | 2,358 |
| D Half-Dollars | 2,548 | 3,659 | 4,408 | 4,556 | 4,522 |
| Average Half-Dollars | 1,825 | 2,495 | 3,023 | 3,414 | 3,440 |

*Rounded to nearest whole dollar

# Appendix VI

## Order Blank for Coin Preservation
## Starter Pack

## ORDER YOUR COIN PRESERVATION
## STARTER PACK NOW

MAIL TO:

**Jefren Publishing Company**
**1216 Holy Cross**
**Monroeville, Pennsylvania 15146**

Please send me a COIN PRESERVATION STARTER PACK which includes:

- 1 pair of cotton gloves

- 100 sheets of VCI paper

- 100 sheets of aluminum foil

- supply of silica gel (sufficient to protect 5 one gallon cans of coin rolls)

- 100 pressure-sensitive coin roll identification labels

- 10 AAPP Calculator Charts

I have enclosed $8.00 to cover all costs including postage and handling.

PLEASE
PRINT
OR TYPE

Name _____

Address _____

City _____

State _____ Zip _____

*Void after December 31, 1977*

# Index